LINCOLN'S
LAST SPEECH

THE "RAIL SPLITTER" AT WORK REPAIRING THE UNION.

Pivotal Moments in American History

SERIES EDITORS

David Hackett Fischer

James M. McPherson

David Greenberg

LINCOLN'S LAST SPEECH

Wartime Reconstruction and the Crisis of Reunion

Louis P. Masur

OXFORD
UNIVERSITY PRESS

OXFORD
UNIVERSITY PRESS

Oxford University Press is a department of the
University of Oxford. It furthers the University's objective
of excellence in research, scholarship, and education
by publishing worldwide.

Oxford   New York

Auckland   Cape Town   Dar es Salaam   Hong Kong   Karachi
Kuala Lumpur   Madrid   Melbourne   Mexico City   Nairobi
New Delhi   Shanghai   Taipei   Toronto

With offices in

Argentina   Austria   Brazil   Chile   Czech Republic   France   Greece
Guatemala   Hungary   Italy   Japan   Poland   Portugal   Singapore
South Korea   Switzerland   Thailand   Turkey   Ukraine   Vietnam

Oxford is a registered trade mark of Oxford University Press
in the UK and in certain other countries.

Published in the United States of America by
Oxford University Press
198 Madison Avenue, New York, NY 10016

Library of Congress Cataloging-in-Publication Data
Masur, Louis P.
Lincoln's last speech : wartime reconstruction and the crisis of reunion / Louis P. Masur.
pages   cm
Includes bibliographical references and index.
ISBN 978-0-19-021839-3
1. Reconstruction (U.S. history, 1865–1877)   2. Lincoln, Abraham,
1809–1865—Views on reconstruction.   3. United States—Politics and government—
1861–1865.   I. Title.
E668.M375   2015
973.8—dc23   2014031019

1 3 5 7 9 8 6 4 2
Printed in the United States of America
on acid-free paper

For Ron Spencer

"When lenity and cruelty play for a kingdom, the gentler gamester is the soonest winner."

Shakespeare, *Henry V*, Act 3, Scene 6

CONTENTS

On the misty evening of April 11, 1865, a huge crowd gathered on the north lawn of the White House and spilled out onto nearby streets to hear President Abraham Lincoln speak about the impending end of the Civil War. General Robert E. Lee had surrendered his army to General Ulysses S. Grant two days earlier. The Northern people had been celebrating ever since, and had not yet run out of energy. All Washington was ablaze with lights to herald the Union triumph. The festive throng expected a triumphant speech from the commander in chief whose armies had won the war.

They should have known better. Lincoln was not given to exultant sentiments. He began with a brief reference to the satisfactions of victory and a call for national thanksgiving. But he quickly changed the mood by launching into a disquisition on the challenges of reconstructing a Union ravaged by four years of war. The crowd quieted. They showed a polite interest in the question of the future status of Louisiana and the other Confederate states now that the war was over, but that was not what they had come to hear. When the president expressed his preference that literate black men and those who had served as Union soldiers should be granted the right to vote, some in the audience nodded in approval but other shook their heads in dissent. One of the latter turned angrily to his companion. "That means nigger citizenship," growled John Wilkes Booth. "Now, by God, I'll put him through. That is the last speech he will ever make."

Booth was the only person who knew that this speech would be Lincoln's last. Knowing as *we* do that it was indeed his last speech, we search it today for clues to Lincoln's intended policy for the problem of reconstruction that consumed the nation during the next several years. The people who came out to hear Lincoln on April 11 expected an address that would mark a pivotal moment between war and peace, disunion and reunion. In one sense, that was the speech they heard, but it took an unexpected form. Louis Masur takes a leaf from Lincoln's actual speech, and analyzes it as a pivotal moment for the meaning of the freighted word "reconstruction" and the tortuous process described by that word.

"Reconstruction" was used for the first time during the secession crisis of 1860–1861. It described the efforts at a compromise that would reconstruct the Union by luring back the seceded states. In that meaning, reconstruction was rejected both by committed disunionists and by Republicans who opposed surrender to disunionist demands. Once the war began, reconstruction evolved from something analogous to "restoration" of the Union as it had existed before 1860 to a full-scale rebuilding of the nation without slavery and the plantation society it had sustained. For some Republicans, reconstruction by 1865 had come to mean full or (in Lincoln's case) partial enfranchisement of freed slaves.

The arguments for these various kinds of reconstruction generated several constitutional theories. Thaddeus Stevens maintained that Confederate states should be treated as "conquered provinces." Charles Sumner contended that they had committed "state suicide." Both theories insisted that the states had reverted to territories that could only be reconstructed as states on conditions laid down by Congress. The basis for the Union war effort, however, was the Northern conviction that states could *not* leave the Union; it was a rebellion by individuals, not states. Thus the process of reconstruction involved the establishment of new state governments formed by citizens loyal to the Union. How to do this, of course, was the subject of endless debate. The devil was in the details.

Lincoln tried to cut through what he called the "pernicious abstractions" of diverse theories about the legal status of Confederate states with a plan to bring them back into their "proper practical relation" to the United States. With great clarity and precision, Masur traces Lincoln's policy from the plan he announced in his Proclamation of Amnesty and Reconstruction on December 8, 1863, through the implementation of that policy in Louisiana, Arkansas, and Tennessee, to congressional rejection of the new governments in these states, and to Lincoln's defense of the policy in his "last speech," which concluded with a promise of a "new announcement to the people of the South." John Wilkes Booth robbed the South—and the nation—of that announcement. But we can surely agree with Masur's conclusion that if Lincoln had lived beyond April 15, 1865, "his humanity might have led the nation toward the righteous peace that he envisioned for all Americans."

James M. McPherson

LINCOLN'S
LAST SPEECH

Prologue

"Gladness of Heart"

Through the cool evening mist of Tuesday, April 11, 1865, darkness gave way to light. The White House was "brilliantly illuminated" and the reflection revealed a "vast throng" assembled to hear the president speak. Throughout the city bonfires blazed and celebratory rockets whistled.[1]

Crowds had gathered outside the White House the previous day, expecting a triumphal speech in the aftermath of Robert E. Lee's surrender to Ulysses S. Grant at Appomattox on April 9. A procession of some two thousand Navy Yard workmen, dragging six boat howitzers, trekked through the city. The gathering had swelled on its march to call on the president. Bands played and people sang the "Star-Spangled Banner," "Hail Columbia," and other patriotic tunes. First to be sighted at the mansion's second-floor window was not the president, but his twelve-year-old son. Tad couldn't resist the parade and, encouraged by the crowd's cheers, he waved a captured rebel flag. Quickly, according to one reporter, "he was lugged back by the slack of his trousers by some discreet domestic."[2]

Abraham Lincoln had appeared twice on the 10th. In the early afternoon "an agitated sea of hats, faces and men's arms" greeted him. "I am greatly rejoiced that an occasion has occurred so pleasurable that the people can't restrain themselves," he said, to boisterous cheers. "I suppose arrangements are being made for some sort of formal demonstration, perhaps this evening or to-morrow night."

"We can't wait!" the crowd roared.

"If there should be such a demonstration, I, of course, will have to respond to it and I will have nothing to say if you dribble it out of me."

Many in the throng laughed and someone shouted, "We want to hear you now!"

Lincoln used the occasion to ask the band that had assembled to play a song. His choice was "Dixie," and he joked that the Union would reappropriate it as a captured prize of war. Some listeners may have wondered whether, in selecting the song ("one of the best tunes I ever heard," he announced), he was signaling eventual reconciliation with rather than mocking the defeated Confederacy. In any case the band played "Dixie" with "extraordinary vigor." "The President understands well the power of national songs," observed the *Daily National Intelligencer*, "and what is better, he uses it in the right time and for a good purpose." Lincoln proposed three cheers for General Grant and his forces, and three more for the navy, and retired from the scene to work on his remarks for the following day.[3]

At 5:30, again on the 10th, another crowd called on Lincoln to speak, but again the president demurred, saying that he planned to wait until the following evening, when he "would be then that much better prepared to say what I have to say." After all, he observed, everything he said found its way into print and he did not want to make a mistake that would create confusion.

"You have made no mistakes yet!" someone shouted. One reporter thought Lincoln's remarks as "unresolvable as the riddle of Sphinx…so carefully did he restrain from any opinion."[4]

The next day, people were waiting "anxiously for the speech which the President has promised to make." The afternoon edition of the April 11 *Daily National Republican* announced that the event was planned for eight o'clock. The notice presumed that bands again would be present. "But the music most desired by the nation at this hour of the country's trial," noted the writer, "is a speech from the president. If he speaks tonight he will speak to the people of the whole country who are anxiously listening to hear something from him."[5]

As darkness fell, lights illuminated the city. At the War Department, every window was "ablaze with light" and the building decorated with large flags. A transparency with the word "Grant" flapped beneath a wreath of evergreens. The Treasury Department featured a sign that read, "U.S. Greenbacks and U. S. Grant—Grant gives the greenbacks a metallic ring." The State Department, "brilliantly lighted and festooned with flags," displayed a banner that read, "the Union saved by faith in the Constitution, faith in the people, and trust in God."[6]

The north portico of the White House was also brightly lit. Men and women gathered and stood in ankle-deep mud from the April rains. They not only filled the grounds in front of the White House but spilled over onto the sidewalks from Fifteenth to Seventeeth Streets. Banners streamed and bands played. At last Lincoln appeared and was greeted with "tremendous and continued applause." Mrs. Lincoln and some friends could be seen in an adjoining window. Noah Brooks, the Washington correspondent for the *Sacramento Daily Union*, observed later that "there was something terrible about the enthusiasm with which the beloved Chief Magistrate was received—cheers upon cheers, wave after wave of applause rolled up, the President modestly standing quiet until it was over." Writing several years afterward, Elizabeth Keckley, Mary Todd Lincoln's black seamstress, recalled a vast mass of heads like "a black, gently swelling sea.... Close to the house the faces were plainly discernible, but they faded into mere ghostly outlines on the outskirts of the assembly; and what added to the weird, spectral beauty of the scene, was the confused hum of voices that rose above the sea of forms." Lincoln chose to read from a prepared manuscript, "evidently so that there should be no chance for misconception of his views enunciated," thought one reporter.[7]

"We meet this evening, not in sorrow, but in gladness of heart," he began. Petersburg and Richmond had been evacuated. Only a week earlier, the president had walked through the streets of Richmond and had sat in Jefferson Davis's chair at the Confederate White House. Lee's army had surrendered. "Hope of a righteous and speedy peace" now abounded.[8]

The word "righteous" invites attention. It was not a word Lincoln employed frequently, but its appearance here echoed earlier usage. In the speech that helped make him a candidate for president, Lincoln told the crowd at Cooper Union on February 27, 1860, that those who seek to preserve the Union by yielding to those who were clamoring for disunion reverse the divine order of things and call "not the sinners, but the righteous to repentance." He repeated the formulation several times in his speaking tour through New England that followed.[9]

The cause of Union was the righteous cause; the next time he would use the word in his writings, it was for the cause of emancipation, also deemed "righteous." In response to a letter from two Iowa Quakers commending him for issuing the Emancipation Proclamation on January 1, 1863, Lincoln wrote, "it is most cheering and encouraging for me to know that in the efforts which I have made and am making for the restoration of a righteous peace to our country, I am upheld and sustained by the good wishes and prayers of God's people."[10]

The religious overtones of the righteous cause, and by extension all measures necessary for victory, were made clear in Lincoln's second inaugural address on March 4, when he quoted Psalms 19:9, "'the judgments of the Lord, are true and righteous altogether.'" Following that line, Lincoln memorably concluded with a sentence calling for "a just, and a lasting peace." Perhaps he did not say "righteous" because he had used it in quoting Psalms. More likely, in keeping with the overall content of a soaring conclusion that begins "with malice toward none, with charity for all," Lincoln wanted to signal fairness and even-handedness. On March 4, the war still was not over; on April 11, it essentially was.

Lincoln not only sought justice, he also desired mercy. His generosity and magnanimity would come to distress his party's radicals, though he never wavered from what he declared in his second inaugural: "judge not that we be not judged." Indeed, he repeated the injunction several times in April 1865. There would be occasion to debate how best to unify the nation, but Lincoln began that speech on April 11 by reasserting the righteousness of the Union cause and calling for a day of national Thanksgiving. "He, from Whom all blessings flow, must not be forgotten," he said.[11]

Lincoln then turned to the subject of his speech: reconstruction. This word, too, is not without its ambiguities. It is common to contrast "reconstruction" with "restoration," and to suggest that the former entailed a more or less radical remaking of southern society whereas the latter simply meant returning the states to full political membership in the nation. Some Democratic newspapers in 1865 were careful to distinguish between the two words. Some historians argue that Lincoln's ideas shifted from "restoration" to "reconstruction," but the president's uses of the words suggest something different. He told the crowd on that misty night, "the re-inauguration of the national authority—reconstruction—which has had a large share of thought from the first, is pressed much more closely upon our attention." Here, Lincoln defines "reconstruction" simply: the states submitting to federal authority and returning to the nation.[12]

When Lincoln used "restoration," he tended to do so in the context of the return of peace or, as he put it in 1862, "the speedy restoration of our Union." But the terms were fluid. Either "restoration" or "reconstruction" could signify simultaneously the process of establishing civil government in the states themselves and the process of the states returning to the nation. Lincoln himself acknowledged the fluidity and imprecision of the nomenclature when, in his Annual Message to Congress in 1863, he spoke of "maintaining the political framework of the States on what is called Reconstruction." Nearly three months earlier, in a letter to Andrew Johnson, then still the military governor of Tennessee, he declared, "let the reconstruction be the work only of such men as can be trusted for the Union."[13]

Under the terms of "*a plan of government*" that he had proposed in his Proclamation of Amnesty and Reconstruction, issued on December 8, 1863, the work of reconstruction had advanced during the war in several states, including Louisiana, Arkansas, and

Tennessee. That plan provided for states in rebellion to be reorganized and restored to the nation once persons equaling one-tenth of the number of eligible voters who had participated in the election of 1860 established a loyal government and adopted a state constitution that abolished slavery. The plan was well received at the time, and Lincoln held out hope for the speedy restoration of these states.

He was especially eager to have Congress recognize reconstruction efforts in Louisiana, the only Deep South state that had taken the necessary steps as outlined by the December proclamation. From the moment New Orleans had surrendered on April 28, 1862, Lincoln had seized the opportunity to establish a loyal state government in Louisiana. Throughout the war, he had monitored developments and encouraged military and civil leaders to organize a loyal government and adopt a new state constitution. They had done so. Nonetheless in February 1865, Congress had refused to seat the representatives elected from the state.

Three times in one paragraph (and six overall) in his April 11 speech he used the phrase "proper practical relation" to characterize the return of seceded states to the Union. Lincoln abjured abstract, theoretical debates. Politicians, jurists, and editors avidly debated the status of the rebellious states but Lincoln himself never recognized the legitimacy of secession (time and again he insisted on referring to the "so-called seceded states"), and instead held to the theory of an indissoluble union. As far as he was concerned, the eleven Confederate states had never left. Some radical Republicans, however, offered different ideas, as embodied in the terms "state suicide" and "conquered territory." Under these notions of the status of the rebellious states, more could be demanded as the price for readmission, because in seceding they had forfeited any rights guaranteed to them by the Constitution. In the hands of some radicals, these demands included universal male suffrage and the confiscation of large estates. But Lincoln had no patience for such arguments and dismissed them as "a pernicious abstraction."

Displeased by the Congress's refusal to act, and appealing directly to the people, Lincoln devoted the speech on April 11, what would turn out to be his final speech, to the case of Louisiana. Twelve thousand voters there had sworn allegiance to the Union, held elections, organized state government, and adopted a constitution that abolished slavery and even provided for public schooling for blacks as well as whites. Lincoln admitted that "we, the loyal people, differ" in thoughts about how best to reconstruct the nation, and he affirmed his willingness to consider all plans and not be entrapped by some "exclusive, and inflexible plan" that would apply to all the former rebel states. Yet what could possibly be accomplished, he wondered, by discarding the new state government of Louisiana? How could this serve the public interest?

Lincoln conceded that the Louisiana government was only at the beginning of what it could become. He publicly acknowledged for the first time a preference for giving the vote to freedmen who were educated or had served as soldiers, a provision not included in Louisiana's constitution (though it did authorize the legislature to enfranchise blacks at its discretion). By 1865, suffrage had become a vital issue, pressed by radical Republicans and abolitionists alike. Lincoln had not pleased these groups when in 1864 he pocket vetoed a bill proposed by Senator Benjamin Wade and Representative Henry Winter Davis. Their bill (which did not include a provision for black suffrage) offered a congressional alternative to the president's plan of reconstruction, one that would have slowed the process and imposed more stringent requirements for readmission. The brouhaha after Lincoln had explained the reasons for his veto, and Wade and Davis published a manifesto that denounced Lincoln's plan of reconstruction, contributed to the desire on the part of some Republicans to replace Lincoln as the party nominee in the election of 1864. Perhaps now, with his public endorsement of qualified voting rights for black men (previously he had offered support only in private correspondence), he was signaling a shift toward the radicals, one that might make them more amenable to readmitting those states that had formed new governments and ratified new constitutions under Lincoln's plan.

Lincoln's endorsement of limited black suffrage signified something else as well: reconstruction would entail more than merely the restoration of the political status quo before the war. For many Republicans, it would not suffice simply to require white Southerners living in Confederate states to take an oath of allegiance, form a new loyal government, and adopt a state constitution that abolished slavery. Reconstruction would also have to address the social transformation of Southern society in the aftermath of emancipation. The transition from slavery to freedom for millions of blacks and the role of the federal government in that transition were widely debated and, as the war progressed, the lives of the freedmen could not be separated from discussions of reconstruction.

Whatever the state of affairs in Louisiana on April 11, Lincoln suggested that the new state government was "only to what it should be as the egg is to the fowl," and asked whether "we shall sooner have the fowl by hatching the egg than by smashing it?" Lincoln loved metaphors and once told a New York legislator that "common people... are more easily influenced and informed through the medium of a broad illustration than in any other way." The egg-fowl analogy captured the public's attention and allowed him to defend his policy in simple terms easily understood by anyone. Broken eggs could not be mended, he declared on more than one occasion. The war had cracked the Union, but not smashed it. Would the turmoil over reconstruction, however, destroy in peace what had been won in war?[14]

The minister Henry Ward Beecher had warned Lincoln in February, six weeks or so before the April 11 speech, that "it is more dangerous *to make peace than to make war.*" "Making peace" had preoccupied Lincoln from the start. He knew it was an enterprise "fraught with difficulty." Reconstruction did not begin once the war ended. Indeed, it had begun even before the first shots were fired on Fort Sumter, initially in the ways some Southerners discussed reconstruction as a rewriting of the Constitution to protect slavery. As important as the debates over reconstruction throughout the war were to shaping what came after, they were also central to the war itself. For Lincoln, reconstruction was not simply an end, but also a means toward winning the war and reuniting the nation. Each state that could be restored while the conflict still raged was one state fewer that remained part of the Confederacy. Each restored state brought the Union one step closer to victory.[15]

In this last speech, which he did not know of course would be his last, Lincoln reminded his audience of what had been done and what was being argued over. He invited them to look with him to the future when the "present *'situation'*" required action. Now that it was certain the United States would endure, reconstruction, both political and social, was the only question, and it was a momentous one. The ongoing debates over how to reestablish state governments and provide for the needs of the freedmen informed his April 11 speech, which brought listeners back to the beginning of the war and invited them to gaze into the future.

Lincoln's last speech was a speech about reconstruction, but not the reconstruction that has become reified as a textbook chapter title referring to 1865–1877. Throughout the war, the fluid term shifted meanings and came to be used synonymously with restoration and reunion. To understand what happened with postwar Reconstruction we need first to look hard at what Lincoln meant by wartime reconstruction, and at the speech that defined it more fully than anything else he ever wrote or spoke.

At the time, the speech perplexed and disappointed those listeners who did not appreciate its importance as a statement of the goals of wartime reconstruction and the necessity of taking immediate steps toward reunion. Noah Brooks observed that the speech was "longer and of a different character from what most people had expected." Others, however, grasped all too well Lincoln's vision of the future, one simultaneously magnanimous and transformative.[16]

As Lincoln spoke, two men, lingering toward the front of the grounds, felt nauseated by what they heard. John Wilkes Booth tried to persuade Lewis Powell to shoot the president as he stood in the window, but Powell refused to take the chance. They departed. As they walked away, Booth remarked, "that is the last speech he will ever make." Three days later, he made good on his threat. We can never know what would have happened had Lincoln lived, but one writer was not alone when he predicted, "the development of things will teach us to mourn him doubly."[17]

Chapter 1

"A Large Share of Thought from the First"

"For the present at least we repudiate this term. We strike it from our vocabulary." The word that so inflamed the pro-Union editors of the *Louisville Journal* on February 5, 1861, was "Reconstruction." "Words are sometimes things," continued the editorial, "and this word 're-construction,' now flowing so glibly from the lips and pens of precipitators here, is that hideous thing DISUNION: nothing less."[1]

At the beginning of the secession crisis, before years of war and discussions of how to restore the Union, "reconstruction" was the term used to consider ways of retailoring the Constitution so as to prevent states in the Border and Upper South from seceding and entice states in the Lower South to return to the Union. One Northern editor believed the strategy of the secessionists was "for their States to secede—to go out of the Union, and wait to be invited back by the people of the free states—then to dictate their own terms and reconstruct the Union to suit themselves." Some pro-secession editorials suggested that citizens approve the "idea of forming at some future period another and a better Union, upon a basis of complete equality [of the states], and with inviolable constitutional guarantees. The reconstruction of the government hereafter is by no means chimerical....If the Southern States are left to the peaceable exercise of their sovereignty, there will be no insurmountable objection to another Union." The New Orleans *Daily Picayune* insisted, "the only process of reconstruction, short of subjugation which involves the extinction of the Saxon race South, must commence by a candid, bona fide recognition of the Confederate States, as an independent power."[2]

Many Southerners had their doubts there was any room for reconsidering the nature of the Union. No matter how completely the old Union was remodeled, argued the *Montgomery Weekly Post*, "to our mind there is no more prospect of a reconstruction of the old Government than there is a return of Northern arrogance and fanaticism to right reason and self-sacrificing justice." Do not even bother, thought the editor, to hold out any false hopes to Northerners that even with "recognition of our rights" the seceded states would return. A new Confederate Constitution had been adopted and the new nation should now find its own place in history. "We look upon a reconstruction of the Union," proclaimed the *Charleston Mercury*, "as inevitable destruction.... We look upon a Southern Confederacy as the thing to be desired." Secession was not a means to negotiate for a union under different terms; it was an end.[3]

Talk of a fundamental rewriting of the United States Constitution appalled most Republicans, who took every opportunity between December 1860 and April 1861 to denounce it. In an editorial titled "Secession and Reconstruction," the *New York Times* saw in secession a strategy by the seceding states to destroy the current Union and form a new one. "Until that is done disunion is incomplete. Reconstruction is the indispensible task, which the Southern seceding states have immediately before them." But, even if desired, this could never be accomplished: "the parts of a ship once dashed to pieces on the breakers can never be replaced." The author of a letter to the *Richmond Whig* agreed: "*Dissolution is revolutionary* and reconstruction afterward is hopeless, if not impossible." In an editorial titled "Reconstruction Not Practicable," the *Chicago Tribune* denounced "the pretence that a re-construction of the Union on terms more satisfactory to the South" was a "bald and shallow lie.... The present Union is the only one possible between the free and slave States."[4]

The abolitionist Frederick Douglass professed his astonishment at the idea of a national convention designed to make the Constitution "the express image of Slavery itself": "The old Constitution is found after all, to be deficient in pro-slavery provisions, ... [it] does not answer the purpose of the human flesh-mongers who delight in the blood and tears of their victims, so they must have another." Douglass declared, "The calamity of permanent disunion, great as it is, is nothing to this proposed plan of Reconstruction." William Lloyd Garrison, editor of the *Liberator*, endorsed the view that "Reconstruction can mean nothing else than either the surrender of the rebels and the destruction of slavery, or the surrender of the North and the slaughter of the Abolitionists." A contributor to the *Baltimore American* declared, "We have politicians, not statesmen, who propose the retirement of all the southern states in a mass and then, after a certain time, to work up a reconstruction of the Federal Government. This is either a great absurdity or a great crime.... When the burning torrent of revolution has blighted the land, and humanity, and liberty, reconstruction becomes a phantom."[5]

How would President-elect Abraham Lincoln respond to secession and would he support an attempt at a negotiated settlement? "The country has been waiting with great interest for the president's opinions on the important subject of reconstruction," wrote the *Chicago Tribune* in December. In hopes of finding answers, the public scrutinized the statements he made between election and inauguration day. Lincoln chose to remain silent. "I feel constrained," he wrote in a private letter to former Connecticut senator Truman Smith, "to make no declaration for the public." What he said publicly was innocuous enough: "Let us at all times remember that all American citizens are brothers of a common country, and should dwell together in the bonds of fraternal feeling."[6]

One reason for Lincoln's reticence was his anxiety over whether the electors would meet to confirm his election. He told Senator William H. Seward, "it seems to me the inauguration is not the most dangerous point for us. Our adversaries have us more closely at disadvantage on the second Wednesday of February, when the votes should be officially counted.... I do not think that this counting is constitutionally essential to the election, but how are we to proceed in absence of it?" Not until February 13, 1861, when the ballots were officially tallied, much to Lincoln's relief, was the election made official.

Of course, other reasons for his reticence, particularly not providing the secessionists with any ammunition, remained in force.[7]

While Lincoln would not speak publicly on secession and compromise, privately he made his position perfectly clear: he would not support a constitutional amendment that protected slavery by restoring and extending the Missouri Compromise line to the Pacific. That line emerged in 1820 when Congress admitted Missouri as a slave state and Maine as a free state, and included a provision that forever excluded slavery from the territories of the Louisiana Purchase north of the latitude 36°30′. The Kansas-Nebraska Act of 1854 in effect repealed the line, and the Dred Scot decision in 1857 found that Congress could not bar slavery from the territories. Now, in the crisis winter of 1860–1861, proposals were surfacing to appease Southern secessionists by allowing for the expansion of slavery.[8]

On December 10, Lincoln wrote to Illinois senator Lyman Trumbull, "Let there be no *compromise* on the question of *extending* slavery. If there be, all our labor is lost, and, ere long, must be done again.... The tug has to come, & better now, than any time hereafter." He repeated the message to other Republican politicians in letters marked "*private & confidential.*" He was especially direct with Seward, who was playing a lead role in congressional deliberations. On February 1, he told Seward that he was "inflexible" on the question of extending slavery: "I am for no compromise which *assists* or *permits* the extension of the institution on soil owned by the nation."[9]

At the same time, Lincoln acknowledged that the Constitution had to be enforced and that meant accepting the fugitive slave clause of Article IV, Section 2, and enforcing the Fugitive Slave Act of 1850, which had put the federal government in the business of returning runaway slaves to their masters. He also told Seward that as far as a bevy of other issues went—slavery in the District of Columbia, slave trade between states, even the status of New Mexico, whose admission to the Union as a slave state was being debated— "I care but little, so that what is done be comely, and not altogether outrageous."[10]

With respect to the Fugitive Slave Act, much as Lincoln disdained it, he could not call on secessionists to stand by the Constitution if he himself was willing to abrogate it. But he also would not have the Constitution revised to prevent secession. "I do not desire any amendment of the Constitution," he wrote on December 28 to Duff Green, whose *United States Telegraph* once served as the political organ for Andrew Jackson before Green came to support John C. Calhoun and nullification. Yet should the American people express a desire to amend the Constitution, he believed it was not in his authority to stand in their way as long as it was pursued "through either of the modes prescribed in the instrument."[11]

Lincoln had sent the letter to Green through Lyman Trumbull, with directions for him not to deliver it if he concluded that it would prove harmful. But Green must have seen it given that on January 7 he wrote to Lincoln and expressed his regret that the president-elect was unwilling "to recommend an amendment to the constitution which will arrest the progress of secession."[12]

Republicans were thrilled with the way Lincoln was handling the situation. Carl Schurz, a German immigrant who played a critical role in the formation of the Republican Party in Wisconsin, wrote his wife, "Lincoln has sent letters which have given a new spirit to even the most timorous. 'Old Abe' so far is splendid, and it would not surprise me if his administration were to determine the future development of the Republic."[13]

Lincoln's private thoughts made their way to the various members of the Senate and House who were considering proposals for compromise. The chief compromise plan had come on December 18 from Senator John J. Crittenden of Kentucky, a craggy-faced septuagenarian. Crittenden took the "Great Compromiser" Henry Clay as his model, believing compromise was possible and to that end he proposed six constitutional amendments and four congressional resolutions. If adopted, his amendments and resolutions would have revived the Missouri Compromise line, prevented Congress from abolishing slavery in those places where it had the power to do so, such as in the District of Columbia or on military posts in slave states, forbidden Congress from interfering in the interstate slave trade, and reinforced the Fugitive Slave Act. A clause that applied to territory "hereafter acquired" especially disturbed Lincoln, who saw it as a justification for filibustering expeditions and a demand to annex Cuba. Crittenden also included an amendment that stated no future amendment could change these proposed amendments or ever empower Congress to interfere with slavery. Nearly everything in Crittenden's proposal seemed like a concession to the South. For most Republicans, this was not compromise; it was surrender.

In the Senate, a Committee of Thirteen, established on the same day Crittenden introduced his plan, debated the proposals. On a separate track in the House, a Committee of Thirty-Three, created on December 4 and comprising one representative from every state, also began work on a proposed constitutional amendment that would protect slavery where it existed and permit New Mexico to enter the Union as a slave state. Another effort to resolve the secession crisis began on February 4, 1861, when more than one hundred politicians, representing fourteen free and seven slave states, held a "Peace Conference" in Washington and also proposed a constitutional amendment that contained multiple provisions.[14]

Time and again, moderate and radical Republicans denounced as misguided any of these attempts at preserving the Union. Seward, who as a member of the Committee of Thirteen had voted against the Crittenden proposal, delivered a speech on January 12 that received widespread attention. The silver-haired, cigar-smoking senator, "small in stature, big as to nose, light as to hair and eyes," had been the front-runner for the Republican nomination. However, speeches he had given in the 1850s that called the North–South conflict "irrepressible," and invoked a "higher law" than the Constitution, had made him seem too radical. Ironically, his would in the main be a conservative voice in Lincoln's cabinet. While Seward supported certain concessions, such as enforcement of the Fugitive Slave Act, he opposed any constitutional amendments except one, prohibiting congressional interference with slavery in states where it existed. Beyond that "I do not agree," he insisted, "with those who, with a desire to avert the great calamity, advise a conventional or unopposed separation, with a view to what they call reconstruction. It is enough for me, first, that in this plan, destruction goes before reconstruction; and secondly, that the strength of the vase in which the hopes of the nation are held consists chiefly in its remaining unbroken."[15]

Senator Charles Sumner of Massachusetts was not happy with Seward, who called for a national convention at some point in the future, after a cooling-off period, to discuss a possible compromise. Sumner told Salmon P. Chase, former governor of Ohio and Lincoln's choice as secretary of the Treasury, "I deplore S's speech," and said he had begged him "with all the ardor of my soul, to change his tone & especially to abandon every proposition of concession." He declared, "I am against any offer now, even of a peppercorn." Any concession or compromise would acknowledge "secession as a constitutional right." To John Andrew, governor of Massachusetts, Sumner declared, "we can offer no terms of Concession, or Compromise, in order to please the border states. The question must be met on the constitution *as it is & the facts as they are*, or we shall hereafter hold our Govt. subject to this asserted right of secession."[16]

Carl Schurz was also dismayed by Seward's speech. "He bows before the slave power," he wrote to his wife. "He has trodden the way of compromise and concession.... This is the time that tries men's souls, and many probably will be found wanting. Lincoln still stands like a stone wall. Every report from Springfield confirms my faith in him."[17]

Republican congressmen also rose up in January and February 1861 to denounce any compromise schemes and the absurdity of reconfiguring the relationship between the states. James H. Campbell of Pennsylvania warned that "*Reconstruction* implies previous *destruction*; and any party, or combination of men, that propose to destroy the American Union, must and will fail." Sidney Edgerton of Ohio, an abolitionist who carried a cane with a hidden sword in the event he was attacked (as Sumner had been, viciously, in the Senate), declared, "We hear much talk here about reconstruction, that the seceding States may come back with new constitutional guarantees to slavery. Let no one deceive himself with such a fallacy. The State which really gets out of this Union will never return.... And should any get out, when they attempt to return, they may realize the truth of the old poet: 'To go to hell is easy; but to come back again, *that* is labor, *that* is toil.'"[18]

No one was more prescient than Pennsylvania's Thaddeus Stevens, who, after the war, would press for a radical transformation of Southern society. Stevens was a power in the House. In a profile, Noah Brooks, the Washington correspondent for the *Sacramento Daily Union*, claimed, "whatever he opposes is well-nigh predestined to die, and whatever he supports is almost certain to go through." Nearing seventy, Stevens wore a dark brown wig and hobbled on a deformed foot. His thick eyebrows hid his eyes. "When he rises to speak," Brooks added, "he locks his hands loosely before him, and never makes a gesture but calmly, slowly, and ponderously drops his sentences as though each one weighed a ton."[19]

Stevens thundered:

> Let no slave State flatter itself that it can dissolve the Union now, and then reconstruct it on better terms. The present Constitution was formed in our weakness. Some of its compromises were odious, and have become more so by the unexpected increase of slaves, who were expected soon to run out. But now, in our strength, the conscience of the North would not allow them to enter into such partnership with slaveholding. If the Union should be dissolved, its reconstruction would embrace one empire wholly slaveholding, and one republic wholly free. While we will religiously observe the present compact, not attempt to be absolved from it, yet if it should be torn to pieces by rebels, our next United States will contain no foot of ground on which a slave can tread, no breath of air which a slave can breathe. Then we can boast of liberty.[20]

Stevens's fellow radical George W. Julian of Indiana put the matter simply: "the rebels have demanded a 'reconstruction' on the basis of slavery; let us give them a 'reconstruction' on the basis of freedom."[21]

With President-elect Lincoln steadfastly opposed to any compromise that altered the Constitution to protect slavery and allow for its expansion, and Republican politicians largely in agreement, all proposals failed. Some of the prolonged discussion was little more than a delaying tactic on the part of Republicans who awaited Lincoln's inauguration. After all, the seven states that had seceded between December 20 and February 1 did not participate in compromise discussions. When plans for the Peace Conference in Washington emerged, Governor Oliver P. Morton of Indiana wrote to Lincoln and explained the strategy for Republican participation: "Another reason is that time wears out revolutions. It might be a measure of procrastination, to delay fatal action, until the dead points of danger, the counting the votes, and the inauguration, were passed." Carl Schurz thought it important to participate because "it shows the South our desire to meet its complaints. It enables us to cultivate good relationships with the border slave states—Virginia, Kentucky, Tennessee, etc.,—to quietly discuss the causes of dispute, tell them the truth, prolong the debate and, what on our side is of critical importance, *gain time.*" The strategy succeeded. Writing to Morton from the conference, Indiana delegate Godlove S. Orth reported, "we have thus far done all in our power to procrastinate, and shall continue to do so, in order to remain in session until after the 4th of March. For after the inauguration we shall have an honest fearless man at the helm, and will soon know whether the honest masses of the People desire to preserve and perpetuate our Government."[22]

On March 4, Lincoln delivered his inaugural address and at last spoke freely in a voice that, according to one eyewitness, "rang out over the acres of people before him with surprising distinctness." He assured "the people of the Southern States" that he stood by what he had already said many times over. Indeed, he quoted himself: "I have no purpose, directly or indirectly, to interfere with the institution of slavery in the States where it exists. I believe I have no lawful right to do so, and I have no inclination to do so." He proceeded to deny any constitutional grounds for secession. "The Union of these States is perpetual," he insisted. "No State upon its own mere notion, can lawfully get out of the Union.... The Union is unbroken." Secession, he observed, "is the essence of anarchy." His administration would continue to execute the laws of the United States and there would be no violence unless "it be forced upon the national authority." Toward the end of the address, he appealed to common institutions and traditions, "bonds of affection" and—famously—the "mystic chords of memory," to the reality that, "physically speaking, we cannot separate. We cannot remove our respective sections from each other, nor build an impassable wall between them."[23]

Lincoln's inaugural is seldom read for insights into his approach to saving and restoring the Union as opposed to its resolute stand against its dissolution, yet several aspects of the address are telling. Most significant is the idea of the indissoluble union. If the Confederate states never left the union because secession was unconstitutional, the residents of those states were still entitled to their rights as citizens even though they were in rebellion. The states would resume their place through the establishment of legitimate state governments by loyal citizens. Soon enough, radical Republicans would oppose this theory of indissoluble union and offer other ways of viewing the Confederate states, ways that would justify making greater demands on them, not only politically but also socially before they could be restored.

When toward the end of the inaugural Lincoln called upon his countrymen to "think calmly and *well*, upon this whole subject," he was expressing a central element of his temperament. Lincoln was a patient man whose careful deliberations often infuriated those who thought of him as stubborn and obdurate. By nature he was a gradualist, willing to let time itself act as the central agent of change. "Nothing valuable can be lost by taking time," he advised. This too would characterize his approach to preserving the nation, which would evolve, but only after he allowed various initiatives to run their course.[24]

When four months later Lincoln sent a message to Congress in special session, secession had become war. Eleven slave states, with a total population of nine million, some three and a half million of whom were enslaved, formed the Confederacy. Four border slave states—Delaware, Maryland, Kentucky, and Missouri—remained in the Union. The Union consisted of twenty-three states, with a population of almost twenty-two million, a half million of whom were slaves. Soon after the firing on Fort Sumter on April 12, Lincoln summoned seventy-five thousand men to put down the insurrection and imposed a naval blockade on all Southern ports.

Lincoln described to Congress what had been his approach to resolving the crisis peacefully prior to Fort Sumter: "relying … on time, discussion, and the ballot-box." But "the seceded states, so called," wanted to dissolve the Union and this, as president, he would not allow. Secession, he proclaimed, was "an ingenious sophism" for rebellion, trying to give legitimacy to a scheme for "the complete destruction of the Union." Lincoln gave voice to what the war was truly about: its aim was to preserve the Union. In time, emancipating the slaves would become both a means of accomplishing that goal and an end in itself. Trumping both, however, was the question of democracy. Anticipating what he would state even more powerfully at the close of his Gettysburg Address on November 19, 1863, Lincoln told Congress that secession "presents to the whole family of man, the question, whether a constitutional republic, or a democracy—a government of the people, by the same people—can, or cannot, maintain its territorial integrity, against its own domestic foes." He went on to ask, "Must a government, of necessity, be too *strong* for the liberties of its own people, or too *weak* to maintain its own existence?" For him, democracy was a form of government that allowed people to rise in the world, its aim "to elevate the condition of men—to lift artificial weights from all shoulders—to clear the paths of laudable pursuit for all—to afford all, an unfettered start, and a fair chance, in the race of life." Lincoln was more than a year away from deciding to issue an emancipation proclamation, but beliefs such as these smoothed his journey to abolition.[25]

Remarkably, in that message to Congress Lincoln discussed what would happen once the rebellion was over. Perhaps he could do so in July because the war had not begun in earnest and no one in mid-1861 could have imagined what was to come. He could do so as well because of his firm belief that everywhere but in South Carolina "the Union men are the majority." Much of his thinking toward eventual reconstruction hinged on providing Southern unionists with the opportunity and means to reclaim control of their state governments. That meant fulfilling the Constitution's mandate that "the United States shall guarantee to every State in this Union a republican form of government." The citizens, in other words, governed themselves by virtue of electing those who made and administered the laws. "The course of the government, towards the Southern States, *after* the rebellion shall have been suppressed," he said, would be guided "then, as ever," by the Constitution.[26]

The issue of reunification was not merely theoretical because developments in Virginia had already provided the first opportunity for Lincoln to consider a state's return to the Union. Until Fort Sumter and Lincoln's call for seventy-five thousand troops to put down the rebellion, delegates to the Virginia state convention that convened in Richmond on February 13 had tilted against secession. Indeed, of the 152 delegates who had been chosen, only about one-third consisted of determined secessionists. On April 17, however, by a vote of 88–55, delegates passed an Ordinance of Secession that repealed the state's ratification of the Constitution. What tipped the balance, in the aftermath of Fort Sumter, was the belief that the federal government had no right to coerce a state militarily. A referendum on the ordinance would be held on May 23.

Three days after the Richmond convention acted, John S. Carlile hurried to Washington to meet with Lincoln. Carlile had been a delegate to the convention from Harrison County in the western part of Virginia, where Unionist sentiment ran high. A former state senator and United States congressman, Carlile was also a slaveholder, but he believed the institution would survive only if Virginians remained in the Union and accepted at face value Lincoln's assurances not to interfere with slavery where it already existed. "It is nothing but the prestige and the power of the General Government now that guarantees to the slaveholder his right," he argued.[27]

After Lincoln encouraged Carlile to rally unionist support in western Virginia, some twelve hundred citizens met in Clarksburg and called for a convention in Wheeling to "determine upon such action as the people of Northwestern Virginia should take in the present fearful emergency." Most delegates thought it best to wait and see whether Virginians approved the Ordinance of Secession on May 23, but not Carlile, who went so far as to propose the breaking off of the state's Trans-Allegheny counties from the eastern ones and the creation of a new state to be called New Virginia. (He would change his mind, but others would not be dissuaded from moving toward forming a new state.) Following Virginia's ratification of the secession ordinance, a second Wheeling convention met on June 11. Carlile wrote a "Declaration of the People of Virginia" that denounced the secession convention, which "has attempted to transfer the allegiance of the people to an illegal confederacy of rebellious States, and required their submission to its pretended edicts and decrees." On June 19, the Wheeling convention delegates voted unanimously to reorganize the government of Virginia. This new government was known as the Restored Government of Virginia, and Francis Pierpont, a prominent attorney and pro-Union activist, was unanimously elected governor. Carlile was elected United States senator to replace R. M. T. Hunter, and Waitman Willey to replace James Mason.[28]

Whether the Senate would accept their credentials led to a brief but volatile debate. Senators James Bayard and Willard Saulsbury, Democrats from Delaware, opposed seating the men, arguing that doing so would be a step toward unifying the nation "under a military despotism," that the men were not elected by representatives of a majority of the counties of Virginia, and that technically the seats to which they were elected were not vacant, since at the time Hunter and Mason had yet to be expelled. In response, Senator John P. Hale of New Hampshire argued that because "the Union loving men of Virginia yet recognized the United States government, and asked to be represented," the election was legal and constitutional, and that elections were always held while an incumbent occupied a seat, so the question of vacancy was moot. Both Carlile and Willey were seated when, by a vote of 35–5, the Senate refused to refer the matter to the Judiciary Committee.[29]

There were dangers in rushing to acknowledge all claims to office. Where there was opportunity, there was always the potential for fraud. On the Outer Banks of North Carolina, which came under Union military control in August 1861, Charles Henry Foster got himself elected to the U.S. House of Representatives after a half-dozen delegates to a convention appointed a provisional governor and held an election. Foster was a character out of a Herman Melville short story, a con artist of the first order. Born in Maine and a graduate of Bowdoin College, Foster was an abolitionist until he moved to Norfolk, Virginia, and then Murfreesboro, North Carolina. He married a slave owner's daughter, and became a Democrat. With secession, he found it expedient to declare for the Union, and wrote to Lincoln to request a meeting and then announced his intention to run for public office. On four separate occasions Foster claimed to have been elected to Congress, once with a total of 268 votes. The House of Representatives put an end to the farce on December 18 when it definitively rejected his claims.[30]

Much as Lincoln sought the election of representatives by loyal citizens, he could distinguish between the travesty of events in North Carolina and the legitimacy of events in Virginia. On June 21, Pierpont wrote to Lincoln and requested "a military force to aid in suppressing the rebellion." That force was already at work under the command of George B. McClellan, whose military success in western Virginia in June and July elevated him to national attention and command of the Army of the Potomac. Union control of northwestern Virginia would prove of strategic importance. One historian notes that it provided a buffer for Ohio and Pennsylvania, offered cover for the western flank of Union armies in the Shenandoah Valley, and denied the Confederacy access to valuable natural resources. Lincoln understood that any possibilities for restored or reorganized governments elsewhere would be contingent on Union victories and the ability of the army to keep Confederate forces in check.[31]

Secretary of War Simon Cameron responded to Pierpont's letter: "the President directs me to say a large additional force will soon be sent to your relief" and that Lincoln "never supposed that a brave and free people, though surprised and unarmed could long be subjected by a class of political adventures always adverse to them; and the fact that they have already rallied, reorganized their government, and checked the march of these invaders, demonstrates how justly he appreciated them." When the Restored Government of Virginia met in Wheeling in July, Pierpont happily announced that Lincoln had offered "full protection" to the citizens of western Virginia.[32]

In his July 4, 1861, message, Lincoln told Congress that "the course taken in Virginia was the most remarkable—perhaps the most important" resurgence of Union sentiment. Lincoln proclaimed, "those loyal citizens, this government is bound to recognize and protect, as being Virginia." Lincoln deleted from the final text a response to anyone who wondered who was the rightful governor of Virginia. The original passage read: "Suppose two respectable gentlemen, both of whom have sworn to support the constitution of the United States, shall each, at the same time, claim to be Governor of Virginia. Which of the two should this government recognize? Him who disregards, or him who keeps, his oath, in this respect?" The logic seemed both simple and irrefutable.[33]

The issue of the Restored Government of Virginia would become more complicated over the next two years as delegates met in constitutional convention to create a new state to be named, after much debate, West Virginia ("Kanawha," "Allegheny," and "Columbia" were among the alternatives). Article IV, Section III, of the Constitution provides that while new states may be admitted by Congress no new states "shall be formed or erected within the jurisdiction of any other state; nor any state be formed by the junction of two or more states, or parts of states, without the consent of the legislatures of the states concerned as well as of the Congress." The Restored Government of Virginia passed an act in May 1862 that consented to the creation of a new state.

Through 1862, both the Senate and the House vigorously debated the question of West Virginia. One issue was whether admitting this new state was constitutional; the other concerned the status of slavery within its borders. Disavowing any idea of legal or constitutional right, Thaddeus Stevens argued, "we may admit West Virginia as a new state, not by virtue of any provision of the Constitution but under the absolute power which the laws of war give us." At the precise moment in December 1862 that Stevens invoked the war powers, Lincoln was weeks away from issuing his Emancipation Proclamation that was based on his powers as commander in chief and the idea of military necessity.

The West Virginia bill that came before Lincoln in late December included a provision for gradual emancipation of those slaves under the age of twenty-one, depending on when they were born. Stevens supported the bill and argued that the "Union shall never with my consent be restored under the Constitution as it is with slavery to be protected by it; and I am in favor of admitting West Virginia because I find here a provision which makes it a free state." Radicals such as Sumner saw the slavery issue differently, voting against the bill because it did not abolish slavery immediately in West Virginia. Sumner denounced the gradual emancipation provision, which "proposes to recognize the existence of slavery during the present generation. Short as life may be it is too long for slavery. If this condition be adopted, and the bill becomes a law, a new slave State will take its place in our Union."[34]

Both the Senate and House passed the bill, and it came before Lincoln for his signature. On December 15, Orville Browning, senator from Illinois and a close friend of Lincoln's, said the president "was distressed at its passage and asked me how long he could retain it before approving or vetoing." Browning told him ten days, and to give the president more time he gave him only a copy of the bill to examine and did not officially present it until the following week. On December 23, Lincoln asked his cabinet for written opinions on two questions: whether admission of West Virginia was constitutional and whether it was expedient.[35]

Of the seven members of Lincoln's cabinet three were in favor of West Virginia statehood and three against. (Interior Secretary Caleb Smith, about to leave office, to be replaced by John Palmer Usher, did not offer an opinion.) Edward Bates, the attorney general, argued the bill was unconstitutional because Congress could only "admit" states and not "form" them. It was inexpedient as well, because admitting West Virginia "may disjoint the fabric of our national government, and destroy the balance of power in Congress." Montgomery Blair, the postmaster general, argued that the Restored Government of Virginia did not satisfy the constitutional requirement of consent. "The Federal Government," argued Secretary of the Navy Gideon Welles, "is not authorized to divide or dismember a state."[36]

Countering his colleagues, Seward argued that the Restored Government of Virginia had standing to give the necessary constitutional permission: "So long as the United States do not recognize the secession, departure, or separation of one of the States, that State must be deemed as existing and having a Constitutional place within the Union, whatever may be at any moment exactly its revolutionary condition." On the issue of expediency, Secretary of the Army Edwin Stanton "thought it politic and wise to plant a Free state south of Ohio." Although he privately told Lincoln that he opposed the provision for gradual emancipation, preferring instead immediate, compensated emancipation, Chase thought the act of "vital importance" and believed there was "no valid constitutional objection."[37]

On December 31, Lincoln decided in favor of West Virginia statehood. With an eye toward affirming the measure's constitutionality, he asked, rhetorically, "Can this government stand, if it indulges constitutional constructions by which men in open rebellion against it, are to be accounted, man for man, the equals of those who maintain their loyalty to it?" As for expediency, he argued that it depends on whether the act would "tend the more strongly to the restoration of national authority throughout the Union." He believed that it would. And in response to those who claimed that by admitting West Virginia, the government was in effect promoting secession, he observed, "Well, if we call it by that name there is still difference enough between secession against the constitution, and secession in favor of the constitution."[38]

West Virginia officially entered the Union on June 20, 1863. The gradual emancipation provision rankled radicals and abolitionists, but what Lincoln most cared about at this point was that emancipation would occur, not when and how it took place. Freedom would not come to some eighteen thousand slaves in West Virginia until February 1865, when the governor signed an act that immediately abolished slavery in the state. Having helped create West Virginia, Pierpont's Restored Government would continue through the war to operate from Alexandria as the recognized state government of Virginia. Southern Unionists would not carve any new states out of the Confederacy, but the actions of Unionists in the western counties of Virginia provided a model that Lincoln hoped pointed the way to the establishment of loyal civil governments in other seceded states. There would be no reconstruction of the nation as secessionists had envisioned it. But a different reconstruction, led by Southern Unionists and supported by Lincoln, might help end the war and save the country.

Chapter 2

"Proper, Practical Relation"

Buoyed by the Restored Government in Virginia, and eager to help promote restoration elsewhere, between March and November 1862, Lincoln appointed military governors in Tennessee, North Carolina, Louisiana, Arkansas, and Texas. Though the specific wording of the commissions varied, their responsibility was to "re-establish the authority of the Federal Government" and provide protection for Unionists in their efforts to establish civil government. The results varied, depending on a variety of factors, including military success, the actions of the individual military governor, and the nature and extent of Southern Unionism in the five states. But Lincoln's intentions were clear and the story of the military governors is pivotal to understanding wartime reconstruction.[1]

Tennessee

Tennessee became the first state with a military governor when, on March 3, Lincoln appointed Senator Andrew Johnson to the position, with the rank of "brigadier general." It is too easy now to see Johnson only as a reprehensible politician whose presidency ended in disarray, but in 1862 he was viewed as a Union hero for refusing to abandon his Senate seat when Tennessee opted for secession. Poor and uneducated, he rose to serve as a congressman and as governor of Tennessee before becoming a senator. He was a Southern Democrat of the Jacksonian persuasion and a slaveholder who opposed Lincoln's election, but who believed passionately in the Union and opportunities for the common man.[2]

Johnson's return to Nashville was made possible by surprising Union triumphs at Forts Henry and Donelson in February 1862 and the costly victory at Shiloh in April. The Union controlled much of western and middle Tennessee, but it was eastern Tennessee that was most strongly Unionist. Here, however, the Confederate army maintained control. Even before Johnson's appointment, Lincoln stressed to General Don Carlos Buell, who commanded Union forces in middle Tennessee, the significance of east Tennessee, where "our friends... are being hanged and driven to despair, and even now I fear are thinking of taking rebel arms for the sake of personal protection. In this we lose the most valuable stake we have in the South."[3]

Johnson would continue to press Lincoln to launch a military operation to liberate east Tennessee, and he often clashed with Buell. The conflict highlighted the tension in overlapping authorities between the military governor and military commanders in the field. Lincoln tried to assuage Johnson by reassuring him that he had control "in your own localities." He also reminded Henry Halleck, on the same day he appointed him general-in-chief of Union forces, "The Gov. is a true, and a valuable man—indispensable to us in Tennessee."[4]

Lincoln in turn pressed Johnson to hold elections: "If we could, somehow, get a vote of the people of Tennessee and have it result properly it would be worth more to us than a battle gained." Wartime reconstruction, Lincoln understood, was a means of hastening victory. "How long before we can get such a vote?" he asked on July 3, 1862. But Johnson believed he could not proceed without east Tennessee in the fold. He responded, "as soon as the Rebel army can be expelled from East Tennessee there can & will be an expression of public opinion that will surprise you." The liberation of east Tennessee would continue to be the stumbling block. A year later, Lincoln heard from General Stephen Hurlbut that although Tennessee was ready to repeal the act of secession and establish gradual emancipation, action would have to wait for the liberation of east Tennessee.[5]

Upon arriving in Nashville, Johnson issued an "Appeal to the People of Tennessee." Dated March 18, 1862, it is a cogent statement of the administration's approach to restoration at that point. Johnson declared that the national government, which has been challenged by a "rebellious, armed force," remained committed to its constitutional obligation "to guarantee to every State in this Union a republican form of government." As military governor, his responsibility was "to preserve the public property of the State, to give the protection of law actively enforced to her citizens, and, as speedily as may be, to restore the government to the same condition as before the existing rebellion." He assured the people that all state offices would be filled by those who bore allegiance to the Constitution and to the government of the United States and that "the erring and misguided will be welcomed on their return." Indeed, "a full and complete amnesty for all past acts and declarations is offered, upon the one condition of their again yielding themselves peaceful citizens to the just supremacy of the laws."[6]

In practice, Johnson was not as conciliatory as he sounded in his initial message. Citizens who refused to take an oath of allegiance were imprisoned; he muzzled newspapers, assumed control of the Bank of Tennessee, and authorized seizure of Confederate property; he even had clergymen who supported the Confederacy arrested. Johnson said he punished these men not because of religion, but because "they are traitors and enemies of society, law and order."[7]

At the same time, he reassured slaveholders that the war was not being fought to abolish slavery. In a lengthy address in Nashville delivered in March, Johnson told Unionist slaveholders that they were secure in their property. "Where has the institution of slavery been invaded?" he asked. Pandering to his audience, with whom he shared racial antipathies, Johnson said he often asked the administration if the war was being fought against slavery. Their response, he said, was "we've got more niggers at home than we want; d—n the niggers. When we have established the rightful power of the Government, we mean to return to our homes and our avocations." The Constitution, he argued, was the best security for preserving slavery. "If you want to enjoy your slave property unmolested," he advised, "seek to restore the protection of the Government."[8]

Yet even as Johnson spoke, Lincoln had begun to move against slavery. On March 6, he had offered the first emancipation proposal ever submitted to Congress by a president. He asked Congress to provide financial aid to any state that would adopt a gradual plan of abolition. He had in mind the Border States, and hoped that if these states moved against slavery it would dampen the hopes of secessionists to one day create a united Confederacy of slave states. Sumner read a draft of the proposal and was shocked by one sentence that Lincoln had included: "Should the people of the insurgent districts now reject the councils of treason, revive loyal state governments, and again send Senators and Representatives to Congress, they would, at once find themselves at peace, with no institution changed." Soon enough, Lincoln would no longer envision the restoration of the nation with slavery possibly intact. He deleted the sentence. Frederick Douglass thought he understood clearly where the president was headed: "a blind man can see where the President's heart is."[9]

Still, Lincoln moved cautiously and deliberately, preferring gradual emancipation and desiring not to alienate Southern Unionists unnecessarily. On July 22, 1862, he informed his cabinet of his decision to issue an emancipation proclamation, but withheld it until after the Union victory at Antietam on September 17. The preliminary Emancipation Proclamation of September 22 gave notice that on January 1, 1863, the slaves of those held in states, or parts of states, in rebellion shall be "forever free." Lincoln was acting out of military necessity and in conjunction with the Second Confiscation Act that had been passed by Congress. Areas under Union control that had elected representatives to Congress would be exempted from the proclamation. Compensation would be given to those who had remained loyal throughout the rebellion "upon restoration of the constitutional relation between the United States, and their respective states, and people."[10]

Many leading Tennessee Unionists were appalled and asked Lincoln to exempt Tennessee from the Emancipation Proclamation. Johnson was among the signatories of a petition dated December 4 that explained the delays in holding any elections: rebel forces needed to be expelled and "the minds of the people quieted before we can have any-thing like a fair expression of the wishes of the people." Intent on not alienating Unionists in Tennessee, and hopeful that elections would soon be held, Lincoln duly exempted Tennessee from the Emancipa-tion Proclamation, even though the state did not meet the requirement for exemption that it have elected representatives to Congress.[11]

Within a year, Johnson converted to emancipation. He freed his slaves on August 8, 1863, and began to give speeches denouncing slavery. He even went so far as to tell a black audience, "I will indeed be your Moses and lead you through the Red Sea of war and bondage to a promised future of liberty and peace." After the war, blacks would be sorely disappointed with Johnson, who in reality cared little about their future, held racist beliefs about their capacity and place in the United States, and would take actions as president that would erode black freedom.[12]

Whatever Johnson's motivation in turning against slavery, no one was more delighted than Lincoln, who wrote on September 11, 1863, "I see that you have declared in favor of Emancipation in Tennessee, for which, may God bless you. Get Emancipation into your new State government—Constitution—and there will be no such word as fail in your case." Lincoln again pressed for elections and advised Johnson, "let the reconstruction be the work of such men only as can be trusted for the Union." His message came just days after Union forces, under Ambrose Burnside, entered Knoxville and sought to liberate east Tennessee. The year was nearing its end and Lincoln would soon issue a major proclamation on reconstruction, but despite these developments restoration in Tennessee was still far away.[13]

North Carolina

Far less successful than efforts in Tennessee was the attempt to restore North Carolina. As would be the case wherever wartime reconstruction was to occur, Union military victories set the stage for the experiment. Between February and June 1862, Burnside conducted a successful expedition in eastern North Carolina, with victories at Roanoke Island, New Bern, Fort Macon, and Tranter's Creek. Burnside took control of Albermarle and Pamlico Sounds, the strategically important town of New Bern, and Fort Macon, which commanded the channel that led to Beaufort. Prior to the firing on Fort Sumter, North Carolina, like Virginia, had opposed secession; as a result Lincoln, as well as many others, overestimated the extent of Union fervor in the state, which, unlike western Virginia or eastern Tennessee, did not have a concentrated population of Unionists.[14]

On May 26, Lincoln appointed Edward Stanly as military governor of North Carolina. Stanly, born in New Bern in 1810, served as a Whig in Congress from 1837 to 1843. He moved to California in 1853 where he practiced law and, in 1857, ran unsuccessfully for governor of the state as a Republican. Stanly was a staunch Unionist but no abolitionist, and almost from the start his actions with respect to blacks raised the ire of radicals in Congress. Although he later denied or tried to explain away his actions, he opposed the opening of a school for black children and had a fugitive slave returned to a Unionist in New Bern. Stanly's approach, as explained in a letter to Edwin Stanton, was to assure North Carolinians that "this is a war of restoration and not abolition and destruction."[15]

Word of Stanly's actions reached Washington, and Sumner took to the Senate floor to denounce the military governor and demand from Stanton a copy of Stanly's orders. A few days later, he raised questions about military governors in general—"a post unknown to the Constitution and laws of the Union"—and suggested that the subordination of civil to military authority was in "derogation of the powers of Congress." Who would rightfully establish policies to govern reunion, the president or Congress, was on the mind of at least one radical Republican.[16]

On July 7, Stanly wrote to Lincoln that, "my conduct has been so much misunderstood, and so many exaggerated reports have appeared in the newspapers, of the declarations of members of the Cabinet, that my influence is weakened. Reports are rife that I am soon to be removed." Stanly still had the support of Stanton and Burnside and, on September 29, Lincoln told him that his conduct "has my entire approbation." He added, "I shall be much gratified if you can find it practicable to have Congressional elections held in that State before January—It is my sincere wish that North Carolina may again govern herself conformably to the Constitution of the United States."[17]

Stanly made little progress in restoring civil government, in part because the military situation remained tenuous, but to a greater degree because a strong nucleus of Unionist leaders did not emerge. Pressed by Lincoln, Stanly scheduled an election for January 1, though he also helped make certain that the winner was his preferred candidate, Jennings Pigott, a former Whig and Washington slave owner (who petitioned for compensation after the District of Columbia abolished slavery in April 1862). His opponent was none less than Charles Henry Foster, the man who had previously claimed to have been elected. The House refused to seat Pigott, despite the fact that he had received 595 of 864 votes. The ballots cast came from only three of the eleven counties in the district. In one of those counties, only one precinct voted. If this was the restoration of civil government, it was a farce.[18]

Stanly soon resigned as military governor (the Emancipation Proclamation, issued on January 1, was anathema to him) and returned to California, where he waged a campaign against abolition. In supporting George McClellan in the election of 1864, Stanly argued that the Emancipation Proclamation "has driven hundreds of thousands of men from their advocacy of the restoration of the Union." In 1865, he published *A Military Governor among the Abolitionists*, a screed directed as an open letter to Charles Sumner in which he denounces the senator's "malice" and "holy indignation." Stanly's failure in North Carolina would leave Lincoln reluctant to try again to restore the state. Before breaking entirely from the president, Stanly wrote in January 1864 that there seemed to be movement among Unionists for a state peace convention. Lincoln had heard similar rumors, but was noncommittal: "I am unable to suggest anything definite upon the subject."[19]

Arkansas

Lincoln also placed some hopes in the Arkansas Unionists who had avidly resisted secession. Union general Samuel R. Curtis led the Army of the Southwest into northwestern Arkansas and won a key victory at Pea Ridge on March 7, 1862. The victory gave Union forces control of the Missouri River and secured the state of Missouri against the threat of Confederate invasion. Curtis would later march across northern and central Arkansas. Helena, taken over by Union forces in July 1863, served as base for an assault on Little Rock.

Nearly a year earlier, on July 19, 1862, Lincoln had appointed John S. Phelps as military governor. Stanton's instructions to Phelps stated, "the great purpose of your appointment is to re-establish the authority of the Federal Government." Born in Connecticut, Phelps moved to Missouri when he was twenty-six and began a legal practice. From 1845 to 1863, he served as a Democrat in the House of Representatives. When war came, Phelps enlisted, rising eventually to rank of colonel. He even organized a regiment called Phelps's Regiment, Missouri Volunteer Infantry, which fought at Pea Ridge. Phelps, according to one report, was "struck by bullets five times within less than twenty minutes" and contracted malaria from the swamps of the lower Mississippi.[20]

Phelps, a slaveholder, had written Lincoln on November 18, 1861, to complain about the actions of Union soldiers in Missouri. Some of the soldiers, he reported, were "averring *the war is prosecuted to liberate the slaves.* This must be stopped. The war is waged for no such purpose. I am as much entitled to the protection of my slaves as I am entitled to the protection of my dwelling house. The Secessionists & rebels did not rob any one in South West Mo or in this state as far as I know of their slaves."[21] What was the use of any government that robs its citizens?

Lincoln had recently dealt with General John C. Fremont, who had issued a proclamation that imposed martial law and declared slaves of rebels free. Lincoln ordered Fremont to amend the proclamation. The general had no authority to free slaves in a Confederate state, much less one that remained in the Union. To now learn that the slaves of loyal, Unionist citizens were being freed not only violated Lincoln's understanding of constitutional protections but also posed a challenge to the belief that restoration would come by assuring Southern Unionists in the border states that their property was secure.

Upon arrival in Helena, Phelps, too, was unhappy. He complained bitterly to Stanton that military efforts were not being made to extend Union authority over larger portions of Arkansas. He was also disgusted to learn that rather than fight, Union officers had remained in Helena to speculate in cotton, and even reported that one colonel had exchanged two contrabands, the term widely used for slaves who ran away and presented themselves to Union lines, for a bale of cotton. He called for the appointment of a new departmental commander and an increase in the fighting force. If the establishment of civil government depended on continued military success, the situation in Arkansas did not look promising.[22]

Nonetheless, Lincoln urged in November 1862 that elections be organized in Arkansas. "In all available ways give the people a chance to express their wishes at these elections," he wrote to Phelps. "Follow law & forms of law as far as convenient, but at all events get the expression of the largest number of people possible. All see how such action will connect with and affect the proclamation of September 22." Here Lincoln was referring to the offer made in the preliminary Emancipation Proclamation: that any states or portions of states that elected representatives to Congress would be exempt from its provisions when he issued the final Proclamation on January 1.[23]

With Phelps ill and soon to be convalescing in St. Louis, Lincoln asked William M. McPherson to arrange elections. McPherson reported he was "greatly encouraged at the prospect of getting an election *if* the people can be sufficiently protected by the movements of the army." This would prove to be a recurring problem for Lincoln: however much territory Union forces controlled, there was always more to be taken, and often in places where Unionist sentiment ran highest. McPherson was negotiating with Lincoln for a delay in having the terms of the Emancipation Proclamation apply to Arkansas: "Can I give the people assureance [*sic*] that if they act in good faith and elect a member within the month of January it will save them?" McPherson also wrote Montgomery Blair, the postmaster general, and asked him to bring these views before the president. Finally, on Christmas day, McPherson told the president, "the Union men urge that more time should be allowed them before they are brought under the provisions of the proclamation." He has also concluded "that it is impracticable to hold an election at present because we do not hold any Country in the Eastern part of the state outside of the camp lines at Helena."[24]

The military successes that Phelps and McPherson saw as a prerequisite for success arrived in September 1863, when Frederick Steele, placed in command of the Army of Arkansas, captured Little Rock (McPherson had urged the appointment in his Christmas Day letter, arguing that Steele "is neither mixed up with cotton speculations or meddleing [*sic*] with the nigger question"). No elections, however, were held.[25]

Lincoln chose not to exempt Arkansas from the Emancipation Proclamation. Perhaps a letter he had received from Benjamin Gratz Brown persuaded him. Brown, an influential lawyer and a founder of Missouri's Republican Party, told Lincoln he had "grave doubts" about initiating elections before the Emancipation Proclamation went into effect. Brown, more radical than the president on the issue of emancipation (he thought it should apply to Missouri as well), argued, "I can see very good reason why Arkansas should not be an exception." He pointed out that Goveror Phelps—"who is hostile to the whole policy of the Admn on the slavery question"—had given aid to proslavery rebel sympathizers and will "*of course* do nothing to advance the views of the government." Phelps's appointment was revoked on July 9, 1863, and the office of military governor in Arkansas abolished.[26]

At the same moment, a new opportunity in Arkansas came to Lincoln's attention. Apparently, William K. Sebastian, who had served in the U.S. Senate since 1848 and resigned when Arkansas seceded, wanted to return to Washington and reclaim his seat. One writer informed the president, "I believe Judge S. to be a consistent Union man." Lincoln was intrigued and wrote to General Stephen Hurlbut, who commanded the XVI Corps and was based in Memphis, where Sebastian had moved after Federal forces occupied Helena.[27]

Lincoln began by acknowledging that it was entirely up the Senate whether to readmit Sebastian (he had been formally expelled on July 11, 1861, along with other senators who vacated their seats to join the Confederacy) but also confessed, "I should feel great interest in the question. It may be so presented as to be one of the very greatest national importance." Lincoln hoped Sebastian would propose a plan of gradual emancipation, which, he believed, "would be better for black and white." The previous month, with respect to a proposed plan for Missouri that, if passed, would not begin for seven years, Lincoln had written, "*gradual* can be made better than *immediate* for both black and white," but he hoped that the period of gradual emancipation would be "comparatively short."[28]

Lincoln told Hurlbut, "the emancipation proclamation applies to Arkansas. I think it is valid in law, and will be so held by the courts. I think I shall not retract or repudiate it. Those who have tasted actual freedom I believe can never be slaves, or quasi slaves again." If Sebastian would take the lead in moving his state toward emancipation, Lincoln wanted Hurlbut to assure the former senator that he took great interest in his case and that Sebastian would have the satisfaction of knowing that "a single individual will have scarcely done the world so great a service." Hurlbut, however, was skeptical: "I doubt if Sebastian has nerve enough, to accept the necessities of the times."[29]

Indeed, Sebastian did not act. But other developments among Arkansas Unionists in fall 1863 seemed more promising. On October 30, delegates to a meeting at Fort Smith called for a state constitutional convention to meet in January 1864. Hurlbut wrote in December, "I am and have been thoroughly convinced that Arkansas can by vote of its people be brought into the Union without slavery, by simply encouraging & sustaining the 'Unconditional Union' men of that State, and by so directing military operations as to give them the opportunity of Action." The convention would meet, adopt a Free-State constitution, and elect representatives to Congress. Nonetheless Arkansas would become embroiled in 1864 in a growing battle between Lincoln and Congress over reconstruction.[30]

Texas

In Tennessee, North Carolina, Louisiana, and Arkansas, appointment of a military governor followed Union military victories. In Texas, Lincoln first appointed a military governor and then began to plan military operations. The person he chose, Andrew Jackson Hamilton, met with him in October and November 1862; by that point, Hamilton had become the poster boy for hardships endured by Southern Unionists at the hands of treacherous Confederates. He was also feted for having been a one-time slaveholder who now fully embraced abolition of the institution.

Born in Alabama in 1815, Hamilton moved to Texas in 1846 and practiced law. He served as attorney general and a member of the state House of Representatives before being elected to the Thirty-Sixth Congress in 1859. Hamilton served on the Committee of Thirty-Three that had sought compromise during the secession winter of 1860–1861. In a speech delivered on February 1, the day a Texas convention approved separation from the Union, he denounced any right of secession and defended the Constitution as "complete and perfect." Hamilton also supported an extension of the Missouri

Compromise line and argued that the Constitution protected slavery. Back home, his opposition to secession resulted in warnings from fellow Texans. In July, death threats compelled him to flee to Mexico, from where he traveled first to New Orleans and then New York to begin a campaign for the liberation of his home state.[31]

In October, Hamilton spoke at the Brooklyn Academy of Music and the Cooper Union in New York. He cut quite a figure, being over six feet tall and possessed of a booming "Jupiter voice." Vilified as a traitor and forced to take flight from his home, Hamilton offered an escape narrative that thrilled audiences. He had had, he said, "to traverse two hundred miles of desert prairie" while assassins shot at him. Nonetheless he had survived to deliver the message that there were many Union men in Texas seeking an opportunity to over-throw Confederate rule. The rebellion, he told a packed house at Cooper Union, was aimed to destroy democratic government and *"to depress the masses and to elevate the few."* In choosing between de-mocracy and slavery, Hamilton chose democracy. The audience cheered when he declared that the moment secession "sought to tear away from me the only protection I ever had, or hope to leave my posterity—the flag of my fathers—for the purpose of building an-other government upon slavery" he had had a revelation. No longer would he just sympathize with abolition; secession made him "*an active, practical abolitionist.*"[32]

The Cooper Union speech, sponsored by New York's National War Committee, was widely reprinted. The *Daily Intelligencer* in Wheeling, West Virginia, called it "masterful." "No candid man can listen to him and not be convinced of the atrocious character of the Southern rebellion," advised the *New York Tribune*. The *New York Times* labeled Hamilton "one of the most earnest prophets the South has yet given to the Union." With his message that a majority of South-erners were opposed to secession, and that "the scales have fallen from the eyes of thousands who were in the beginning duped into treason, and that they stand ready to espouse the cause of the old govern-ment," Hamilton, appointed military governor and commissioned brigadier general in November 1862, became Lincoln's choice to engineer restoration in Texas.[33]

Stanton's orders to Hamilton directed him "to re-establish the authority of the Federal Government in the State of Texas and to provide the means of maintaining peace and security to the loyal inhabitants of that state until they shall be able to establish a civil government." General Nathaniel P. Banks, he was told, had been placed in command of an expedition to liberate Texas. Lincoln appointed Banks a major general because of his political credentials as onetime Speaker of the House (chosen on the 133rd ballot) and governor of Massachusetts. Stonewall Jackson had defeated Banks at the battles of Winchester and Cedar Mountain in May and August 1862. Lincoln then gave Banks command of the Department of the Gulf in December 1862.[34] There were reasons to invade Texas that went beyond alleviating the plight of Southern Unionists. Economically, there were millions of dollars' worth of cotton to be controlled and traded; diplomatically, the French had invaded Mexico and Lincoln's administration feared the establishment of a monarch who would support, even recognize, the Confederacy.

Nonetheless, whatever hopes Hamilton had for a rapid Union invasion of Texas were not to be. An expedition that departed on December 3 for New Orleans was ordered to remain there. However important Texas was, opening the Mississippi was more pressing. Banks did launch an expedition to Galveston, which Union forces had taken on October 2, but the three companies of Massachusetts men dispatched by Banks to reinforce the position failed, and Confederates retook Galveston on New Year's Day.[35]

Hamilton returned to the North to continue his campaign to build public support for an invasion of north Texas. He wrote Lincoln, urging the creation of a separate Texas department and the authorization to raise volunteers (a request not acted on). In April 1863, he delivered an address at Faneuil Hall in Boston. In order for secessionists to overthrow the government and rebel against democracy, Southerners had first had to have been "deluded." He added,

"They were really, at heart, on the side of the Government; and, I may add, this night, their hearts are with the Government of the United States." This was greeted with loud applause. Two years into the war, it was becoming increasingly difficult to make the case for Southern Unionism, but Hamilton did it with zeal.[36]

He also offered a ringing defense of the Emancipation Proclamation. The president, he argued, possessed the "power to strike the shackles from the limbs of the slaves, and reduce the rebels to the last extremity by dispossessing them of this property, so valuable to them." On the other hand, no one had the power "to make a slave of one solitary freeman." Hamilton declared himself an abolitionist and his resolute opposition to slavery, which, he argued, created despotism, degraded free labor, and destroyed free speech: "*I hate it, and ought to hate it, and I will fight against it while God grants me life.*"[37] Hamilton concluded with an extensive defense of Lincoln's policies overall and asked the audience to continue to support the president. He never mentioned Texas; he didn't have to. He would publicly endorse Lincoln and hope, in turn, that the president would support the liberation of Texas.

In July 1863, with Ulysses S. Grant's victory at Vicksburg and control of the Mississippi secured at last, Hamilton knew an opportune moment had arisen again, not only to plead the case of Southern Unionists but against any compromise that would leave slavery intact and repudiate the Emancipation Proclamation.

Hamilton requested a meeting with Lincoln on July 25, and then published a pamphlet entitled *Letter of Gen. A. J. Hamilton of Texas, to the President of the United States,* dated July 28, 1863. The parallels between Hamilton's letter and Lincoln's famous letter to James C. Conkling, written a month later, are noteworthy. Hamilton wrote, "If your proclamation was not then a mere assumption of power, but a valid act, done in the exercise of constitutional discretion, what power can abrogate or annul it?" Lincoln would write to Conkling, "but the proclamation, as law, either is valid, or is not valid. If it is not valid, it needs no retraction. If it is valid, it can not be retracted, any more than the dead can be brought to life." (One opposition paper responded "the logic…is another instance of the application of the pettifogger to momentous questions of state policy.") Hamilton discussed the actions of black soldiers who "have already, on historic battle-fields, vindicated their right to freedom by their heroic defense of the flag of the free." Lincoln, too, spoke of the service and sacrifice of black men in his letter to Conkling.[38] Hamilton also warned that not only were "domestic foes" endangering "the cause of nationality and free government" but foreign ones as well. The fall of Mexico might result in an alliance between Texas rebels and Louis Napoleon. Indeed, he reported, negotiations were pending. The Union could take action now, or have to take action later when "we will at no distant day be standing upon the law of force and the preparation of the nation for warfare to save us from intervention."[39]

What Hamilton warned of was on the president's mind. On June 7, the French army had entered Mexico City and forced Benito Juarez into exile. On July 29, Lincoln asked Secretary of War Stanton, "can we not renew the effort to organize a force to go to Western Texas?" In response to a letter forwarded from Francis P. Blair Sr., Lincoln wrote to Blair, "yesterday I commenced trying to get up an expedition for Texas." The letter, from William Alexander, a Unionist Texas lawyer, questioned whether the president would keep his promise to raise an expedition to Texas. Lincoln's tone turned querulous. "Who is the great man Alexander, that talks so oracularly about 'if the president keeps his word,'" he wrote Blair. "How has this Alexander's immense light been obscured hitherto?"[40]

John Hay, one of Lincoln's secretaries, noted in his diary that Lincoln was "very anxious that Texas should be occupied and firmly held in view of French possibilities." On August 5, Lincoln wrote to General Banks and advised that "recent events in Mexico, I think, render early action in Texas more important than ever." He also wrote to Grant, who wanted to move against Mobile, that "in view of recent events in Mexico, I am greatly impressed with the importance of re-establishing the national authority in Western Texas as soon as possible."[41]

The expedition organized by Banks sailed from New Orleans on September 4, 1863. The next day, Banks wrote Lincoln, expressing confidence that proceeding through the Sabine Pass and Sabine River troops would march to Houston and Galveston. Lincoln wrote Banks on September 19 and expressed the "strong hope that you have the old flag flying in Texas" and informed him that Hamilton was being sent to act as military governor. "I really believe him to be a man of worth and ability," one who "can scarcely fail to be efficient in re-inaugurating the National authority." What Lincoln did not yet know was that on September 8, a Confederate force of forty-four men at Fort Griffin defeated the Union flotilla of four gunboats and seven troop transports.[42]

In November, Banks sent a much larger expedition to the Rio Grande, some six thousand troops. They took control of Brazos Santiago, and in December Hamilton traveled to Brownsville where, at last, the military governor in exile sought to execute his orders. He accomplished little except to make some impolitic speeches about the French presence in Mexico. It didn't matter. By the following summer military setbacks forced Union forces out of mainland Texas. Hamilton returned to New Orleans. There would be no restored government in Texas. Hamilton would henceforth devote himself to speaking on behalf of Lincoln's reelection and return again in 1865 as provisional governor, appointed by Andrew Johnson. He remained in office a year, unable to do much to curb the violence that exploded in north Texas, and was content to drift toward a more conservative position on rights and race than he had expressed while military governor.

Louisiana

The surrender of New Orleans on April 28, 1862, was the most important Union victory to that point, and it set the stage for an attempt at wartime reconstruction that would dominate discussions during the war and carry through to Lincoln's final speech roughly three years later. Early on April 24, Admiral David G. Farragut's Gulf Expeditionary Force, consisting of seventeen wooden warships, ran past Forts Jackson and St. Philip and moved up the Mississippi. Several days later, the forts surrendered to General Benjamin Butler, who arrived with three regiments and took command of New Orleans, the largest city in the Confederacy and one that was unlike any other. A substantial number of residents, many of them planters who had been former Whigs, had opposed secession, and the population of New Orleans included a well-educated free black community of ten thousand.

On June 20, Lincoln appointed George F. Shepley, a forty-two-year-old widower, military governor of Louisiana. A colonel in the Twelfth Maine Infantry Regiment, Shepley, a Democrat, had once served in the Maine Senate (his father had been a U.S. senator) and as U.S. district attorney for the state. At Butler's request, Shepley's regiment had been part of the New Orleans expedition; the two men had become friends as delegates to the Democratic Convention in 1860. It was Butler who suggested that Shepley be appointed.[43] Stanton's instructions to Shepley mirrored those given to other military governors. The purpose of the appointment was to reestablish Federal authority and aid Unionists in endeavors to establish civil government.[44]

Promoted to brigadier general, Shepley did not have an easy time implementing his orders. Butler's harsh actions as commander in New Orleans had alienated Unionists and led Confederates to revile him. He silenced newspapers and arrested anyone suspected of smuggling. He had a civilian executed for tearing down an American flag. Most notoriously, he issued an order that any woman who insulted a Union soldier "shall be regarded and held liable to be treated as a woman of the town plying her avocation"—in other words, a prostitute. His actions earned him the nickname "Beast." Suspected of corruption (his brother Andrew was said to have made a fortune off illicit trade in cotton), Butler also antagonized British and French foreign consuls in New Orleans. By December, Lincoln had had enough and replaced Butler with Nathaniel Banks.[45]

In the summer and fall of 1862, Lincoln was eager to see elections organized in districts under Union military control. He was growing tired of Southern Unionists who complained and wanted their property, particularly slaves, protected but who seemed unwilling to take action to restore a loyal government. Lincoln's exasperation boiled over and he expressed himself candidly in several letters written within a week of one another.

The first was in response to a letter written on July 16 by Reverdy Johnson, who was in New Orleans at the behest of William Seward to resolve diplomatic disputes over the seizure of foreign property by General Butler. Described as "short, stout, and round-shouldered," Johnson represented Maryland in the Senate from 1845 to 1849. He had become a Democrat and served as the state's delegate to the Washington Peace Conference. In his letter, Johnson warned Lincoln that if the purpose of the government was to force the emancipation of slaves, "this State can not be, for years, if ever, re-instated in the Union." He complained specifically about the actions of General John W. Phelps, who wanted to organize fugitive slaves into armed regiments.[46]

Lincoln responded on July 26 that the actions of Phelps were a "false pretense" not to organize a loyal government. The president never intended "to touch the foundations of their society," but the way to avoid it was not to complain but "simply to take their place in the Union upon the old terms. If they will not do this, should they not receive harder blows rather than lighter ones?" As for "professed friends," their appeal that he take a conservative path in fighting the war and restoring the Union "has paralyzed me more in this struggle than any one thing."[47]

Two days later, Lincoln wrote Cuthbert Bullitt, a New Orleans Unionist, about a letter Bullitt had received and shared with the president from Thomas J. Durant, a lawyer who would later play a key role as a radical in attempts to write a new state constitution.

Lincoln began by acknowledging Durant's claim that it is "probably true" that the secession ordinance of Louisiana was "adopted against the will of a majority of the people." But if so, these loyalists seem to be willing to do nothing except demand that the government "not strike its open enemies, lest they be struck by accident." Some complained about how the presence of the Union Army in New Orleans "disturbed ... the relation of master and slave," but Lincoln (who had only days earlier announced to the cabinet his decision to issue an Emancipation Proclamation) warned the "pressure in this direction" toward acting against slavery as a military necessity was strong. "The rebellion will never be suppressed in Louisiana," he argued, "if the professed Union men there will neither help to do it, nor permit the government to do it without their help." It would not suffice for them "to touch neither a sail nor a pump, but to be merely passengers,—dead-heads at that—to be carried snug and dry, throughout the storm, and safely landed right side up." Lincoln assured Bullitt that "the people of Louisiana who wish protection to person and property, have but to reach forth their hands and take it. Let them, in good faith, reinaugurate the national authority, and set up a State Government conforming thereto under the constitution." He concluded, "I shall do nothing in malice. What I deal with is too vast for malicious dealing." The letter would make its way to public attention. And it would resonate after Lincoln's death. On May 7, 1865, the *New York Times* published it under the headline "Letter of President Lincoln—the Duty of Southern Union Men."[48]

A few days after the letter to Bullitt, Lincoln wrote to the New York financier August Belmont in reaction to a letter written by someone in New Orleans that asked why the North would not simply make clear officially "what it wishes for the restoration of the union as it was." The phrase "the Constitution as it is—the Union as it was" was being employed by Northern Democrats to express their desire for an eventual restoration of the Union with slavery intact. One politician put it bluntly: "the Constitution as it is—the Union as it was, and the niggers where they are." Responding to the slogan, one essayist noted, "the Union 'as it was' is a thing that never can be again."[49]

Lincoln had his own unique way of putting the issue: "broken eggs cannot be mended," he explained. "Louisiana has nothing to do now but take her place in the Union as it was, barring the already broken eggs. The sooner she does so, the smaller will be the amount of that which will be past mending." But Lincoln also warned that "this government cannot much longer play a game in which it stakes all, and its enemies stake nothing. Those enemies must understand that they cannot experiment for ten years trying to destroy the government, and if they fail come back into the Union unhurt." There would be a price to pay. Lincoln already knew that price would be the end of slavery, but the terms under which emancipation would occur were still up for negotiation.[50]

On October 14, Lincoln pressed Butler and Shepley to arrange elections. More than a month later, he was annoyed to learn that nothing had been done. He wanted elections for congressmen to be held and emphasized that it had to be a movement led by the people, "not a movement of our military and quasi-military, authorities." There needed to be evidence that respectable Southern citizens would swear allegiance and accept election to Federal office. To elect Northern men as representatives, at bayonet's point, "would be disgusting and outrageous." "Do not waste a day about it," he demanded. He wanted the results of elections to be determined before January 1, so he would know whether the Union-occupied portion of the state qualified for exemption from the Emancipation Proclamation.[51]

On December 3, elections were held, under a special proclamation issued by Shepley, for the First and Second Congressional Districts of Louisiana. With more than twenty-six hundred votes in the first and five thousand in the second, the turnout was 60 percent of the 1860 vote. Benjamin Flanders, a Unionist lawyer and editor, and Michael Hahn, a German immigrant and Democrat turned Republican, were elected. Shepley informed Lincoln that the election had gone well and that those elected were Louisiana citizens unconnected to the army and represented "the free and unbiased choice of the people of their respective districts." Butler wrote Lincoln to say they were both *unconditional Union men* who would support the administration.[52]

The question remained whether the two men would be seated, and in February the House engaged in a protracted debate in Congress about whether to accept their credentials. Part of the debate concerned the validity of the civil functions of a military governor. Republican Henry Dawes of Massachusetts argued that there was no way other than by a military governor who abided by all the same procedures required of an elected, civil governor to "draw anew law and order" from anarchy. "I am not an advocate of the authority of military governors," acknowledged Dawes. "The presence of that authority, one inch beyond where it is necessary, does not meet my approval." There could be, however, "no better method, no healthier method" for the restoration of government under the sanction of the Constitution, which, under Article IV, Section IV, guaranteed to states a republican form of government. Those who opposed seating Flanders and Hahn resented what they saw as executive usurpation of authority over congressional prerogatives, "a grand gigantic system of Executive domination." According to Indiana Democrat Daniel Voorhees, Shepley was a military commander assuming authority to act as governor of Louisiana. "By virtue of what clause in the Constitution," he asked, "by virtue of what rule of law the President of the United States has authority to appoint any human being 'military governor'? He has not got it. It is nowhere given to him. It is an assumed power." The only responsibility of the military governor was to keep the peace, not to organize an election. Remarkably, Michael Hahn was invited to address the House. Acknowledging the truism that "he who pleads his own case has a fool for a client," Hahn reassured House members of the loyalty of the citizens of New Orleans, tens of thousands of whom had taken oaths of allegiance. Shepley, Hahn insisted, acted only after the Union associations of New Orleans asked him to, and the elections were fairly held. Hahn and Flanders were seated by a vote of 92–44. But the debate was a flash point that anticipated future conflict over the question of presidential versus congressional initiatives on reconstruction.[53]

With the representatives seated, the next step in restoring Louisiana would be election of members to a state convention to adopt a new constitution. In June, Lincoln responded to a petition from a committee representing the planters of Louisiana that asked the president to authorize an election under the terms of the state constitution as it was before secession. That constitution included slavery. Lincoln responded that "a respectable portion of the Louisiana people" desire to amend the constitution and hold a convention for that purpose. It was to those efforts that Lincoln gave his support.[54]

On August 5, 1863, he wrote to Banks to specify what he would like to see accomplished in Louisiana. "I would be glad for her to make a new Constitution recognizing the emancipation proclamation," he said, "and adopting emancipation in those parts of the state where the proclamation does not apply." Looking beyond political reconstruction, he then turned to the question that was only beginning to draw attention: how would emancipation alter social relations between blacks and whites? "And while she is at it," Lincoln observed, "I think it would not be objectionable for her to adopt some practical system by which the two races could gradually live themselves out of their old relation to each other, and both come out better prepared for the new." Perhaps by this Lincoln meant new wage labor relationships. It certainly meant education for black children. What was needed to begin the process was the election of delegates to a constitutional convention.[55]

Three months later, Lincoln wrote Banks that the lack of any action "disappoints me bitterly." Banks must have wondered how much the president thought he could do. Only recently he had been ordered to arrange for an invasion of Texas. Furthermore, there was confusion as to who was supposed to organize the process, Shepley or Banks. (It was Shepley who had received orders from Stanton on

August 24 to proceed with elections.) Perhaps Thomas Durant, the head of the general committee representing various Union associations in New Orleans, had a role to play. (Durant had told Lincoln that, contrary to the president's belief, he was not supervising the registration of voters.) No matter, Lincoln wanted them all "to go to work and give me a tangible nucleus which the remainder of the State may rally around." Time, he thought, was critical. "Professedly" loyal men were acting to establish a government that would be contrary to his wishes, one that repudiated the Emancipation Proclamation and reestablished slavery. Such a government he would not recognize.[56]

At the same time, Lincoln said he would not object to some sort of "reasonable temporary arrangement, in relation to the landless and homeless freed people," as long as it was clear that permanent freedom was the end result. He made it clear that he did not insist on some sort of apprenticeship system to ease the transition from slave to free labor, but only that "it would not be objectionable to me."[57]

General Banks responded on December 6, mortified that Lincoln should hold him accountable since he thought he was not charged with the responsibility for organizing a government in Louisiana. If Lincoln wanted him to take charge, he would, though he did not covet the power ("I have enough before, me, to satisfy my ambition"). Banks agreed completely with Lincoln as to the necessity of moving forward: "The first and greatest step in this direction, now, lies in the reconstruction of States. If we cannot re-organize, we cannot Conquer—Military success is not enough! You must open the eyes of the world to another result." Banks thought successful reorganization in a single state would help bring the rebellion to a close, and no state was more important than Louisiana, which "will make a more powerful impression upon the world because it is better known to Europe" and identified with the policies and interests of the Confederacy.[58]

Lincoln no doubt appreciated Banks's perspective. Just as emancipation was both a means to an end (winning the war) and an end in itself (the abolition of slavery), so too was reconstruction a means toward bringing the war to a close and an end that would result in the Union once again becoming a nation. Much work was yet to be done in Louisiana, and elsewhere, and through 1864 the remaining military governors and commanders would be guided by the conditions Lincoln outlined on December 8 in his annual message and Proclamation of Amnesty and Reconstruction.

Chapter 3

"A Pernicious Abstraction"

By fall 1863, pressure was mounting for Lincoln to proclaim formally a plan for reconstruction and amnesty. It came from multiple directions at once. In an article titled "The 'Reconstruction' Discussions," the *Harrisburg Patriot and Union* reported in September, "Most of the leading newspapers of the country are discussing with more or less ability and much earnestness, the basis, method, and terms of a reconstruction of the Union."[1]

What people envisioned of the reunification of the North and the South depended on their politics. For example, some Northern Democrats thought that, in the aftermath of Gettysburg and Vicksburg, Lincoln "should at once second the recent victories of our armies by a proclamation of amnesty" though without reference to slavery. By comparison, some moderate and radical Republicans took comfort in Lincoln's defense of the Emancipation Proclamation in his public letter to Conkling, but they also wanted him to go further and state unequivocally that no state would be restored with slavery intact. Rumors spread that the president had already prepared a proclamation of amnesty, and that the cabinet was discussing the matter. Lincoln responded privately to a suggestion from General William S. Rosecrans to offer a general amnesty to officers and soldiers in the rebellion: "I intend doing something like what you suggest whenever the case shall appear ripe enough to have it accepted in the true understanding, rather than as a confession of weakness and fear."[2]

Pressure for a formal statement intensified when multiple newspapers published a supposedly confidential exchange of letters between Lincoln and Fernando Wood from December. Wood, a New York

Democrat with strong Confederate sympathies, informed the president that it was his understanding "that the Southern States would send representatives to the next congress, provided that a full and general amnesty should permit them to do so." Wood asked the president to confirm what he had heard.[3]

Lincoln responded that he suspected Wood's information "to be groundless." He then parsed Wood's words:

> Understanding the phrase in the paragraph above quoted "the Southern States would send representatives to the next congress" to be substantially the same as that "the people of the Southern States would cease resistance, and would re-inaugerate [*sic*], submit to, and maintain the national authority, within the limits of such states under the Constitution of the United States," I say, that in such case, the war would cease on the part of the United States; and that, if within a reasonable time "a full and general amnesty" were necessary to such end, it would not be withheld.

Lincoln added, "while there is nothing in this letter which I should dread to see in history, it is perhaps better, for the present, that its existence should not become public."[4]

Whatever Wood's intentions in releasing the exchange, Republicans, at least, believed that the correspondence confirmed Lincoln's public position that no amnesty had ever been offered to the rebels. "Mr. Wood will make very little of this publication," predicted the *New York Tribune*, "and the country will coincide with the President on the propriety and prudence of his reply."[5]

The publication of the correspondence with Wood constituted a small part of a proliferation of public letters and speeches about reconstruction that appeared from July through December 1863. Embedded in these works were various theories of reconstruction and recommendations about how best to restore the Union. William Whiting, the war department solicitor, had argued for Lincoln's authority to structure the terms of reconstruction. Whiting's book *The War*

Powers of the President (1862) would go through many editions, and Lincoln had relied on it for an explanation of the war powers by which he justified the Emancipation Proclamation. Now, in "The Return of Rebellious States to the Union," a July speech to the Union League of Philadelphia, Whiting warned, "do not allow old States, with their constitutions still unaltered, to resume State powers." Doing so would be an invitation for them to continue their opposition to the Constitution of the United States and to pass local laws to exclude "all Northern men, all soldiers, all free blacks, and all persons and things which shall be inconsistent with the theory of making slavery the corner-stone of their local government." The war, Whiting argued, had shifted from a war against persons to a war against a territory. That meant that every person, whether loyal or disloyal, must take an oath of allegiance to regain the rights of citizenship. Such "public enemies" are not restored to their citizenship rights merely because fighting has ceased. The only plan of reconstruction that would render permanent domestic tranquility would be the adoption of new state constitutions "such as will forever remove all causes of collision with the United States by excluding slavery therefrom."[6]

Whiting's argument raised an issue that plagued discussions of reconstruction: were the Confederate states in the Union or not? Had they ceased to be states? Reduction to conquered territories implied they had been independent prior to defeat. If independent, why, for example, couldn't foreign countries recognize the Confederacy? Lincoln's entire theory of secession hinged on the rebellion as a domestic insurrection; he argued repeatedly that the states were still in the Union. But many radical Republicans, Whiting among them, suggested that, for the purposes of reconstruction, war reduced them to territorial status. One Democratic newspaper viewed Whiting as a surrogate for the radical views of Secretary of War Edwin Stanton, who "it would seem...were at the head of a little government of his own." The *New York World* summed up the paradox this way from the perspective of the Confederacy: "if the seceding states claim not to be in the Union, they are; but if they claim to be in the Union, they are not."[7]

Whiting's speech drew much attention. One writer called it "able, eloquent, and ingenious," but also challenged the notion that the rebels were anything but rebels. The laws of nations, he insisted, did not apply between government subjects and government itself. Let the armies finish their work and however the union was restored, he declared, make certain it included "universal emancipation." Speaking for border-state Democrats, who thought the doctrine of reducing states to territories was merely an excuse to abolish slavery, one writer called Whiting "one of the vilest and most shameless radicals of the time."[8]

Gideon Welles, secretary of the navy, also read Whiting's speech and thought little of either the man or the content. He knew Whiting had influence with Lincoln, who favored his views, but in an explosion of adjectives described him as "vain, egotistical, and friendly; voluble, ready, sharp, not always profound, nor wise, nor correct; cunning, assuming, presuming, and not very fastidious." And this before he read the public speech, which did nothing to increase Welles's estimation of Whiting. Welles knew that the condition and future of the nation and slavery were topics about which people held many different opinions, but "no clear, distinct, and well-defined line of policy has as yet been indicted by the Administration."[9]

However fully Welles dismissed Whiting, the speech had him thinking and, on August 19, he returned to the most pressing issue of the day: "What is to be done with the slaves and slavery." Without slavery, reestablishing the Union would not be a problem. Slavery, however, remained and could not be extinguished by pretending that the states in rebellion no longer existed. From Welles's perspective the war remained one against individuals and not states. And even once the rebellion ended, the question of slavery in the four loyal Border States remained.[10]

Several days later, Welles and Salmon Chase took a two-hour carriage ride, the purpose of which was "a consultation on the slavery question, and what in common parlance is called the reconstruction of the Union." Perhaps no two cabinet members looked more unalike. Welles, nicknamed "Father Neptune," had a flowing white beard and ill-fitting grey wig that received frequent comment in the press. Noah Brooks said he had "an apostolic mien," though he was also known for his affability and accessibility. By comparison, Chase, though a "robust man, with handsome features," was also seen as humorless and exuding ambition.[11]

Salmon Chase made clear his position: no retreat from the Emancipation Proclamation and the extinction of slavery as a requirement for the readmission of any rebel state. Welles was noncommittal. He thought that slavery as it was once had all but been ended and was against "intruding speculative political theories in advance to embarrass official action." Welles supported emancipation, but, as a former Democrat, he also favored state power over federal power. ("The States had rights which must be respected, the General Government limitations beyond which it must not pass.") He wondered by what authority the president or Congress could dictate local policy. Chase argued that the seceded states had lost their rights and were conquered. He feared readmitting them without abolishing slavery and placing the government back in the hands of slaveholders. Welles thought this unlikely. There were loyal Southerners and others who evinced hostility to the Confederacy. The key was to act on individuals and not states. What was needed was patience and time: "the reestablishment of the Union and harmony will be a slow process, requiring forbearance and nursing rather than force and coercion." Welles saw Chase as trying to build an alliance with other cabinet members for his position, but the navy secretary was wary of "the intrusion of partyism." Chase, he thought, was warped by his presidential aspirations. His position of denying to the states their sovereign rights under the Constitution was the reverse side of the doctrine of secession by which states claimed they could leave the Union. The states, Welles argued, "cannot secede, nor can they be expelled." While persons who participated in the rebellion had lost their rights, the states had not forfeited theirs. A week later Welles expressed exasperation in his diary: "shall we receive back the Rebel States? is asked of me daily. The question implies that the States have seceded,—actually gone out from us,—that the Union is at present dissolved, which I do not admit."[12]

The issue of how to treat the seceded states, as still within the Union or out, for the purposes of reconstruction, was a threshold question that permeated the arguments offered throughout the fall. The Supreme Court decision in the Prize cases (1863) became part of that discussion. Whiting based portions of his argument on the decision, and Robert Dale Owen began his letter on *The Conditions of Reconstruction* with an account of the judicial ruling as well. Owen, who had been elected to the House as a Democrat in the 1840s, and had helped found the utopian community of New Harmony in Indiana in the 1820s, had written an influential letter on emancipation in September 1862 that had been shown to Lincoln. Now, in August 1863, he addressed a letter to Seward, and made certain to send a copy of the pamphlet to Lincoln.

In a 5–4 decision, the Supreme Court had ruled that Lincoln acted within his powers when he authorized the seizure of vessels prior to July 13, 1861, when Congress declared a state of war. Owen cited Justice Robert Cooper Grier's decision that civil war exists when "the regular course of justice" is interrupted by "revolt, rebellion, or insurrection...and hostilities may be prosecuted on the same footing as if those opposing the government were foreign enemies invading the land." Grier, a Pennsylvania Democrat appointed by Polk and the one Northern justice to support Roger Taney's position about slavery in the territories in the *Dred Scott* case, had helped give the administration an important victory.[13]

Owen argued that once peace came, the administration had the right to determine on what terms constitutional privileges would be restored. While any reconstruction should be without "bitterness, or anger, or rankling animosity," it must make certain to include terms that will prevent another insurrection. The foremost task was to eradicate "the delusion that this Republic may be reconstructed part free, part slave." There were politicians who talked of reconstruction that left the "peculiar institution" of the South in place but such talk was "nothing else but a mischievous mystification." Owen concluded by summarizing: the Confederacy had no right to elect members of Congress until such time as the government restored the right by establishing under what conditions the states would be permitted to return; and the permanent destruction of slavery was nonnegotiable.[14]

A month after his letter to Seward, Owen wrote a fifty-one-page letter to Lincoln headed "The Pardoning Power in Its Relation to Reconstruction." Article II, Section 2, of the Constitution gives the president "the power to grant reprieves and pardons for offenses against the United States," and Owen traced the various arguments for vesting such power in the executive. Notably, he quoted Alexander Hamilton, who in *Federalist* 74 maintained that "the principal argument for reposing the power of pardoning...in the Chief Magistrate, is this: in seasons of insurrection or rebellion there are often critical moments when a well-timed offer of pardon to the insurgents or rebels may restore the tranquility of the Commonwealth." Owen not only assured Lincoln that he was fully within his powers to grant pardons; he also suggested that the recipients should be required to affirm support for all laws passed by Congress as well as any proclamations issued by the president during the rebellion. This is precisely what Lincoln would do.[15]

If Whiting and Owen both believed that the course of reconstruction should be in the hands of the president, Henry Winter Davis had a different idea. The Maryland congressman's failure to support Lincoln in the election of 1860 may have hurt him when his name came up for possible inclusion in the cabinet. A one-time Whig and member of the Know-Nothings, a nativist party with a brief life in the 1850s, he embraced the Republican Party during the war and became one of its most radical members, as well as one of Lincoln's most virulent critics. Davis was described as having a golden tongue but a somewhat odd personality. Noah Brooks reported in 1865 that Lincoln once said of him, "I've been told that insanity is hereditary in his family, and I think we will admit the plea in his case."[16]

But there was nothing irrational about Davis's speech in Philadelphia on September 24, 1863. Governor Andrew Curtin was running for reelection against a Peace Democrat, and Davis was delivering a campaign speech. He reminded voters that Peace Democrats, who wanted to restore the Union with slavery intact, "are very fond of asking who is responsible for the war, and I take great pleasure in responding the Democratic party that ruled the country for thirty years." He denounced all calls for armistice being made by Northern Democrats who opposed emancipation and averred that peace would only come through war. The conservatives, Davis claimed, sought restoration by having the president offer amnesty to individual offenders and "open his arms to receive those who have just now had the sword pointed at our bosoms." Davis imagined a scenario where, under the mildest and most forgiving of terms, restoration would mean literally "the union as it was" with slavery intact and Confederate officials in power in Southern states. He entreated readers to ponder this "gravely." There could never be a Union such as had existed before the outbreak of war: "call the dead to life; clothe his bones with his dissolved flesh; restore the soul to the soulless eyes of the thousands that have fallen martyrs upon the battle-field, and then you can restore the Union as it was."[17]

Davis opposed any doctrine that reduced the Confederate states to territories or that treated the rebels as alien enemies as opposed to traitors. Rather, he relied on the constitutional guarantee of a republican form of government to the states, and the president was fulfilling his executive responsibilities in that regard while it was the duty of Congress to fulfill the legislative. First crush the rebellion, Davis concluded, and then "the Southern planter will make the best terms that he can with his emancipated and armed fellow-countrymen of the African race."[18]

On October 3, Montgomery Blair, the man who beat out Davis for a cabinet position, gave a speech before a sizable crowd at the fairgrounds in Rockville, Maryland. Within days every politician was talking about it, including Lincoln, and it may have contributed a year later to the president's decision to accept Blair's resignation. It certainly widened the rift between radicals, who required emancipation as indispensable to reconstruction and believed the seceded states should be reduced to territories, and conservatives, who worried what abolition might mean for America and thought Lincoln's policy of treating the states as if they had never left was the correct one.

Blair directed his speech at "the ultra-Abolitionists" whose ambition was to amalgamate "the black element with the free white labor of the land." He argued that the plan by which radicals hoped to accomplish their revolution was by abolishing the state constitutions in the rebellious states, as evoked in a recently published piece in the *Atlantic Monthly* under the title "Our Domestic Relations: Power of Congress Over the Rebel States," which argued for giving Congress absolute power over the states that rejoined the Union. "The assumption that certain States of the South are extinct . . . is abhorrent to every principle on which the Union was founded," Blair argued. Blair mocked the concept of "state suicide"—the idea that the states had ceased to exist upon breaking the national compact and seceding from the Union. But how, Blair asked, "can the Union, which is the guaranty of the government of every republic of which it consists, admit, whilst it lives, that any part of it is dead?" The traitors, not the states, had committed political suicide. As far as Blair was concerned, the abolitionists and the nullifiers shared many ideas, including a total disregard for the loyal citizens of the South.[19]

Blair then turned from what he dubbed the "Abolition programme" to Lincoln's plan: he would pursue the rebels but appeal to the loyal Southerners. The president's policy, as evidenced by Tennessee and Louisiana, was to put as quickly as possible the power of government into the hands of loyal Southerners. This was a "safe and healing policy," the only one that could accomplish the eventual restoration of relations between the United States and the states in rebellion.[20]

The denunciations of Blair came in force. Thaddeus Stevens, not surprisingly, wrote to Chase that Postmaster General Blair had made a "vile speech," more infamous "than any speech made by a Copperhead orator." Henry Wilson, senator from Massachusetts, informed Lincoln that Blair was being denounced both for the speech and for "setting men against you." Lincoln must have been especially perturbed that Blair, according to one reporter, was presuming to speak for him and his cabinet, and claiming a "proslavery, states rights theory as being that of the administration." Adam Gurowski, who worked in the State Department, believed that "Blair peddles for Mr. Lincoln's re-election. Blair thus semi-officially spoke for the President, and for the Cabinet." Even the Democratic-leaning *New York Herald* asserted that "Mr. Lincoln should not have entrusted the championship of the conservative cause to such a frail vessel as Montgomery Blair."[21]

Looking ahead to the election of 1864, Noah Brooks wondered whether Lincoln would keep Blair in the cabinet and in the process sacrifice his chances of getting renominated. The Pennsylvania elections of 1863 went to the Republicans, and afterward John W. Forney, secretary of the Senate and influential editor of the *Washington Chronicle*, called on Lincoln to congratulate him. At the same time, he wanted him to know that Governor Curtin believed that had Blair's speech occurred a month earlier than it did the Union ticket might have lost. Blair was in the room, but that did not stop Forney from saying he was astonished that a cabinet member would "utter such sentiments on the eve of important elections in other states." Blair said he only spoke his honest sentiments, to which Forney responded, "why don't you leave the cabinet, and not load down with your individual and peculiar sentiments the administration to which you belong." Brooks, who had earlier described Blair as "repellant," wrote about the incident for the *Sacramento Daily Union*. "The President," he noted, "sat by, a silent spectator of this singular and unexpected scene." Brooks commented that he hoped Lincoln would repudiate Blair "for otherwise he would fall with him." Brooks would later write privately that Lincoln never read Blair's Rockville speech until months later and that he tolerated him in the cabinet because he was good at his job. While it was understandable for some to assume that a member of the cabinet spoke as an authoritative source for the government's policy, the *Boston Daily Advertiser* wisely cautioned, "it will be dangerous for us to assume that the President holds to any theoretical plan, so as to bind him against what he regards as the practical expediency of any particular case."[22]

Everyone knew Blair's target in his Rockville speech had not been the abolitionists in general but one in particular: Charles Sumner. It was Sumner who on February 11, 1862, introduced a set of resolutions with respect to the seceded states. He asserted that upon secession a state had abdicated all its rights under the Constitution and forfeited all powers "essential to the continued existence of the state as a body-politic." The termination of a state under the constitution also meant the "termination of those peculiar local institutions." Slavery no longer had the protection of the Constitution. While Sumner's resolutions were tabled, they were the basis for the idea of state suicide.[23]

The resolutions also triggered a debate over the implications of Sumner's theory about state suicide. "The resolutions," predicted the *New York Tribune*, "are destined ... to engage very thoroughly the public mind." But not everyone was as amenable to the idea of state suicide as the radical Republican press. The conservative *Daily National Intelligencer*, in an article titled "Political Metaphysics," tried to parse the difference between a state and a state government, whereas the radical *New York Evening Post* said Sumner's logic was fallacious. Sumner wrote to Park Godwin, the *Post's* editor and wondered what the difference was between those who say the actual function of the state was annihilated as opposed to those who say states are de facto but not de jure dead as opposed to those who claim that state governments are vanquished. As for himself, "I rejoice to believe that Slavery itself has lost its *slender legality* in this suicide. But you may disown this consequence. I don't think you can disown the statement of position." In May, he declared, "call it suicide if you will, or suspended animation, or abeyance,—they have practically ceased to exist."[24]

Blair had referred to that anonymous *Atlantic Monthly* article but no one doubted that Sumner was the author. In a headnote to Sumner's collected works, the editor reported that it was originally prepared as a speech in support of his February resolutions, titled "State Rebellion, State Suicide, Emancipation, and Reconstruction."[25]

Sumner began the article with a consideration of what Lincoln, quietly, had already done: "he has constituted military governments in the Rebel States, with governors nominated by himself." The senator objected to this "imperatorial dominion," this "military despotism," and argued that such magistrates elevate military over civil rule and are not sanctioned by the Constitution. Lincoln's actions assumed the old state governments would be done away with, and while it was true, it was Congress not the president that should reestablish them. Sumner's analysis rejected any doctrine of states' rights and asserted that the states were subordinate to the national government. He thought it best to "discard all theory" because such discussions "are only endless mazes." What mattered was that as a result of treason "rightful government in the rebel states" had been "vacated." The senator concluded by defending the rightful power of Congress to organize new state governments. He based the authority on necessity, on war powers, and on the constitutional provision that the United States shall guarantee to every state a republican form of government. What Blair made the most of in his Rockville critique of Sumner actually comprised only a small portion of the article. Sumner made it clear, however, that Congress had the jurisdiction to act against slavery and that any plan of reconstruction required that *"Congress should enter and assume the proper jurisdiction."*[26]

After delivering his Rockville speech, Blair wrote the senator to say he did not mean it as a personal attack. Sumner generously responded

that on the constitutional "*principles* involved" there was little difference between them. Blair might have accepted Sumner's gracious
reply and moved on, but instead he further condemned the senator
for his February resolutions. This was too much for Sumner who responded, "you have fallen into a complete mystification." All Sumner
cared about was finding the best means by which to suppress the
rebellion and restore the states and he was adamant that this could
not be done "*constitutionally* by military or presidential power" alone.[27]

At least one reader of the *New York Times* found the battle between Blair and Sumner "a little ridiculous." The letter writer disagreed with Sumner and with Blair. The only policy that made sense
was straightforward and simple: "this Government shall be restored
to every foot of its legal territory, and that Slavery shall, under no
pretence, be restored to political power in the land."[28]

Lincoln, too, found the dispute less than edifying. According to
John Hay, Lincoln called the disagreement "one of mere form and
little else. I do not think Mr. Blair would agree that the states in rebellion are to be permitted to come at once into the political family &
renew the very performances which have already so bedeviled us.
I do not think Mr. Sumner would insist that when the loyal people of
a state obtain the supremacy in their councils & are ready to assume
direction of their own affairs, that they should be excluded." Lincoln
understood that Sumner favored Congress taking from the executive branch power over "insurrectionary districts," but the "practical
matter" was how to keep the rebels from "overwhelming and outvot-
ing the loyal minority."[29]

The president did not mention the issue of slavery; he did not
have to. Blair was swimming against strong currents in his hope that
somehow slavery might survive the war and reconstruction. In November 1863, Andrew Johnson wrote to Blair to say he hoped that
Lincoln would reject the "proposition of States relapsing into territories." The postmaster general must have nodded in agreement as
he read this since he believed the states did not lose their status
through secession. But, then, Johnson's conclusion no doubt disturbed

Blair: "The institution of slavery is gone & there is no good reason now for destroying the states to bring about the destruction of slavery." Whatever theory of the status of the rebellious states to which one subscribed, including that they had never left the Union, slavery would be vanquished.[30]

In December, the *Continental Monthly*, a conservative Congregationalist magazine published in New York, ran an article titled simply "Reconstruction." Written by Edward Everett Russell, who contributed regularly to the periodicals of the day, it began, "Reconstruction is the hope of the Union; and the hope of the Union is the controlling energy of the war."[31] Russell helpfully parsed the three central theories that had been circulating for the previous six months. Two of the theories, he explained, stemmed from a determination to achieve the abolition of slavery. One was the theory of state suicide: "the States in the rebellion have, by the fact of rebellion, forfeited all rights of States." There were distinctions among those who argued this position. Some called it territorialization; others thought state authority was more in abeyance than dead. But whatever the nomenclature, it meant Congress had the authority to dictate the terms of readmission and to act against slavery. Russell opposed this theory as repugnant to the Constitution because it gave Congress too much power, and argued that it was itself revolutionary because it gave credence to the doctrine of secession by regarding the states themselves as independent and sovereign.

The second theory that allowed for the administration or Congress to dictate terms was the idea that the rebellious states were conquered provinces and, as such, "according to the laws of war, the nation may treat them altogether as alien enemies." Here, too, Russell was opposed: "our constitution is, in no sense, a treaty between sovereign States." Only persons, not states, can be called and considered enemies.[32]

The third theory, the one that had shaped the administration's policy in Russell's view, held the "rebellion to be an armed insurrection against the authority of the United States, usurping the functions and powers of various State governments." Reconstruction could only come by ending the rebellion and restoring to loyal citizens control over the apparatus of state government. This has been the course of the administration, and for this "Abraham Lincoln is entitled to the gratitude of the people. His conscientious policy has been the salvation of the Republic," protecting it against armed rebellion while also saving it from antislavery zealots who placed abolition above the higher claims of nation.[33]

As the arguments raged through the fall, Lincoln was beginning to prepare his annual message to Congress. Undoubtedly, he would have to address the administration's approach to reconstruction. Would he follow the approach recommended by Blair or track the paths suggested by Whiting and Owen? Were there elements in Davis's and Sumner's perspective that he could use, while at the same time asserting executive as opposed to congressional authority in the business of reconstruction. Could he find a way to navigate between the demands of the conservatives and the radicals?

One matter seemed certain—he had no use for theoretical debates about the status of the states in rebellion or who would take control of the process. As he would say about the issue in his last speech on April 11, 1865: "I have *purposely* forborne any public expression upon it. As appears to me that question has not been, nor yet is, a practically material one, and that any discussion of it, while it thus remains practically immaterial, could have no effect other than the mischievous one of dividing our friends. As yet, whatever it may hereafter become, that question is bad, as the basis of a controversy, and good for nothing at all—a merely pernicious abstraction."[34]

With the summer's military victories at Gettysburg and Vicksburg, Lincoln believed that peace seemed less distant. Progress had been made in Tennessee and Louisiana, and West Virginia had joined the Union. The fall elections in 1863 had gone well for the Republicans. Looking ahead, politicians already were scrambling for position in the upcoming presidential election. Michigan senator Zachariah Chandler wrote Lincoln in November: "you are today

Master of the situation if you stand firm." "Conservatives & traitors are buried together," Chandler added. "For God's sake don't exhume their remains in Your Message." Lincoln responded, "I hope to 'stand firm' enough not to go backward, and not go forward fast enough to wreck the country's cause." The time had come for Lincoln to declare his plan for reconstruction.[35]

Chapter 4

"A Plan of Re-construction"

"The President quite unwell," John Hay reported on November 26, 1863. Lincoln had contracted varioloid fever, a mild form of smallpox. His illness alarmed Unionists of all political persuasions. The *New York World*, a rabidly anti-administration Democratic paper, paused to comment, "we believe we but echo the feeling of the whole country, without distinction of party, in sincerely hoping that the President will soon be restored to health and strength. Men of his habit of body are not usually long-lived.... His death at this time would be a real calamity to the country."[1]

However ill it made him feel, the smallpox did not impair Lincoln's sense of humor. He observed how "since he had been president he had always had a crowd of people asking him to give them something." He then quipped, "Now, he has something he can give them all." He joked as well about his appearance, saying, "There is one consolation about the matter, ... it cannot in the least disfigure me."[2]

The illness had given Lincoln time to work on his annual message, due to be read by a clerk on December 8, the day after the Thirty-eighth Congress opened. But because of last-minute revisions by John Palmer Usher, the interior secretary, it was held over a day. Hay reported, "Wednesday we went up with the document and it was read. We watched the effect with great anxiety."[3]

The anxiety was not over the first part of the message, where the president reviewed foreign relations, the operations of the Treasury, the conditions of the army and navy, and the status of the territories and settlement of public lands. Lincoln then served as historian of the previous year when "the time of public feeling and opinion, at home and abroad, was not satisfactory." The elections in 1862 had gone against the administration; Europe was threatening intervention on behalf of the Confederacy; there was great anxiety over the Emancipation Proclamation and its announcement of the enlistment of black troops; military setbacks had ushered in "dark and doubtful days."[4]

But since then, the Mississippi had been opened and the Confederacy split; Tennessee and Arkansas were nearly free of insurgent control; citizens who had once owned slaves and defended slavery now "declare openly for emancipation"; some one hundred thousand men who had been slaves now bore arms and the experiment had been a success despite the forebodings of those who believed it would result in violence or insurrection. "The crisis which threatened to divide the friends of the Union is past," Lincoln declared. There was now a "new reckoning."[5]

Lincoln then turned to the rationale for the accompanying Proclamation of Amnesty and Reconstruction that he now saw fit to issue. Lincoln offered "full pardon" to persons who "have, directly or by implication, participated in the existing rebellion." There were, to be sure, several categories of exceptions: Confederate civil or diplomatic officers or agents; all who left seats in Congress, or judicial stations, to aid the rebellion; officers above the rank of colonel in the army and lieutenant in the navy; anyone who treated prisoners of war, white or black, unlawfully. The pardon would be granted, "with restoration of all rights of property, except as to slaves and in property cases where the rights of third parties shall have intervened," to persons who took an oath to "faithfully support, protect and defend the Constitution" and "abide by and faithfully support all acts of Congress passed during the existing rebellion with reference to slaves," as well as "all proclamations of the President made during the existing rebellion having reference to slaves," as long as the Supreme Court did not overturn them. Lincoln's proclamation also declared that whenever a number of persons "not less than one-tenth in number of the votes" cast in the presidential election of 1860 take the oath and "re-establish a State government which shall be republican," that government "shall be recognized as the true government of the State" and receive the full benefits provided by the Constitution. Thus far the proclamation provided details. Toward the end, Lincoln relied on double negatives, passive voice, and third person to make two important additional points. Any plans with respect to the freed people that "shall recognize and declare their permanent freedom, provide for their education, and which may yet be consistent, as a temporary arrangement, with their present condition as a laboring, landless, and homeless class, will not be objected to by the national Executive." Finally, the proclamation presents a "mode" whereby national authority and loyal state government can be reestablished. "While the mode presented is the best the Executive can suggest, with his present impressions," concluded Lincoln, "it must not be understood that no other possible mode would be acceptable."[6]

In the last portion of his annual address, Lincoln provided some explanations for the proclamation. "Nothing is attempted beyond what is amply justified by the Constitution," he declared. The Constitution authorizes the executive to grant or withhold pardons; the oath required is voluntary, not forced, and serves as a "sufficiently liberal" test to separate those whose continued "hostility and violence" would be a bar to the revival of state government.[7]

Lincoln went on to explain why an oath to uphold the "laws and proclamations in regard to slavery," in addition to the Constitution, was necessary. They were enacted, he argued, to help put an end to the rebellion and "they have aided, and will further aid, the cause for which they were intended. To now abandon them would be not only to relinquish a lever of power, but would also be a cruel and an astounding breach of faith." As he had been doing since January 1, 1863, Lincoln made his commitment to emancipation clear: "I shall not attempt to retract or modify the emancipation proclamation; nor shall I return to slavery any person who is free by the terms of that proclamation, or by any of the acts of Congress."[8]

He explained his "proposed acquiescence" to any "reasonable temporary State arrangement for the freed people." He hoped it might help ease "the confusion and destitution which must, at best, attend all classes by a total revolution of labor." Lincoln had been thinking about the transition from slave to free labor and, while he did not propose any specific plans, he recognized that this would pose one of the great challenges of "what is called reconstruction." Lincoln emphasized that he was issuing the proclamation as a "rallying point" so that states will know what was expected and under what terms their resumption in the Union would be accepted. The plan proposed was not a fixed one and could be changed to accommodate developments. For example, other groups might be added to the list of those pardoned. "Saying that reconstruction will be accepted if presented in a specific way," he added, "it is not said it will never be accepted in any other way."[9]

In a preliminary draft of the message, Lincoln explicitly addressed the various theories of the status of the states in rebellion: "the question whether these States have continued to be States in the Union, or have become territories, out of it, seems to me, in every present aspect, to be of no practical importance." Hay explained that Lincoln deleted those words because the guarantee clause of the Constitution "empowers him to grant protection to states *in* the Union and it will not do ever to admit that these states have at any time be[en] out. So he erased the sentence as possibly suggestive of evil." In the annual address he said only that his proclamation maintained the "political framework of the States."[10]

Lincoln's proclamation made it clear that there would be no reconstruction without emancipation. It may have shocked those who thought the president was tacking toward a conservative policy that might leave slavery intact, but those who believed so had ignored his many statements to the contrary issued during the previous year: his public letter to James Conkling, his instructions to his military governors, his support of the Free State General Committee in Louisiana, even his Gettysburg Address.[11]

At the same time, he might have gone even further. If he was fully committed to emancipation, and truly had concern that the Supreme Court might overturn the Emancipation Proclamation, he might have at this time proposed a constitutional amendment abolishing slavery. On December 4, Isaac Arnold, Illinois congressman and personal friend of Lincoln's, implored the president to "*complete the work you have begun*" and include in the annual message "a change in the Constitution so as to prohibit slavery in every part of the United States." But Lincoln would not endorse this path until after his nomination for reelection in 1864.[12]

Perhaps more surprising than support for emancipation was Lincoln's decision to require an oath from all Southerners, including those who had remained loyal. While the distinction between loyal and disloyal citizens had been useful in ad hoc attempts to restore state governments, it would create disharmony and confusion in applying the procedures of the amnesty proclamation. The only way to be certain about the future was to require everyone to take the oath. Lincoln explained to Andrew Johnson, "Loyal as well as disloyal should take the oath, because it does not hurt them, clears all question as to their right to vote, and swells the aggregate number who take it, which is an important object."[13]

But many Southern loyalists were unhappy. Lincoln heard from Nathaniel Banks that loyal citizens in Louisiana who had already voted believed they "ought not to be compelled to take an additional oath." One resident of New Orleans wrote, "Citizens who have not sinned cannot honorably accept a pardon." From Nashville, Horace Maynard reported that he heard repeatedly the criticism that the proclamation placed "in the same category repentant rebels & men always loyal."[14]

Lincoln responded to Banks that he had intentionally incorporated into the proclamation language that would permit flexibility. "You are at liberty," he wrote, "to adopt any rule which shall admit to vote any unquestionably loyal free-state men and none others." To one Louisiana conservative he wrote, "I deem the sustaining of the emancipation proclamation, where it applies, as indispensable." But other than that, and his hope that emancipation would extend to those places exempted on January 1, 1863, he gave assurance that he did not issue his reconstruction proclamation "as a Procrustean bed, to which exact conformity is to be indispensable."[15] With respect to a letter from a colonel in the Fourth Tennessee Union Cavalry who objected to taking an oath, Lincoln wrote to Stanton, "On principle I dislike an oath which requires a man to swear he *has* not done wrong. It rejects the Christian principle of forgiveness on terms of repentance. I think it is enough if a man does no wrong *hereafter*." But oaths would be required, except in those individual cases where discretion suggested that an exception be made.[16]

If the commitment to emancipation and the requirement that all white residents of the rebellious states take an oath seemed radical to some, other elements appeared less so. Lincoln did not adopt the doctrine of state suicide (state name, boundaries, constitution, and laws would "be maintained," except as modified by the requirements of the proclamation), though some conservatives would read the proclamation as if he had. And while the figure of 10 percent would later engender controversy between Lincoln and radicals in Congress who proposed 50 percent as the number of voters from 1860 required to reestablish state government, few thought the number problematic at the time. Finally, the list of pardons was if anything seen as too lenient. In March, Lincoln issued another proclamation with regard to amnesty, clarifying that it did not apply to prisoners of war.[17]

For all of Hay's initial anxiety over reactions to the proclamation, the White House could not have been happier with the response. Hay wrote about it effusively: "Whatever may be the results or the verdict of history the immediate effect of this paper is something wonderful. I have never seen such an effect produced by a public document. Men acted as if the Millennium had come. [Michigan senator Zachariah] Chandler was delighted, Sumner was beaming while at the other political pole [Senator James] Dixon and [Senator] Reverdy Johnson said it was highly satisfactory.... [Massachusetts senator] Henry Wilson came to me and laying his broad palms on my shoulders said 'The President has struck another great blow. Tell him from me God bless him.'" The effect, Hay reported, was much the same in the House. George Boutwell, a radical from Massachusetts, said, "it is a very able and shrewd paper." Illinois abolitionist Owen Lovejoy said it was "glorious." Michigan Republican Francis Kellogg "was superlatively enthusiastic. He said, 'the President is the only man. He is the great man of the century. There is none like him in the world. He sees more widely and clearly than anybody.'"[18]

Inside Lincoln's cabinet there seemed to be unanimity, except for Salmon Chase. Asked if because of the commitment in the proclamation to emancipation Blair and Bates, the most conservative cabinet members, would resign, Lincoln responded, "both of these men acquiesced to it without objection. The only member of the Cabinet who had objected to it was Mr. Chase." In saying so, Lincoln seems to have ignored the opening line of Chase's letter to him on November 25, in which he made suggestions after seeing a draft: "the conclusions you have come to concerning the reconstruction of the rebel States give me very great satisfaction." But Chase pressured Lincoln to revoke the exceptions that had been included in the Emancipation Proclamation. He also advised against making any reference to apprenticeship plans in the transition from slavery to freedom.[19]

Lincoln's patience with Chase was severely tested. In September, he had written Chase a forceful letter explaining why the exceptions could not be revoked: "If I take the step must I not do so, without the argument of military necessity, and so, without any argument, except the one that I think the measure politically expedient, and morally right? Would I not thus give up all footing on the Constitution and law? Would I not thus be in the boundless field of absolutism?"[20]

Chase was nothing if not stubborn and, privately at least, he criticized the proclamation. He told Henry Ward Beecher, "I really expected that he would have revoked the exceptions," and that he was "a good deal disappointed" by the suggestion of "qualified Involuntary Servitude." But, he concluded, "I suppose I must use the Touchstone's philosophy & be thankful for skim milk when cream is not to be had." In a war of tortured metaphor, Beecher responded, Lincoln's "bread is of unbolted flour & much straw, too, mixes in the bran & sometimes gravel stones—Yet, on the whole the loaf will sustain life, tho' it makes eating a difficulty—rather than a pleasure."[21]

Outside Washington's inner circle, private reaction mirrored Hay's enthusiasm. The writer and editor Charles Eliot Norton observed, "Once more we may rejoice that Abraham Lincoln is President. How wise and how admirably timed is his Proclamation.... Lincoln will introduce a new style into state papers; he will make them sincere, and his honesty will compel even politicians to like virtue." Unitarian minister Edward Everett Hale praised the proclamation as "sublimely practical." And New York lawyer George Templeton Strong recorded that "Uncle Abe is the most popular man in America today. The firmness, honesty, and sagacity of the 'gorilla despot' may be recognized by the rebels themselves sooner than we expect, and the weight of his personal character may do a great deal toward restoration of our national unity." John Bennitt, a surgeon with the Nineteenth Michigan, spoke for his regiment: "We are very well pleased with the President's message & think there is light ahead. Lincoln is *the* man yet."[22]

Lengthier evaluations came from the partisan press, which was predictable in its reaction. "Suffice it to say," observed one writer, "that the administration journals generally commend the views of the President, while those of the opposition express various dissentient opinions."[23]

No reporter was more proadministration than *Sacramento Daily Union* journalist Noah Brooks. The proclamation, thought Brooks, is "temperate, wise, statesmanlike and broad in its proposed treatment of the vexed questions of this hour and of the coming hour." Brooks admired Lincoln's political acumen and praised him for having "pleased the radicals and satisfied the conservatives." The arch Democratic *New York World* saw the same quality, but didn't admire it. The proclamation, observed the paper, "is so skillfully devised and so curiously phrased that it equally admits of an interpretation which ought to please the radicals, and of an interpretation which can be accepted by such Republicans as are not extremists." However even-handed the proclamation, Brooks thought Lincoln did it in an original way by taking "bold, high and original ground" and disregarding "the claims of either of the great factions which profess to own the President and the next Presidency."[24]

The *New York Times* proclaimed, "Abraham Lincoln is one of the few men who believes that words stand for things; he economizes them accordingly.... The process of reconstruction, as the President puts it, is simple and yet perfectly effective.... He gives no countenance to the project, which has been so vehemently advocated, of reducing the redeemed States to a territorial condition." A month later, the paper tied Lincoln's plan to his reelection: "unquestionably one of the strongest causes of the popular manifestations for the re-election of President Lincoln, is the fact that he most directly represents an acceptable policy in regard to reconstruction."[25]

The *Tribune* praised the terms of the proclamation and asked, "how can any one who means to be loyal at all, object to these conditions?" The paper also noted that under these terms, Tennessee, Louisiana, and Arkansas might be quickly restored to the Union. Most important, reunion would come without slavery: "in no metaphoric or poetic sense, the Union and Liberty are henceforth inseparable." Employing an extended metaphor of rebuilding the nation's foundation, the *Chicago Tribune* described Lincoln as "determined, if possible, that there shall be no timber in the new edifice shaky or rotten with slavery, and no stone cracked or crumbling from treason."[26]

At the same time, the more conservative *Daily National Intelligencer* gave credit to Lincoln for considering the feelings of Southerners in his willingness to consider "a temporary arrangement" in the transition to freedom. The *Massachusetts Spy* found in Lincoln "a heart incapable of conceiving or of cherishing malice." The amnesty "is not an iron hand under a silk glove, but a warm human hand carrying reconciliation and peace."[27]

The 10 percent provision seemed eminently fair to one editor, who argued "one loyal man in a rebel State is certainly entitled to as much consideration as nine traitors.... The proposition does not prohibit the nine from qualifying themselves to vote. If they decline the terms, it is their own fault." But the *New York Herald* snorted, "we dare say that our Father Abraham's 'one-tenth' proposition was suggested by this proposition from the original Father Abraham of ten righteous men in Sodom, and we fear that the result will be the same—that the righteous men required to save the rebellious States from a destructive storm of fire and brimstone will not be found."[28]

Religious publications expressed enthusiasm without resorting to biblical texts. The *Christian Examiner* noted that the proclamation was "a generous alternative" to destruction. The radical *Independent* was thrilled that Lincoln sustained his commitment to emancipation, but the editor wondered about the arbitrary number of one-tenth of the voters and noted, "the readmission of states cannot take place on arithmetical grounds. It is a moral question to be decided by the discretion of the Government." The paper also expressed concern with Lincoln's proposed oath that provided for support of the Emancipation Proclamation unless "modified or declared void" by the Supreme Court. The editor, with the *Dred Scott* decision obviously in mind, noted wryly that the Court "has not of late years laid the country under any obligations of gratitude for its sympathy with the doctrine of liberty." Nonetheless, "the President has presented to the country a *practical* issue, instead of a sentiment of theory." The *Evangelist* proclaimed that the proclamation, "like everything else which comes from Mr. Lincoln, ... is simple and clear in its statements, lenient and forbearing in the feelings expressed and strongly marked by his characteristic honesty and firmness." Readers were reminded that the 10 percent threshold was only a minimum intended to accelerate the process of reconstruction and make it "a practicable measure." Lincoln, the editor concluded, "carries a steady and even hand, turning neither to the right nor to the left."[29]

Whereas most Republicans showered Lincoln with praise, many Democrats denounced him. Deploring his use of executive power, those speaking for them labeled the proclamation a "Despot's edict." They strenuously opposed the requirement of emancipation. "The President's message," howled the *World*, "settles the question that the war during his administration is for the abolition of slavery." The *New York Journal of Commerce* observed, "It is plain that what Mr. Lincoln wants is peace and abolition. He does not take into consideration at all the question of peace without abolition. In this respect he lends himself entirely to the radical abolitionists." The *Daily Age* marveled, "For Mr. Lincoln . . . to compel the people of the South to swear that they will 'abide by and faithfully support all proclamations having reference to slaves' is not less arbitrary and unreasonable than to force them to give in their allegiance to his creed about spirit-rapping." The editor concluded, "it is now clear that so long as the present administration is in power, the abolition of slavery will be made paramount to the restoration of the Union."[30]

According to the *Old Guard*, whose editor adamantly opposed the war and militantly defended slavery, the proclamation asked Southerners to help the Republicans "murder and rob your neighbors, then you shall have our gracious pardon." The *World* found the amnesty provision galling: "it seeks out the sorest, the most inflamed, the most sensitive spot in the southern mind, and applies to it a burning brand." The staunchly Democratic *Republican Farmer* in Bridgeport, Connecticut, whose offices were once mobbed for its opposition to the war, claimed the document teemed "with deceit, falsehood, a suppression of facts, and a course of policy worthy only of a man who has been schooled in the wiles and trickery of obscure Western politicians. . . . It offers to the Southern people no alternative but complete submission—their utter degradation and humiliation."[31]

Because Lincoln's proclamation required adherence to the Emancipation Proclamation, and the only way, according to conservatives, that he could interfere with slavery in the states was if he no longer recognized the state's constitutional authority to organize its own domestic institutions, some editors argued that the president had nearly embraced the doctrine of state suicide. "The general scope of the President's plan may be said to be of the extreme radical sort," argued the *Journal of Commerce*. "He almost, but not quite, recognizes Mr. Sumner's State suicide theory. He ignores the present existence of State governments, regards them as defunct, and anticipates a sort of territorial reorganization. In this view, he is neither sound nor consistent." According to the *New Haven Daily Register*, "Mr. Lincoln adopts the extreme Radical theory that the State governments were dissolved by the insurrection." Even the proadministration *Springfield Republican* thought the "theory of state suicide...obtains considerable countenance from the message and proclamation," and lamented "alas that it be so."[32]

Although Lincoln certainly did not endorse the doctrine of state suicide, Charles Sumner, who did, nonetheless expressed satisfaction with the proclamation. Noah Brooks claimed that Sumner was irate because Lincoln's magnanimous offer of amnesty did not echo the senator's beliefs. But Sumner wrote to John Bright, British radical and member of the House of Commons, that "the Presdt's proposition of reconstruction has *two* essential features—(1) The irreversibility of Emancipation,—making it the 'corner-stone' of the new order of things, (2) the reconstruction or revival of the States by a *preliminary* process before they take their place in the Union— I doubt if the details will be remembered a fortnight from now." Sumner cared far less about Lincoln's theory of the state than the question of the role of Congress in the reconstruction process.[33]

The most sustained critiques of Lincoln's proclamation came not from conservatives but from radicals. Adam Gurowski, the minor State Department functionary who cut so terrifying a figure as he trooped about Washington that one of Lincoln's friends said the president felt threatened by him, thought the proclamation "corresponds to a Ukase—all confusion. The validity of the proclamation, and the oath prescribed by it, are submitted to the judicial decision. And if a Taney and such ones invalidate all, what then? A tenth part of the voters are to organize a State—altogether against the paramount principle of majority. And when the remaining nine-tenths oppose, what then?"[34]

One of the most independent of radical voices belonged to Orestes Brownson. Born in Vermont in 1803, Brownson was one of those searching intellectuals New England seemed to produce in abundance. He made his way from Presbyterianism through Universalism and Transcendentalism before converting to Catholicism in 1844. An avid supporter of the labor movement and the abolition of slavery, he started *Brownson's Quarterly Review* and wrote extensively about religious doctrine as well as political and social issues. Sumner was one of his readers. In October 1863, the senator praised Brownson for adopting the doctrine that the states should be made territories and readmission left to Congress.[35]

Brownson argued that Lincoln's plan for reconstruction was unconstitutional, and possibly as dangerous to the Union as the "southern rebellion itself." His central criticism was that the executive did not have the authority to do what Lincoln proposed, and that the power to organize a state government belonged to Congress alone. Brownson explained his position: if the seceded states are still states, the executive has no power, whether justified under war or peace powers, to establish government within their limits; if they are not states, "their reorganization is the work of congress under its peace power." Brownson also objected to offering terms of amnesty and pardon, which he recognized were within Lincoln's powers. "Submission first, is our rule," he proclaimed. "When rebels have submitted and thrown themselves on the mercy of the government, we will then offer terms and treat them humanely." He was skeptical of oaths of allegiance, which would "have no binding force on the rebel conscience."[36]

Brownson did not understand how newspapers such as the *New York Times* could claim that the proclamation discarded the doctrine

of state suicide: "will they tell us on what principle the president authorizes one-tenth of the legal voters under the constitution to organize and assume to be a state, if the old state is still a state in the
Union?" Lincoln's proposal "can be defended only on the ground
that the old state is dead." Even if Congress, which had the authority,
sought to implement Lincoln's plan, Brownson objected to the idea
that one-tenth of the eligible voters was sufficient: it was neither just
nor fair to exclude nine-tenths of a state's population.[37]

Unlike most opponents of slavery, including Sumner, who believed
the proclamation "fastens Emancipation beyond recall," Brownson
condemned Lincoln for not fully embracing abolition. What did it
mean, he wondered, that the oath to support emancipation applied
only if the Emancipation Proclamation was not set aside at some
future date? No one, he said, expects the Supreme Court "to sustain
the freedom of slaves under the proclamation." More nefarious was
Lincoln's support for some temporary arrangements. "If the president believes the proclamation really freed the slaves," asked Brownson, "how can he proclaim that he will not object should they for any
reason whatever even for one moment be detained in servitude?"
Lincoln's implied support of gradual rather than immediate emancipation dismayed Brownson. It also contradicted the president's own
Emancipation Proclamation, which used military necessity to justify immediate emancipation. Now, Brownson thundered, Lincoln
issued a proclamation that told the rebels "if they choose to retain
their slaves, that is, the men he had professed to free, in bondage for
a time, he shall make no objection!"[38]

Brownson could only conclude that the proclamation was the
work of a politician, not a statesman, someone more concerned with
looking "to the next presidential election than to the welfare of the
nation." Democrats, in particular, saw the rapid restoration of state
governments as nothing more than a "machination" by which Lincoln
sought to reassure his reelection. The *New York World* argued that
the proclamation was not intended for the rebels, but "to unite the
Republican party upon Mr. Lincoln as a presidential candidate."

Even more conspiratorially, "by setting up...state governments, representing one-tenth of the voters in Arkansas, Louisiana, Tennessee, and North Carolina" Lincoln could "control as many electoral votes as may be needed to turn the scale." A table published in the *Albany Atlas and Argus* calculated that, under the 10 percent plan, it would take only 84,680 votes for Lincoln to secure eighty-two electoral votes in ten states (South Carolina was excluded because its electors were chosen by the legislature). The insinuation that Lincoln's proclamation was devised solely with a view to the upcoming presidential election led the *Tribune* to counter, "his plan of reconstruction has no designed or necessary connection with the Presidency in prospect, and should be judged entirely by its intrinsic merits."[39]

Although antislavery, Brownson had no more use for radical abolitionists than he did for extremist Northern Democrats. At war's end, Brownson declared, "Wendell Phillips is as far removed from true Christian civilization as was John C. Calhoun, and William Lloyd Garrison is as much of a barbarian and a despot in principle and tendency as Jefferson Davis." It came as a surprise to some that even though Lincoln had stood fast by emancipation, these abolitionists vilified the proclamation. Garrison's *Liberator* regarded "this Amnesty as uncalled for, and anti-republican and perilous in some of its features." In the paper's view, Lincoln was too magnanimous and in his proclamation was simply "giving over the sheep to the guardianship of wolves." Leaving the former slave "betwixt bondage and manhood" was as cruel as slavery. "Has the President so soon forgotten his noble speech at Gettysburg?" wondered Wendell Phillips Garrison, the editor's son. "We can never have a Republic so long as we deny to any of our fellow-creatures rights inherent in their humanity."[40]

Garrison's editorial in the *Liberator* received little attention compared with a speech delivered by Wendell Phillips at the Cooper Union in New York. Phillips had left a career in law to become an abolitionist and he had worked closely with Garrison for decades. Before a crowded house on a wintry Tuesday evening, Phillips took to the stage to condemn the president. He spoke without notes, and without a lectern. Nothing could separate him from his audience. A listener once recalled, he looked "like a marble statue, cool and white, while a stream of lava issued red hot from his lips."[41]

Phillips denounced Lincoln for abandoning the freedmen and demanded more than simply saying that the oath would require Southerners to abide by the Emancipation Proclamation unless modified by the Supreme Court. Such an avowal made the Emancipation Proclamation largely hollow. Phillips noted, "The meaning of that proclamation nobody knows until the Supreme Court has settled it.... God help the Negro if he hangs on Roger B. Taney for his liberty!" The idea of a "temporary arrangement" from slavery to freedom appalled Phillips, who asked, "how long does that mean—fifty years?" The apprenticeship system in Jamaica, where an Act of Parliament abolished slavery in 1833, lasted for years. All the plan did was put the slave back where he had been and "furnish Jefferson Davis with sixty or ninety representatives in Congress." What was needed was a greater commitment to abolition and the lives of the freedmen. Phillips added, "As commander-in-chief, he has *freed slaves*. I ask the *Nation to abolish slavery*," and he urged Lincoln to propose a constitutional amendment doing so. More needed to be done as well: "The nation owes to the negro not merely freedom; it owes him land, and it owes him education also." Lincoln, Phillips argued, "is antislavery. He does not believe in a nation 'being half slave and half free'—but he is a Colonizationist and does not believe in a nation half black and half white." Unless he did so, his reconstruction plan would fail.[42]

Both the radical *Tribune* and conservative *Herald* critiqued Phillips's speech, which also drew the attention of the Confederate press. "Lincoln—radical as he appears to us," reported the *Richmond Examiner*, "is not, in Phillips' opinion, the man for the times." The lesson for the Confederacy was to realize that Northern opinion was radicalizing; with conservative views at war's beginning, Northerners now accepted emancipation and the use of black troops. Could confiscation of land and "complete dominion over the lives" of

Southerners be far behind Lincoln's announced policy, which was bad enough?[43]

Confederate reactions to Lincoln's proclamation ran a predictable course: newspapers denounced him as a tyrant. The *Richmond Enquirer* thought, "recovering out recently from an attack of smallpox, some excuse may be given for the Message. It is but another example of his weakness and folly." Augusta's *Daily Constitutionalist* believed that the smallpox must have impaired the president mentally. The 10 percent provision was "tantamount to erecting an oligarchy," wrote one editorialist. "He makes his forgiveness dependent upon terms," charged the *Richmond Sentinel*. "We have only to swear obedience to his will. We have to swear *that the proclamation of emancipation which he issued last year* ... shall be submitted to by us. Our society is to be uprooted." In the Confederate Congress, Henry Foote, who had been a U.S. senator from Mississippi, offered a resolution that denounced the "imbecile and unprincipled usurper who now sits enthroned upon the ruins of constitutional liberty in Washington City."[44]

Neither the severe criticisms of Democrats, nor the condemnations of abolitionists, nor certainly the demagoguery of the Confederates diminished the initial enthusiasm for Lincoln's plan among most Republicans. Even the conservative *St. Louis Republican*, a voice for the Border States, observed, "it must be remembered that the South has sinned against the Union, and who ever sinned without having to pay some penalty for it?"[45]

It helped that, almost immediately, Lincoln's plan seemed to reap dividends when a former Confederate general asked for a pardon from Lincoln. Edward W. Gantt, a wealthy Arkansas lawyer and slave owner, had been elected to Congress in 1860. A fiery secessionist, he never took his seat. Instead, he was elected colonel of the Twelfth Arkansas Infantry. Appointed brigadier general in early 1862, Gantt was among the seven thousand Confederates who surrendered to Union forces and relinquished Island No. 10 in the Mississippi River. Imprisoned in Fort Warren, in Boston, he was released in a prisoner exchange in August 1862 and returned home, awaiting further orders that never came.

In June 1863, Gantt surrendered to Grant. General Stephen Hurlbut brought him to the attention of Lincoln, and said he "desires to be instrumental to his full capacity" in putting the rebellion down. In July, Gantt met with Lincoln and afterward wrote a well-meaning but confused letter to the president, assuring him, "I can offer no better proof of my sincerity than that I have cut myself loose from home friends kindred fortune & prejudices to follow in what I conceive to be the path of duty." He averred, "My only object is to induce the withdrawal of my state from its allies in rebellion & its reentry into the Federal union. Its geographical position & the state of public feeling at this time among its citizens convince me that it is the first state among those which clearly seceded that can be induced to return to its allegiance." Lincoln liked what he heard.[46]

Whatever Gantt's motivations (he had a reputation as a drinker and a womanizer and knew that after his surrender at Island No. 10 he had no future in the Confederate army), he became a zealous spokesman for restoration and Union. The *New York Times* reported his October speech in Little Rock as "Repentance and Confession of a Rebel Officer." "After two years of strife," he told the citizens of Arkansas, "we awake from a fearful baptismal of blood to the terrible truth that the shadow of the despotism which we fled from under Mr. Lincoln dissolves into nothingness, compared to the awful reign of tyranny that we have groaned under at the hands of Jefferson Davis and his minions." Gantt asked the citizens to accept slavery's end. "Reunion is certain," he proclaimed, "but no more certain than the downfall of slavery.... We fought for negro slavery. We have lost."[47]

Following the Proclamation of Amnesty and Reconstruction, Gantt became the first Confederate officer to be pardoned by Lincoln. He lectured widely and worked zealously for the restoration of Arkansas under Lincoln's 10 percent plan. Others followed Gantt's lead, and newspapers circulated reports of responses to the proclamation. In a piece titled "How Amnesty Works," the *New York Times* reported news from North Carolina that a number of Confederate officers and soldiers had sought pardon and that thousands in Arkansas

were "securing oblivion" of their past actions in support of the Confederacy. "We know that one swallow don't make a Summer," observed the *Times*, but only three weeks had passed since Lincoln's
message and, while it will take time, Southerners now knew "there
will be a general escape [from the slave power] through the wide and
safe gate this Amnesty Proclamation will always keep open."[48]

Lincoln sought to spread word of the proclamation through the
Confederacy. He even appointed Russell Alger, an attorney and colonel in the Fifth Michigan Cavalry, a special commissioner in charge
of distributing copies of the proclamation. Among Alger's ideas: "let
scouts carry it within the enemy's lines; let cavalry expeditions be
sent out, supplied with it: leave copies at every house possible, and
scatter wherever the enemy will be likely to find it."[49]

In February 1864, Lincoln asked General Judson Kilpatrick to
use his cavalry forces to distribute copies of the proclamation. A raid
intended to liberate Union prisoners of war held at Belle Island and
Libby Prison in Richmond provided an opportunity to circulate the
proclamation, but the raid on Richmond proved disastrous. It accomplished none of its objectives and resulted in the death of Ulric
Dahlgren, son of Rear Admiral John A. Dahlgren and a war hero
whose foot had been amputated in the aftermath of Gettysburg.[50]

Nonetheless, Union troops were so effective at distributing the
proclamation that Confederate general James Longstreet wrote in
protest to General John G. Foster, who commanded Union forces in
Knoxville. "I find the Proclamation of President Lincoln of the 6th
of December last, in circulation in handbills among our soldiers,"
reported Longstreet. "The immediate object of this circulation appears to be to induce our soldiers to quit our ranks and to take the
oath of allegiance to the United States Government." Longstreet declared that it was improper to communicate with the soldiers directly and that those likely to respond are of such debased character
"they can do your cause no good, nor can they injure ours." Foster
could not resist some sarcasm in his response: "I accept...your suggestion, that it would have been more courteous to have sent these

documents to you for circulation, and I embrace with pleasure the opportunity thus afforded to enclose to you twenty (20) copies of each of these documents, and rely upon your generosity and desire for peace to give publicity to the same among your officers and men." Lincoln, who first saw the correspondence reprinted in newspapers, asked Foster, "is a supposed correspondence between Gen. Longstreet and yourself, about the amnesty proclamation, which is now in the papers, genuine?" Foster responded that it was.[51]

Lincoln wasted no time trying to advance the election process. On Christmas Day 1863, Hay reported, he "got up a plan for extending to the people of the rebellious districts the practical benefits of his proclamation." He was sending record books to keep track of the administration of the oath, the first of which went out to Governor Pierpont in Virginia. The next would go to Arkansas. He also decided to commission Hay a major and send him to Florida with an oath book to try and "get the matter going there." A military expedition, led in part by the black troops of the Fifty-fourth Massachusetts, succeeded in retaking Jacksonville (which had first been occupied in March 1862), and Hay had copies of Lincoln's proclamation posted about town. Although he reported to Lincoln, "I have the best assurances that we will get the tenth required," the defeat of Union forces at Olustee on February 20, 1864, effectively put an end to reconstruction efforts in Florida. It also provided political fodder for his opponents. The *New York Herald* accused Lincoln of "executive intermeddling" with military affairs and reported rumors "that the expedition was intended simply for the occupation of Florida for the purpose of securing the election of three Lincoln delegates to the National Nominating Convention, and that of John Hay to Congress."[52]

By March, Hay was back in Washington. Congress was debating its own reconstruction proposal, and Louisiana and Arkansas were organizing for elections and constitutional conventions. For all his faith that with Lincoln's proclamation the millennium had come, Hay, for one, now knew that the restoration of the Union remained far off in the distance.

Chapter 5

"We, the Loyal People, Differ"

The winter of 1863–1864 was the coldest winter in memory. Some days the temperature fell to five degrees below zero. Thick ice covered the Potomac clear across to Alexandria. Citizens slipped on the frigid streets; horses struggled to pull carriages along frozen tracks; ferryboats were locked in place. On a "fearfully cold and windy" New Year's Day, people still crowded the White House to be received by the Lincolns. A year earlier, the president had signed the Emancipation Proclamation, his hand shaking not from cold or nerves but from having been on the receiving line all morning. Now Lincoln was recovering from varioloid and he looked much improved. Noah Brooks reported, "his complexion is clearer, his eyes less lackluster, and he has a hue of health to which he has long been a stranger."[1]

After receiving Lincoln's annual message, Congress had referred various provisions to relevant congressional committees. It was Thaddeus Stevens, as chairman of the House Ways and Means Committee, who offered the resolutions on December 19. The last of twenty-three resolutions read, "that so much of the President's message as is contained in the proclamation, and as refers to the conditions and treatment of the rebellious States, be referred to a special committee of nine, to be appointed by the Speaker."[2]

It seemed innocuous enough, except Representative Henry Winter Davis had an amendment to introduce. He wanted the resolution to read instead, "that so much of the President's message as relates to the duty of the United States to guarantee a republican form of government to the States in which the governments recognized by the United States have been abrogated or overthrown, be referred to a select committee of nine, to be named by the Speaker; which shall report the bills necessary and proper for carrying into execution the foregoing guarantee." Davis defended his motion as containing greater specificity than the original resolution. He supposed Stevens's motion "intended to point to what, in the very inaccurate phraseology of the day, is known as the question of reconstruction." But Davis rejected that term: "There has been no destruction of the Union, no breaking up of the Government." Davis was also rejecting the idea of territorialization, as well as Stevens's concept of conquered provinces, and instead, as he had in his September speech in Philadelphia, was relying on the language of the Constitution to restore republican governments to states in rebellion. The Illinois radical Owen Lovejoy agreed: "I do not believe, strictly speaking, that there are any rebel States. I know there are States which rebels have taken possession of and overthrown legitimate governments for the time being."[3]

Davis's amendment passed 91–80 with all but three Republicans voting for it. While this particular amendment did not signal a breech between Congress and the executive (among those voting aye were Lincoln's most avid supporters), it certainly foreshadowed a tempestuous session ahead as congressmen offered various proposals on how to organize state governments and readmit them to the Union. Indeed, Henry Dawes of Massachusetts observed, "everybody abounds in schemes for settling the troubles in the rebel states, and at least six plans a day are offered in the House in the shape of a Bill."[4]

Resolutions poured forth, including several uncompromising proposals from Democrats, none of them going anywhere except to the oblivion of being held over or tabled. Aaron Harding of Kentucky proposed "that the Union has not been dissolved" and that when the rebellion ended states would be restored to all rights and privileges. When George Yeaman of Kentucky resolved, "a formal return or readmission into the Union is not necessary," Owen Lovejoy jumped up and shouted that he hoped no one would second the resolution. As various bills came forward in Congress, Senator John Conover Ten Eyck, Republican from New Jersey, praised Lincoln

who, "with practical good sense, has, in his message and accompanying proclamation, 'hit the nail upon the head' and opened a way."
The specifics of what that way would be, and the rationale, were up
for debate. Representative James Ashley of Ohio presented the first
major reconstruction bill on December 21.[5] One writer called Ashley
"the best looking man, physically, on the floor of the House." He also
said he was "a hare-brained abolitionist."[6]

In most respects, Ashley's bill was consonant with Lincoln's
proclamation and sought to provide mechanisms to implement it.
He rejected territorialization and referred to "States which have abrogated the State governments recognized by Congress." Relying on
the guarantee clause, Ashley's bill directed that after the rebellious
states had been brought back into line Congress "provide by law for
the internal government of such States." The bill also accepted the
figure of 10 percent of the aggregate vote in 1860 as a precondition
for calling an election for delegates to a constitutional convention.
Ashley provided for establishing military governments, intended to
give Lincoln authority that he had already taken, in part, in 1862.
Indeed, the measure was entitled "A Bill to Provide for the Establishment of Provisional Military Governments."[7]

Ironically, it would seem that Lincoln himself had moved beyond
a commitment to military governors—after Edward Stanly in North
Carolina and John Phelps in Arkansas resigned, they were not replaced. Part of the problem, Lincoln had come to see, was the tension over who was in charge: the military governor or the military
commander in the region. He explained to an Arkansas delegation,
"there was constant conflict between military governors and military commanders." The situation became especially problematic in
Louisiana, and a few weeks after issuing his proclamation, which
said nothing about military governors, Lincoln wrote to General
Banks that he had intended for Shepley only to assist him and that
"you are master while you remain in command of the Department."[8]

With respect to the freedmen, Ashley's bill went beyond Lincoln's
proclamation. Both insisted that those taking the oath of loyalty

abide by provisions of the Emancipation Proclamation and that any new constitution forbid slavery. But Ashley's bill also declared void any state laws that barred black people from testifying, serving on juries, or being educated. He said nothing about transitional stages from slavery to freedom that might involve some sort of apprentice-ship scheme. Most significantly, Ashley's bill provided the vote for black men over the age of twenty-one.

One writer praised Ashley's plan for fulfilling Lincoln's plan. Another observed that while it "seems based mainly upon the Presi-dent's Amnesty Proclamation," he thought it unwise to disenfran-chise every soldier who fought against the Union because after having "extracted the poison of slavery," Southerners must be trusted to govern their own affairs. The *New York Tribune* called the bill a "very radical and thorough" measure that applied the tests for readmission proposed by Lincoln. By comparison, the *Weekly Patriot and Union* in Harrisburg thought the bill went far beyond radical: "it is as un-constitutional, arbitrary, cruel, and revolutionary as the most ardent disciple of the treasonable school of Garrison could desire."[9]

If Northern Democrats and conservative Republicans despaired over Ashley's plan, they must have combusted over Thaddeus Ste-vens's proposal. His bill referred to "the conquered territory of the Confederate States" which "can claim no protection nor invoke in their defence any of the provisions of the Constitution or the laws of the United States, but are subject to the laws of war and the law of nations alone." Accordingly, Congress would enact legislation that would abolish slavery in those conquered territories or provinces and require the abolition of slavery before any of them could become a state in the Union. Stevens's conquered provinces doctrine, even more extreme than Sumner's state suicide concept, would gain no traction, but his remarks reminded his congressional colleagues that perhaps they should not rush into reconstruction.[10]

On January 22, Stevens used the occasion of a debate over con-fiscation to return to the subject of the relation of the seceded states to the United States. He disparaged the idea that the rebel states still enjoyed the same privileges and immunities as loyal states and that whenever "those 'wayward sisters' choose to abandon their frivolities and present themselves...we must receive them." This belief, Stevens declared with disgust, meant that the rebel states, after years of bloody and expensive war, might simply stop fighting, elect representatives to Congress, and continue as if nothing had happened. Instead, he argued, the Confederacy is "a distinct and hostile government" and in its defeat its component parts should be treated as "conquered provinces" on which the victor may impose whatever terms it chooses. Stevens believed these terms should include punishing the leading traitors, seizing their lands and estates, and selling them to help defray the cost of the war. "Above all," he proclaimed, we "will forever exclude the infernal cause of this rebellion—human bondage—from the continent of North America." Orestes Brownson called the speech "able, straightforward, and manly," but the *New York Herald* could only hear in it "an insane fanatic of the Danton, Marat and Robespierre type."[11]

On February 15, a third bill was introduced that tacked between the Ashley and Stevens bills. Henry Winter Davis introduced it, and it served as the basis for the Wade-Davis reconstruction bill that would eventually pass on July 2. Davis's was a bill "to Guarantee to Certain States Whose Governments Have Been Usurped or Overthrown, a Republican Form of Government." The title itself incorporated a theory of secession whereby the states had not committed suicide or been conquered, they were still in the Union, but their governments had been subverted. The bill authorized the president to appoint a provisional governor to oversee civil administration and enroll all loyal white male citizens age twenty-one or older who took an oath to support the Constitution. The oath would not be the one Lincoln specified in his Proclamation of Amnesty and Reconstruction, but rather one adopted by Congress on July 2, 1862. The oath required the person to swear, "I have never voluntarily borne arms against the United States" and "I have voluntarily given no aid, countenance, counsel, or encouragement to persons engaged in armed hostility thereto." The oath would come to be known as the "ironclad oath" for its rigorous, uncompromising test of what constituted loyalty.[12]

As with Ashley's bill (and Lincoln's proclamation), Davis's proposed law required that 10 percent of voters take the oath as a precondition for the election of delegates to a constitutional convention. Among the provisions the convention was required to adopt were that "involuntary servitude is forever prohibited, and; the freedom of all persons is guaranteed in said state." In order to protect the free labor rights of the freedmen, Davis also included a section that provided for harsh fines and prison terms for anyone who restrained the liberty of individuals with the intent to hold or reduce them to involuntary servitude. Following the adoption of an approved new constitution, the state could then hold elections preparatory to regaining representation in Congress.[13]

With its emphasis on guaranteeing a republican form of government, appointing provisional governors, requiring 10 percent of the electorate to initiate the process, outlawing slavery, and limiting the franchise to white males, Davis's proposal fit snugly with Lincoln's. According to the *New York Evening Post*, "It reduces to a practical form the plan proposed in the President's Amnesty Proclamation." Yet at this same moment in early 1864, tensions between Congress and the president on the issue of reconstruction began to grow worse. In January, the fearsome Adam Gurowski wrote in his diary, "reconstruction is the order of the day," and observed that Lincoln's 10 percent proposal had its opponents in Congress who "wish to keep this whole question in suspense, rather than see it pressed, and thus bring it to an issue between Congress and Mr. Lincoln." He added more emphatically, "What Congress intends" differs diametrically "from what Lincoln attempts." The *Independent* reported that those ready to stymie the president's proclamation were "the very men who at first were loudest in praise of that policy." It was more than the details of Lincoln's Proclamation of Amnesty and Reconstruction that led Congress to oppose Lincoln (after all, the bills of both Ashley and Davis had followed the president's ideas closely);

problems with attempts to restore Louisiana and Arkansas to the Union helped bring Congress to a boiling point.[14]

Shortly after issuing his proclamation, Lincoln tried to reenergize efforts in Louisiana by putting General Banks fully in charge of establishing a loyal government. The work of Shepley and Durant seemed at a standstill. Moreover, the president was unhappy with a spurious November election in Louisiana that chose three conservatives for Congress, including one who had signed Louisiana's ordinance of secession. (The House report that denied them seats could not determine how many votes were actually cast and noted that in one district only two precincts participated.) Lincoln told Banks that he had always intended him to be "*master*," in both organizing civil government and directing military affairs. To emphasize his point, Lincoln used the word "master" three times in a two-page letter.[15]

Banks responded quickly to Lincoln's desires and assured the president that rapid progress would be made. Lincoln was thrilled: "the words '*can*' and '*will*' were never more precious." Banks issued an order calling for an election of state officers on February 22, 1864. This raised two interrelated problems. First, it alienated the Free State Committee, whose members had been working toward organizing a loyal government and now saw their plans undone. Second, by calling for elections before the state constitution had been revised to prohibit slavery, Banks seemed to be supporting Louisiana's proslavery faction. The Unionist lawyer Benjamin Flanders, who was up for election, informed Lincoln, "the Free State men are bitterly disappointed by the course of Gen Banks in ordering an election for State Officers and in his not ordering an election for a Convention." It disturbed him that despite the new oath Lincoln had not abolished slavery but only emancipated slaves in a portion of the state: "There is nothing to prevent the continuance of this as a Slave State if the pro slavery party get control."[16]

Flanders would have been even more disturbed had he known that Lincoln treated the oath prescribed in the proclamation as flexible. Banks informed the president on January 22 that "prominent

Union men" who had voted in the previous election that had elected Flanders and Michael Hahn did not want to take the oath. "Having been established in their rights as citizens," Banks reported, "they should not be compelled to take an additional oath." He added, "The exception taken refers of course, to the clauses referring to the laws of Congress, &c. relating to Slavery."[17]

In response, Lincoln told Banks, "you are at liberty to adopt any rule which shall admit to vote any unquestionably loyal free-state men and none others." He added, "and yet I do wish they would all take the oath." It was typical Lincoln. Desperate, perhaps too much so by some lights, for a loyal government to be established in Louisiana, he was willing to compromise on requirements while at the same time wishing he could have both politics and principle.[18]

Banks's decree, observed the *Springfield Weekly Republican*, "suits neither the radicals nor conservatives" in Louisiana. Radicals were unhappy because state officials would be elected before the adoption of a new state constitution whereas conservatives saw an expansion of a policy of emancipation.[19]

Both groups also lamented military interference with civilian matters. In addition to his fear that the conservative planter class would regain political power, Thomas Durant of the Free State Committee wondered why Lincoln had handed the power of civil reorganization exclusively over to the military. Durant thought a state created by military power "not in accordance with your Proclamation." At the other end of the political spectrum, the Democratic *New York World*, having learned of Lincoln's letter to Banks making him "master," called it "an astounding announcement" that showed the commander in chief giving to one of his generals "the power (which bayonets fully give him) of moulding the future condition" of affairs in Louisiana. Henry Winter Davis proclaimed in Congress what both sides of the political spectrum could endorse: "the President has called on General Banks to organize another hermaphrodite government, half military, half republican, representing the alligators and the frogs of Louisiana, and to place that on the footing of a government of a State of the United States." And furthermore Banks, "an adroit politician" who "covers his tracks with Indian skill," was not to be trusted.[20]

Despite the objections to Banks's having taken control, elections were held on February 22. Michael Hahn, the moderate candidate who had served briefly at the end of the Thirty-seventh Congress, won the gubernatorial race, defeating the more radical Flanders, the choice of the Free State Committee, and J. Q. A. Fellows, the conservative candidate. Other state officers were also elected. Banks reported to Lincoln that the election "was conducted with great spirit and propriety. No complaint is heard from any quarter so far as I know, of unfairness or undue influence on the part of the officers of the Government."[21]

Banks may have heard no complaints, but Lincoln certainly did. Durant wrote to say that Hahn was elected only because he was supported by the military authority. Conservative citizens also wrote to Lincoln. Banks, according to one voter, "enslaved the loyal press that he intimidated and corrupted the loyal voters." But Lincoln was content that some eleven thousand people voted, twice the number required to reach the 10 percent threshold, and that every voter, according to Banks, "accepted the oath prescribed" by the amnesty proclamation.[22]

On March 11, Banks issued an order calling for the election of delegates to a constitutional convention that would begin on April 6. Banks himself was overjoyed by the prospect. He wrote to John Hay, a little giddily, "we have changed all the elements of society—in labor, trade, social organization, in the church, and in the army. The revolution is complete." Voters had created a foundation for a state government "based upon the idea of the utter extinction of slavery." Banks had no doubt as to the outcome of the convention to rewrite the state constitution: "Rhode Island or Massachusetts is as likely to become a slave state as Louisiana."[23]

On March 11, Lincoln wrote to congratulate Hahn on his election. Anticipating the constitutional convention, he raised the issue of voting eligibility under a new state constitution: "I barely suggest for your private consideration, whether some of the colored people may not be let in—as, for instance, the very intelligent, and especially those who have fought gallantly in our ranks." He added, "this is only a suggestion, not to the public but to you alone."[24]

Lincoln had good reason not to make his preference known. Most Americans viewed extending the vote to blacks as more radical than eliminating slavery. In the election of 1860, for example, New York went handily for Lincoln, but a ballot measure to abolish the requirement that blacks must own at least $250 in order to vote was defeated by nearly 150,000 votes. Apart from New York, the only other states in which blacks were enfranchised (and on the same basis as whites) were the New England states, except Connecticut. Abolitionists and radical Republicans understood the importance of giving the vote to black men. In that speech at New York's Cooper Union on May 21, 1863, Wendell Phillips proclaimed, "give the negro a vote in his hand, and there is not a politician from Abraham Lincoln down to the laziest loafer in the lowest ward in this city, who would not do him honor. . . . [G]ive a man his vote, you give him tools to work and arms to protect himself. The ballot is the true standing ground of Archimedes, planted on which a man can move his world." Salmon Chase argued that peace cannot "be restored on any other basis than entire enfranchisement," and he lobbied for inclusion of the vote in any reconstruction plans that might emerge in Louisiana: "I know of no way to keep the State loyal but to open the elective franchise to the blacks all of whom almost are true friends of the Fed Govt & infinitely superior to the white aristocracy in business capacity & general morality." Chase went so far as to tell Thomas Durant that in December 1863, months before Lincoln's letter to Hahn, he had told the president of Durant's plans to allow native-born free persons of color to vote and that Lincoln said "he could see no objection to the registering of such citizens [or to] their exercise of the right of suffrage."[25]

Lincoln's letter to Hahn may have been prompted by a visit on March 3 from Jean Baptiste Roudanez and Arnold Bertonneau, two prominent free black men from New Orleans. Roudanez was an engineer; Bertonneau a wine merchant who had been commissioned a captain in Louisiana's first black regiment. Both were men of property. They brought with them a petition signed by over a thousand free black men who requested the right to vote. "Having rendered loyal services in the suppression of the rebellion," they asked "also that their electoral franchise shall be recognized." According to Roudanez, the president "listened attentively to our address, and sympathized with our object, but said he could not aid us on moral grounds, only as a military necessity." The *New York Times* reported that Lincoln "declined to act upon their petition, taking the ground that having the restoration of the Union, paramount to all other questions, he would do nothing that would hinder that consummation, or anything that would accomplish it. He told them therefore that he did nothing of matters of this kind upon moral grounds, but solely upon political necessities." Lincoln was talking like a politician, and the political necessities for now cut against him publicly endorsing suffrage for black men. Reelection was on his mind. In April, Chase reported, "the President...seems to think that to give negroes, however intelligent, the right of suffrage would jeopard[ize] the success of the Union Party at the next election."[26]

The state constitutional convention convened in New Orleans on April 6. On May 11, after defeating various resolutions presented by conservatives, including ones that would have provided compensation to slave owners, banished all blacks from the state, forbidden immigration of blacks into the state, and mandated that the legislature "shall never pass any act authorizing free negroes to vote," the convention adopted an ordinance that abolished slavery. Hahn proudly reported the vote to Lincoln: 70–16. The new constitution did not provide for universal black suffrage, but authorized the state legislature to give voting rights to blacks who were literate, owned property, or fought for the Union—authority the legislature was unlikely to exercise.[27]

The convention adjourned on July 25, and Banks wrote Lincoln that the constitution "is one of the best ever penned...composed entirely of men of the People." Banks, perhaps saying what he thought Lincoln wanted to hear, proclaimed black enfranchisement would come: "at the beginning of the session negro suffrage was scarcely mentioned—To-day it may be regarded as secure." He added, "The work of reconstruction in this state is all that you can desire."[28]

Lincoln replied that he was "anxious that it shall be ratified by the people." On September 5, voters approved the constitution by a vote of 6,836–1,566. The total vote, Banks acknowledged, was a disappointment, fewer than the number who had voted for governor in February. Still the vote was "good," "honest," and "respectable." Banks concluded, "history will record the fact that all the problems involved in restoration of States, and the reconstruction of government have been already solved in Louisiana."[29]

There was reason, in the winter and spring of 1864, to be optimistic as well about reconstruction efforts in Arkansas. In early January, the *New York Times* reported, "there seems no reason to doubt that a very remarkable change has occurred in public sentiment in Arkansas, and that this State will speedily resume her position in the Union." In early January, Lincoln sent General Frederick Steele some blank enrollment books to be used to record oaths of allegiance. "I wish to afford the people of Arkansas an opportunity of taking the oath prescribed in the proclamation of Dec. 8, 1863, preparatory to re-organizing a State-government there," he wrote. Lincoln had decided not to appoint a new military governor to replace John Phelps and instead to give Steele authority for both the military and civil administration of the state.[30]

An Arkansas delegation that included Edward Gantt visited the White House and heard Lincoln express his hopes that a new state government would be organized under the terms of the amnesty proclamation. They told him of plans already under way and Lincoln scrambled to make certain there was no clash between his orders to Steele and the progress already being made in Arkansas. Lincoln's only concern was that whatever was done, a Free State constitution "in some unquestionable form" was adopted. Perhaps with affairs in Louisiana on his mind, he warned Steele "of all things, avoid if possible, a dividing into cliques among the friends of the common object. Be firm and resolute against such as you can perceive would make confusion and division." Lincoln wrote William M. Fishback, a lawyer who played a critical role in organizing a loyalist government and would be elected to the U.S. Senate when the new legislature convened in April, "discord must be silenced." He told him that Steele was "master."[31]

On January 19, a convention consisting of forty-five delegates and representing half the counties in Arkansas adopted a constitution that abolished slavery and repudiated secession. An election to ratify the document and choose state officials was scheduled for March 14. Lincoln was determined that it go off without disruption, so much so that General Steele wrote to Banks to explain why transfer of his forces for the impending Red River campaign would be delayed: "an election for State officers is ordered for the 14th proximo, and the President is very anxious that it should be a success." The troops were necessary to hand out poll books, administer the oath of allegiance, and police the voters. When informed of the reasons for the delay, William Tecumseh Sherman told Steele, "if we have to modify military plans for civil elections, we had better go home."[32]

On March 8, Provisional Governor Isaac Murphy informed Lincoln that he expected the vote to exceed 10,000 and that loyal men were enthusiastic about the prospect of voting despite the threats of Confederate guerillas "to hang every one that went to the polls." The Free State constitution passed, 12,430–226. Lincoln told Murphy he was "much gratified to learn that you got out so large a vote" and promised to do all he could to have the army provide protection. The *New York Times* reported, "Arkansas has given a larger vote for the Union than even Louisiana, and is also ahead of her in the adoption of a Free State Constitution.... The President's method of reconstruction ... will soon, we believe, be universally recognized to be the only true way—the way at once perfectly safe and perfectly effective."[33]

However gratified Lincoln felt, he could not have been pleased by the actions of the House in debating whether to accept the credentials of James M. Johnson of the Third Congressional District in Arkansas. He came before the House on February 10 because of a provision in the newly written constitution, not yet ratified, that "no election being ordered in district number three this convention recognizes the election of Col. James M. Johnson as the representative of that district."[34] Henry Winter Davis had asked that the motion referring Johnson's credentials to the Committee on Elections be laid on the table. This was unusual; motions to refer were typically pro forma and the House would discuss the case once it received a recommendation from the committee. On February 16, Davis withdrew his motion so the issue could be discussed.

Henry Dawes, chairman of the Committee on Elections, was shocked that a representative-elect, who has "the honor of bearing here the first free-State constitution out of the fire and smoke of this war," and is "covered with honorable scars won in defense of the flag of his country," should be "denied so much as a hearing." Davis explained he had no intention to insult Dawes or Johnson, but at issue was the question of whether or not to recognize a new state government in Arkansas. Davis had a point because the new constitution had not yet been ratified and a new legislature elected. But Davis was also hunting bigger game. It wasn't enough, he thought, for the president to recognize a new loyal government. Both houses of Congress had to as well. They did so, of course, by seating elected representatives from those states. The discussion digressed into those pernicious abstractions about whether Arkansas was in the Union or out, and Dawes halted it by saying the "House . . . is quite tired of this discussion."[35]

But Davis still was not satisfied and brought up the problem of military rule, particularly Banks's proclamation in Louisiana. "Dangerous doctrines are gaining a hold upon the public mind," he warned.

"I shudder when I find his proclamation summoning the people of Louisiana to an election under a declaration of martial law." Davis also disparaged the idea of a military governor, "a mere agent of the President without any authority of law whatever to appoint him." Davis again moved to table the matter, but the House voted to refer Johnson's credentials to the Committee on Elections. That committee would not report until February 17, 1865. At that time, it recommended that Johnson be seated, but the House did not act.[36]

In June, it was the Senate's turn as the body deliberated whether to seat William Fishback and lawyer Elisha Baxter, who had been chosen in May by the Arkansas Legislature to fill the two Senate seats. The presentation of credentials, wrote the *New York Evening Post*, "opens up the whole *question of the reorganization* of state governments."[37]

Under the best of circumstances admitting the men would have been problematic because Congress was on the verge of adopting its own bill on reconstruction and the radicals, at least, were not about to ratify Lincoln's more moderate and gradual approach by seating anyone. But the possibility was made that much more unlikely because of claims about Fishback. Newspapers reported that he had been a member of the Arkansas secession convention, signed the secession ordinance, raised rebel troops, and took an oath of allegiance to the Confederacy. Others described him more generously as "signer of the ordinance of secession" who "has returned to allegiance and is a radical Union man." The *Springfield Republican* observed, "he is distrusted by some of the radicals on account of this great change of opinion, but it is no greater than must take place in the people of the South generally, or there can be no restoration of the Union. He is in the same category as General Gantt of the same state, to whom the administration, the radicals in Congress, and the people of the North generally have given their faith and most abundant honors." Fishback, for his part, denied the charges.[38]

But it did not really matter. Sumner, in particular, decided to go for the juggler and by slashing Fishback to get at Lincoln. He sharpened his blade by offering a resolution that a state would continue to be regarded as a rebel state "until it has been readmitted by a vote of both Houses of Congress." He argued that only a small minority of voters had participated in the election and that Arkansas's civil government was still very much beholden to military authority. He also believed the organization of the loyal government lacked legality because it resulted from a military order. And those points, he thought, were dispositive, without considering his belief that no claimant can be seated before Congress "has restored the State to its original position." Finally, he stabbed at Lincoln's Proclamation of Amnesty and Reconstruction, a plan, he thought, that was only provisional, intended to offer protection to a minority of loyal voters. But "it does not by any means follow that such local government can be entitled to representation in the National Government." On June 27, the Senate, by a vote of 27–6, agreed with the Judiciary Committee's unanimous recommendation not to seat the two men.[39]

Edward Gantt was furious. In a long public letter to Sumner, he challenged the senators' arguments and said he was appalled that it would turn out to be the abolitionists who opposed the brave work of Arkansas's loyalists: "we are thunderstruck to find you in favor of driving us away, and throwing the victory at last to a handful of Copperheads in Arkansas who hope still to retain Slavery."[40]

Lincoln said nothing except to inform General Steele, "my wish is that you give that government and the people there, the same support and protection that you would if the members had been admitted." He had always recognized the authority of Congress to seat elected representatives, but he had to be disappointed. His reconstruction plan was predicated in part on the idea that the sooner states resumed their place in the Union, the sooner the war would come to an end, that a domino effect might ensue whereby ever increasing numbers of Southerners, inspired by actions of others, took an oath of allegiance. The adoption of a Free State constitution in Arkansas delighted him, and that accomplishment would stand whether or not elected officials were seated. Indeed, he was eager that Louisiana would follow suit. And he was elated that Maryland had adopted a Free State constitution that voters would approve in October.[41]

Slavery was doomed; it would not survive the war. Lincoln knew that. Through the spring he offered ever more emphatic private and public expressions of his convictions. In March, for example, he wrote to John Creswell, congressman from Maryland and a former Democrat turned Republican, that he was "anxious for emancipation to be effected in Maryland in some substantial form," and explained that while he had thought gradual emancipation was preferable because it "would produce less confusion and destitution," he fully supported immediate emancipation. His main concern, which emerged time and again when it came to reconstruction, was that harmony should prevail among the different constituencies: "My wish is that all who are for emancipation *in any form*, shall co-operate, all treating all respectfully, and all adopting and acting upon the major opinion, when fairly ascertained." Lincoln desired consensus and dreaded the "jealousies, rivalries, and consequent ill-blood" that might divide supporters of emancipation and lead to losing "the measure altogether."[42]

Like the letter to Hahn expressing support for black suffrage that he wrote less than a week later, the letter to Creswell was private. A letter to Albert Hodges, former senator from Kentucky and editor of a newspaper in Frankfort, was not. Hodges was part of a border-state delegation that had met with Lincoln and afterward he asked for a copy of the president's remarks. Lincoln wrote that he had said, "I am naturally anti-slavery. If slavery is not wrong, nothing is wrong. I can not remember when I did not so think, and feel." He added that the presidency did not confer "an unrestricted right to act officially upon this judgment and feeling." Within weeks, the letter appeared in Hodges's *Frankfort Commonwealth* and was reprinted in other newspapers. The *New York Tribune*, which often criticized the president for not being radical enough, thought "few men have ever lived who could have better explained and commended his course and attitude with regard to Slavery." Of course, Northern Democrats, who believed Lincoln's actions to be unconstitutional and dictatorial, denounced the letter as an example of "sophistry and pettifogging," filled with "uncouth, distorted, ungainly and crooked utterances." Only "remote posterity will admire the wonderful rhetoric and queer sayings of the great Lincoln."[43]

As the weather warmed, so did Lincoln's public denunciations of slavery. In an address at a sanitary fair in Baltimore, organized to provide support for the soldiers, he offered a parable: "the shepherd drives the wolf from the sheep's throat, for which the sheep thanks the shepherd as a *liberator*, while the wolf denounces him for the same act as the destroyer of liberty, especially as the sheep was a black one. Plainly, the sheep and the wolf are not agreed upon a definition of the word liberty." Lincoln was not making a case for relativism. There was a right and a wrong definition of liberty and fortunately Maryland, in writing a new constitution that abolished slavery, was about to repudiate "the wolf's dictionary." The *Richmond Whig* derisively labeled the president "Shepherd Lincoln."[44]

In June, Lincoln publicly endorsed a constitutional amendment to abolish slavery. Charles Sumner had introduced a joint resolution for such an amendment in February, and the Senate approved it by the requisite two-thirds in April. Lincoln announced, "I approve the declaration in favor of so amending the Constitution as to prohibit slavery throughout the nation." Known for his willingness to be tolerant and patient, Lincoln flashed impatience: "when the people in revolt, with a hundred days of explicit notice, that they could, within those days, resume their allegiance, without the overthrow of their institution, and that they could not so resume it afterwards, elected to stand out, such amendment of the Constitution as now proposed, became a fitting, and necessary conclusion to the final success of the Union cause."[45]

Lincoln was resolute. However qualified, his Proclamation of Amnesty and Reconstruction had made it clear that the price of being restored to the Union was the abolition of slavery. But it seemed that was the only price Lincoln sought to extract, and the terms he offered were generous and magnanimous, too much so for many Republicans in Congress who thought they, not the president, should control reconstruction and make the process more stringent. The result was a bill introduced in the House by Henry Winter Davis and in the Senate by Benjamin Wade and passed by Congress on July 2, 1864.

The final bill called for the appointment by the president, with Senate consent, of a provisional governor for each state in rebellion. Once military resistance had been suppressed, all white male citizens would be enrolled and asked to swear an oath to support the U.S. Constitution. If 50 percent of them took the oath (as opposed to 10 percent, as under Lincoln's plan), the provisional governor would call a constitutional convention. Only those who could take the ironclad oath adopted by Congress on July 2, 1862, could vote for convention delegates or serve as delegates. This disqualified persons who had held "any office, civil or military, state or Confederate," during the war or "voluntarily borne arms against the United States." The bill further mandated that the new constitution must declare that slavery "is forever prohibited," repudiate the Confederate debt, meaning that the Federal government would not pay expenses incurred by the rebellious states, and bar from voting for or serving as governor or state legislator anyone who held civil or military positions, except those that were ministerial or a rank lower than colonel. The governing theory was that the states had always remained in the Union: "until the United States shall have recognized a republican form of state government, the provisional governor in each of said states shall see that this act, and the laws of the United States, and the laws of the state in force when the state government was overthrown by the rebellion, are faithfully executed within the state."

In certain ways, the plan was a moderate one. Indeed, Pennsylvania's William Darrah Kelley, a friend and loyal (though sometimes critical) supporter of Lincoln, complained "the bill…is drawn rather too largely from the President's plan." It did not enfranchise blacks and it did not adopt the theory of territorialization. At first, it even incorporated Lincoln's 10 percent plan. An amendment on May 4, however, created a significant distinction. Rather than 10 percent, 50 percent would be needed to reestablish a state government. The change came out of congressional concern for majority rule and the belief, as Davis put it, that "one tenth cannot control nine-tenths."[46]

Whatever the details, the bill threatened the progress made under Lincoln's Proclamation of Amnesty and Reconstruction. It encapsulated Davis's belief that "it is the exclusive prerogative of Congress—of Congress, and not the President—to determine what is and what is not the established government of the State." Furthermore, the bill would delay reconstruction until after the rebellion had ended. "It is not safe," Davis warned, "to confide the vast authority of State governments to the doubtful loyalty of the rebel States until armed rebellion shall have been trampled in the dust." If Lincoln signed the measure, the result would be the abandonment of progress made in Louisiana and Arkansas and a repudiation of his belief that reestablishing loyal state governments would hasten the end of the rebellion. It would have meant that there would be no reconstruction until the war was over.[47]

Chase saw something else in why Lincoln would not sign the bill: "it was a condemnation of his Amnesty Proclamation & his general policy of reconstruction, rejecting the idea of possible reconstruction with Slavery; which neither the President nor his Chief advisers have, in my opinion, abandoned." How Chase could make this claim is hard to fathom given all that Lincoln had been saying and doing with respect to making certain that new state constitutions provided for emancipation. But Chase and other radicals held onto the idea that Lincoln was not fully committed to abolition and used it as fuel to energize their opposition.[48]

Because the bill was delivered to Lincoln only two days before Congress adjourned, he could kill it simply by not acting on it, a pocket veto. Few expected him to do that. So, according to Chase, when Jesse Olds Norton, an Illinois congressman, heard the news of Lincoln's intention to do exactly that he said, "it was impossible & would be fatal." The pocket veto was rarely used, and through weeks of debate on the bill Lincoln had not expressed any reservations about it.[49]

On the morning of July 4, prior to Congress adjourning at noon, Lincoln was busy in an office at the Capitol signing bills. Sumner was there "in a state of intense anxiety." George Boutwell, the representative from Massachusetts, also paced. Senator Zachariah Chandler of Michigan asked if the bill was signed. Told no, he spoke with Lincoln who, according to John Hay, said, "this bill was placed before me a few minutes before Congress adjourns. It is a matter of too much importance to be swallowed in that way." Chandler thought failure to sign it would hurt Lincoln in the upcoming presidential election. Besides, he said, it prohibits slavery in the reconstructed areas. That was all that should matter. Lincoln responded, "That is the point on which I doubt the authority of Congress to act." But "it is no more than you have done yourself," Chandler exclaimed. "I conceive that I may in an emergency do things on military grounds," Lincoln replied, "which cannot be done constitutionally by Congress." Chandler stormed out. William Pitt Fessenden, Senator from Maine, had arrived. Secretary of the Interior John Palmer Usher was also present. Lincoln explained further that, as he read the bill, it asserted that the states in rebellion were no longer states, and therefore that it made "the fatal admission...that states whenever they please may of their own motion dissolve their connection with the Union." Lincoln's misreading of this aspect of the bill reflected his disdain for theoretical issues. He had "laboriously endeavored" to avoid "a merely metaphysical question," he said, apparently so much so that he saw it even when it was not present. He would not worry about the political consequences of his action, and he would not abandon the efforts at reconstruction begun under his December proclamation. He told Hay, "I must keep some standard of principle fixed within myself."[50]

Given the consternation his actions caused many Republicans, and perhaps hoping to unify the party as it approached the November election, Lincoln decided a few days later to issue a proclamation explaining why he did not sign the bill. Using for the first time the phrase "proper practical relation" to describe the objective of restoring states in rebellion to the Union, Lincoln said he was "unprepared, by a formal approval of the Bill, to be inflexibly committed to any single plan of restoration." He also was "unprepared" to set aside the free-state constitutions in Louisiana and Arkansas. Furthermore, he did not believe Congress had "a constitutional competency . . . to abolish slavery in States," but was hoping for a constitutional amendment to abolish slavery throughout the nation. And yet, he declared, "I am fully satisfied with the system for restoration contained in the Bill, as one very proper plan for the loyal people of any State choosing to adopt it."[51]

With that sentence, Lincoln sounded generous and accommodating, but he knew, of course, that the concession had no meaning: what state would choose sterner measures (an ironclad oath and majority requirement, for example) offered by Congress when the president's plan held out less demanding terms? The *Daily National Intelligencer* marveled at the preposterous logic: "so we have the anomaly presented to the world of a 'very proper plan' involving an unconstitutional feature—a plan which has no legal validity, (because lacking the President's official approval in the only way prescribed by the Constitution,) and yet one under which the people of certain States are invited to act."[52]

As they had since Lincoln issued his proclamation on December 8, some commentators saw electoral politics at work. That Lincoln had been officially nominated by the Republican Party, now calling itself the National Union Party, only weeks earlier in Baltimore lent added vitality to this view. Moreover, Andrew Johnson had been chosen to replace Hannibal Hamlin as vice president, and the convention admitted and gave voting rights to delegates from Tennessee, Louisiana, and Arkansas. The party had, in effect, sanctioned Lincoln's

reconstruction policy. Although the platform did not specifically endorse the policy (how could it with Congress at that moment debating its own measures?), it did approve "the measures and acts
which he has adopted to defend the nation." Thaddeus Stevens expressed the thoughts of many in his reaction to Lincoln's explanation of his actions: "What an infamous proclamation! The Pres is
determined to have the electoral votes of the seceded states—at
least of Tenn Ark—Lou & Flor—Pehaps also of S. Car—The idea of
pocketing a bill and then issuing a proclamation as to how far he will
conform to it, is matched only by signing a bill and then sending in a
veto—How little of the right of war and the law of nations our Prest.
Knows." Stevens concluded his rant, "But what are we to do? Condemn privately and applaud publicly."[53]

Henry Winter Davis did not feel the same way and on August 5,
through the pages of the *New York Tribune*, he and Benjamin Wade
issued a manifesto that denounced Lincoln's pocket veto and proclamation of explanation as "a defeat of the will of the people by an
Executive perversion of the constitution." They denounced the new
governments in Louisiana and Arkansas as shadow governments that
exist as "mere creatures of his will." The rejection of representatives
from these states meant the existence of state government is "conclu-
sively rejected and denied." By killing the bill, Lincoln "holds the electoral vote of the rebel States at the dictation of his personal ambition."
His claim that Congress could not act against slavery was "unintelli-
gible." And his final concession that the plan was proper as a "system of
restoration" was a "studied outrage on the legislative authority of the
people": he defeats the law, and then proposes to act without congressional consultation on a congressional plan. The "authority of Congress is paramount, and must be respected." If not, remedies existed
(in other words, impeachment) for "these usurpations."[54]

Wade and Davis devoted a portion of their manifesto to con-
demning reconstruction in Louisiana. They claimed elections were
held under martial law and that the Union controlled only eleven of
forty-eight parishes. Of the 11,000 votes cast, they suspected at least

4,000 came from Union soldiers under General Banks stationed there. The appointment of Michael Hahn as provisional governor, vested with the power of military governor, was a farce whereby Lincoln made him "Dictator of Louisiana" without legal authorization or Senate consent. They also said that they had been informed by someone on Banks's staff that several moderate senators were working to make certain the reconstruction bill was held back long enough so that Lincoln would not have to formally veto it to defeat it.[55]

Banks was outraged and he responded to the accusations in a long letter to Kansas senator James Lane, who had supported seating the Louisiana delegation at the Baltimore convention. Banks's letter appeared in newspapers in September and was published separately as a pamphlet. Wade and Davis, he wrote, "imperfectly understood the condition of things," and were misled by their informant (who everyone suspected was Durant). In fact, events in Louisiana were in accord with the congressional plan: "every material provision had been anticipated, every substantial guarantee had been recognized and established." Banks provided specifics: thirty-day notice of elections was given; nearly ten thousand voters in just the parish of New Orleans took an ironclad oath; only soldiers who had enlisted from Louisiana were allowed to vote; no one who held office or borne arms against the United States participated; the constitution abolished slavery; Governor Hahn was chosen by the people at a "formal, free election." Banks insisted, "All the substantive, material conditions of the bill passed by the two Houses of Congress have been anticipated and answered in the elections held in Louisiana."[56]

The only group thrilled by the manifesto was the Peace Democrats, who virulently opposed Lincoln and could not get over their good fortune of having two radical Republicans attack him on nearly the same grounds as they did. The *New York Herald* exulted, "nothing… the most venomous of the copperhead politicians have uttered in derogation of Mr. Lincoln has approached in bitterness and force the denunciations which Messrs Wade and Davis, shining lights of the Republican party, have piled up in this manifesto." The *Chicago*

Tribune asserted, "from the fact that it is received with shouts of triumph by the whole Copperhead press, it is safe to say that Wade and Davis have done them some service." Most of the Republican press denounced the manifesto as of "questionable" taste, the "result of soreheadedness," a "treacherous and malignant attempt to stab a President whom they profess to support." The *Albany Journal* argued that "the result of the Manifesto is simply to make still more clear the wisdom of the President's course." Even most of their fellow radicals felt Wade and Davis had gone too far.[57]

Lincoln, for his part, professed that "he had not, and probably should not read it," and had no desire to take part in the controversy. But Seward read it to him, and Lincoln remarked, "I would like to know whether these men intend openly to oppose my election—the document looks that way." He was more agitated than he let on. Former Treasury agent Benjamin Rush Plumly reported that Lincoln's "blood is up on the Wade & Winter Davis protest." Another writer informed Lincoln what he told Wade, who wondered about the president's reaction: "I said I thought you *felt* more than you *said*."[58]

If Wade and Davis believed their actions would give Lincoln pause on reconstruction in Louisiana they were mistaken. Four days after they issued their manifesto, Lincoln wrote to Banks to congratulate him on the adoption of the new Louisiana constitution and to pledge support for its ratification. Reconstruction in Louisiana would remain a battleground between the president and Congress through 1864 and the first months of 1865.

Lincoln's concern in August 1864 was not only reconstruction but also his reelection. Wade and Davis would come back into the fold and endorse the president (prompted in part by Lincoln's purge of Montgomery Blair from the cabinet in September). And he survived an attempt by some Republicans to dump him for another candidate. But moderate Thurlow Weed declared at the end of August, "as things stand now, Mr. Lincoln's re-election is an impossibility." Henry J. Raymond, who chaired the National Union Executive Committee, warned Lincoln "the tide is against us." George Templeton

Strong observed, "Lincoln manifestly loses ground every day. The most zealous Republican partisans talk doubtfully of his chances." Lincoln knew the score. "You think I don't know I am going to be beaten," he was overheard as saying, *"but I do* and unless some great change takes place *badly beaten."*[59]

Lincoln was suffering personally; a visitor described him as "quite paralyzed and wilted down." One reason for his pessimism bordering on despair was the lack of military progress and the resulting low morale of Northerners. In April, the Red River campaign in Louisiana ended in failure (leading to Banks being relieved of field command); in May and early June, Grant's push through Virginia led to a series of battles (among them the Wilderness, Spotsylvania, and Cold Harbor) that resulted in massive Union casualties; at the same time, Sherman's forces seemed bogged down in Georgia north of Atlanta; in early July, a raid on Washington by Confederate General Jubal Early created panic (the city is "in a state of siege," reported Noah Brooks); two weeks later, Confederate cavalry torched Chambersburg, Pennsylvania; and at month's end, four thousand were killed or wounded in a botched attack at Petersburg (Grant called it "the saddest affair I have witnessed in the war"). Lincoln had no choice but to call for five hundred thousand additional soldiers with a draft to follow in September. "War, at the best, is terrible," Lincoln said in a speech at Philadelphia in August 1864, "and this war of ours, in its magnitude and in its duration, is one of the most terrible."[60]

Gideon Welles thought "the slow progress of our armies, the mismanagement of military affairs exemplified in the recent raids, the factious and discontented spirit manifested by Wade, Winter Davis, and others, have generated a feeling of despondency." On July 7, Horace Greeley wrote the president: "our bleeding, bankrupt, almost dying country also longs for peace—shudders at the prospect of fresh conscriptions, of further wholesale devastations, and of new rivers of human blood." Unwisely, Lincoln allowed himself to be drawn in and he authorized Greeley to go to Niagara Falls for possible peace negotiations. He provided a letter for Greeley to give to the Confederate agents that said he would consider "any proposition which embraces the restoration of peace, the integrity of the whole Union, and the abandonment of slavery."[61]

When Lincoln's letter was leaked to the press, War Democrats, who had accepted emancipation only as a war measure and still clung to the illusion that the war could end with slavery intact, reacted with furor. (Edward Bates remarked, "I am surprised to find the Prest. green enough to be entrapped into such a correspondence.") Seeking to limit the political damage, Lincoln drafted a letter to a prominent War Democrat. "Saying re-union and abandonment of slavery would be considered, if offered," he asserted, "is not saying that nothing *else* or *less* would be considered, if offered."[62]

Lincoln showed the draft to several people, including Frederick Douglass, who found the president "in alarmed condition." Douglass recalled, "The country was struck with one of those bewilderments which dethrone reason for a moment. Everybody was dreaming and thinking of peace, and the impression had gone abroad that the President's anti-slavery policy was about the only thing which prevented a peaceful settlement with the Rebels." Douglass warned that the offer "would be given a broader meaning than you intend to convey; it would be taken as a complete surrender of your antislavery policy, and do you serious damage."[63]

Lincoln did not mail the letter; he also decided against sending Henry J. Raymond to Richmond to propose peace negotiations. He despaired over the chances of his reelection and, on August 23, wrote a memorandum that he found a way to seal thoroughly and had cabinet members endorse blindly. It read: "This morning, as for some days past, it seems exceedingly probable that this Administration will not be re-elected. Then it will be my duty to so co-operate with the President elect, as to save the Union between the election and the inauguration; as he will have secured his election on such ground that he can not possibly save it afterwards."[64]

Without reelection, there would be no reconstruction. The sacrifices made to save the union, and to free the slaves, would have been for naught.

Chapter 6

"Fraught with Difficulty"

Only "Divine Providence" could explain it. On September 3, Lincoln and the Union learned that Atlanta had fallen to Sherman's army. "So Atlanta is ours, and fairly won," William Tecumseh Sherman informed General Henry Halleck. Only ten days earlier, Admiral David G. Farrragut's fleet took firm control of Mobile Bay. The two victories immediately reversed the despondency of the summer and brightened Lincoln's hopes for reelection. George Templeton Strong, though worried that reports of "*Atlanta taken at last*!!!" would prove false, thought it couldn't have come at a better moment and was "the greatest event of the war." The *New York Times* exulted, "The skies begin to brighten. The clouds that lowered over the Union cause a month ago, are breaking away."[1]

Rejoicing over the news, Lincoln issued several orders: one calling for a celebration commemorating the two victories, another one to give thanks to Farragut, and yet another to give thanks to Sherman. He also issued a proclamation of thanksgiving and prayer, calling on places of public worship to rejoice in the preservation of "our national existence against the insurgent rebels" and to pray for the soldiers. On September 4, he responded to a letter from Eliza P. Gurney, an English abolitionist and member of the Society of Friends who had written wishing that Lincoln would be strengthened by the Almighty: "We must work earnestly in the best light He gives us, trusting that so working still conduces to the great ends He ordains. Surely He intends some great good to follow this mighty convulsion, which no mortal could make, and no mortal could stay." With so much uncertainty, and so much suffering, there was comfort to be taken in placing outcomes in God's hands.[2]

In the case of Lincoln's Democratic opponent in the upcoming presidential election, it was not providence but politics that furnished a candidate whose nomination improved the president's chances for reelection. At a convention held in Chicago at the end of August, Democrats nominated George B. McClellan. McClellan had led the Army of the Potomac until Lincoln dismissed him in November 1862. McClellan had objected to making the war into anything more than an organized effort to defeat an opposing armed force. "Neither confiscation of property, political execution of persons, territorial organization of states or forcible abolition of slavery should be contemplated for a moment," he wrote Lincoln in July 1862. The general also privately derided the president, calling him "the original gorilla" and "nothing more than a well-meaning baboon."[3]

McClellan's nomination caused the Republicans concern. He was popular with the soldiers and was a War Democrat who supported seeing the ordeal through to ultimate victory. But the Copperhead Peace Democrats controlled the platform at Chicago and resolved "that immediate efforts be made for a cessation of hostilities" to be followed by a convention to create a "Federal Union of the States." The Democrats labeled the war a "failure." Such a platform, Republicans believed, would be rejected by the mass of voters who, regardless of how exhausted and dismayed they were by the war, did not want to see it end without victory.

Adam Gurowski, while not the typical Republican, understood that the actions of Democrats in Chicago played into Lincoln's hands. McClellan, he thought, was "a moral nonentity, neither a man nor a soldier … taken up by the politicians as glue to catch flies" and a gift to the Republicans. As for the platform, "rebels, traitors, and slavery to be saved. That is the spirit and the letter of that platform." He believed the Democrats had no chance.[4] Other writers saw it the same way. A contributor to the *North American Review* proclaimed, "the Resolutions of the Chicago Convention … propose only one thing,—surrender."[5]

The military victories in Atlanta and Mobile seemed to serve as commentary on the Democratic platform. The fall of Atlanta, claimed the *New York Evening Post*, "was not reckoned upon by the sages of Chicago as among those 'immediate efforts' which they 'explicitly declared' ought to be made for a 'cessation of hostilities.'" It exposed the "absurdity and wickedness" of the Democratic platform.[6]

The success of General Philip Sheridan in the Shenandoah Valley added to the rejoicing. In mid-September he won victories at Opequon Creek and Fisher's Hill three days apart. Washington residents were especially thrilled because Sheridan defeated Jubal Early, who had briefly threatened the capital during the summer. Sheridan's triumphs reached a climax on October 19, with a victory at Cedar Creek. Lincoln wrote to Sheridan to offer "the thanks of the Nation," as well as his "personal admiration and gratitude for the month's operations."[7]

"The Chicago platform & our victories have settled the Presidential election beyond question," thought Charles Sumner, "& we all see the beginning of the end." In addition to these developments, Lincoln received good political news when he saw the October election returns for Ohio, Indiana, and Pennsylvania. In Ohio, Republicans gained twelve House seats. That was not a surprise, as many in the state had repudiated the seditious peace activities of Clement Vallandigham, who in a speech had once denounced the war as "wicked, cruel and unnecessary," and received little support when he ran for governor the previous year. But Indiana was a concern, so much so that in September Lincoln asked Sherman to allow Indiana soldiers to go home and vote, because the state constitution forbade them from voting in the field. In 1862, Democrats had a majority of ten thousand votes; now Republicans had a majority of nearly twenty thousand. "Indiana's action astonished everyone," reported the *Atlantic Monthly*. Republicans gained four seats and Republican governor Morton was reelected.[8]

Pennsylvania was more closely contested, but expectations that the soldiers' vote from the field would give Republicans the edge proved accurate. In a letter to his father, the minister to the Court of St. James's, Charles Francis Adams Jr. predicted, "the October vote will foreshadow exactly the November vote. Soldiers don't vote for individuals; they don't vote for the war; they have but one desire and that is to vote against those who delay the progress of the war at home." The *New York Times* believed that come November the soldier vote would again play a pivotal role and swing things to the Republicans. The conclusion drawn from the October elections, and trumpeted widely by Republican supporters, was that "the opponents of Lincoln are everywhere overwhelmingly defeated." San Francisco's *Daily Evening Bulletin* predicted, "Lincoln will be triumphantly re-elected, and if his life is spared will continue at the head of Government until every State is brought to acknowledge his rightful authority."[9]

The allusion to threats to Lincoln's life was not fanciful. Throughout his presidency, Lincoln had received death threats, but with reelection approaching more warnings arrived. One writer implored him, "*Forget* not yourself for *one instant*. Beware of *poison!*—Beware of *assassination!*" Another writer warned of a plot and beseeched Lincoln to keep a gun handy. Someone wrote from West Virginia that he had overheard two men talking, one of whom said, "that if old Abe was Realected we are agointo Kill him and I am the man that is agointo do it with your help." Secretary of the Senate John W. Forney recalled Lincoln saying, "I know I am in danger; but I am not going to worry over threats like these."[10]

The campaign was a vituperative one, filled with racial demagoguery, and Peace Democrats took every opportunity to alarm the public as to what would happen if Lincoln were reelected. Racist pamphlets and broadsides proliferated. The *Lincoln Catechism* dubbed Lincoln "Abraham Africanus the First," and in answer to the question "what is a president?," answered, "a general agent for negroes." A new word was coined, "miscegenation," to describe interracial mixing. The name of the United States, the volume averred, would be changed to "*New Africa*."[11]

The race hatred was a preview of what the nation would face once the war was over, slavery was abolished, and millions of blacks would make the transition from slavery to freedom. The problem of reconstruction, however, played little role in public discourse leading up to the election. Everyone knew what was at stake. Lincoln's position was clear; so was McClellan's: peace followed by discussion of restoring the Union through a compromise that respected states' rights and left slavery intact. But once the election was over, Adam Gurowski predicted, "reconstruction will become more and more the order of the day."[12]

With election day approaching, Carl Schurz took time to explain to a childhood friend who deprecated the president the genius of Lincoln: "He is an overgrown nature-child and does not understand artifices of speech and attitude. But he is a man of profound feeling, just and firm principles, and incorruptible integrity.... He is the people personified; that is the secret of his popularity. His government is the most representative that has ever existed in world history. I will make a prophecy which may perhaps sound strange at this moment. In fifty years, perhaps much sooner, Lincoln's name will stand written upon the honor roll of the American Republic next to that of Washington, and there it will remain for all time. The children of those who now disparage him will bless him."[13]

Schurz's prediction would have proven less meaningful without reelection, and on election day Lincoln anxiously awaited results at the War Department. He told Noah Brooks, "about this thing I am far from certain; I wish I were certain." Apparently, when he expressed his concern about how the soldiers would vote, another journalist told him not to worry, "They'll vote as they shoot." It was a stormy night, and the telegraphic dispatches were slow to arrive. The others present, John Hay, Edwin Stanton, Gideon Welles, Gustavus Fox, and Thomas Eckert, dined on fried oysters and drank coffee. At one point the conversation turned to Henry Winter Davis, who had not been renominated (the lame duck session running from December 5 to March 3 would be his last). Fox said he was happy to see retribution come to Davis. But not Lincoln. "You have more of that feeling of personal resentment than I," he said. "Perhaps I may have too little of it, but I never thought it paid."[14]

By midnight, Lincoln knew he had been reelected. He won 55 percent of the popular vote, and carried the electoral college 212–21. McClellan won only New Jersey, Delaware, and Kentucky. Lincoln received more than 75 percent of the separately tabulated soldiers' vote (nineteen states allowed soldiers to vote in the field, eleven of which tabulated the soldier vote separately). Lincoln felt relieved and Brooks reported that the president appreciated the significance of the mandate that came with an overwhelming victory—"clear, full, unmistakable." That night, Ward Hill Lamon, marshal for the city of Washington and an old Illinois friend who took it upon himself to protect the president, stationed himself outside Lincoln's door and, according to John Hay, spent "the night in that attitude of touching and dumb fidelity with a small arsenal of pistols & bowie knives around him."[15]

The election, claimed George Templeton Strong, was the "most momentous popular election ever held since ballots were invented and has decided against treason and disunion." Adam Gurowski reached new heights of purple prose, even for him: "Slavery and its devoted henchmen, the American political Democracy, are prostrated and crushed, self-government loftily asserted, and its enemies and slanderers bite the dust. The stain on the American escutcheon is blotted out, the sin is atoned, and humanity satisfied.... The people voted for its own duration, for its own life, for its own national integrity and honor. The verdict of the people sounds: *not a State out of the Union, no slavery in the Union.*"[16]

In victory, Lincoln displayed his magnanimity. "I do not impugn the motives of anyone who opposed me," he said. "It is no pleasure to me to triumph over any one." He celebrated the glory of democracy and observed, "we can not have free government without elections; and if the rebellion could force us to forego, or postpone a national election, it might fairly claim to have already conquered and ruined us." In response to a serenade he reflected, "Human-nature will not change. In any future great national trial, compared with the men of this, we shall have as weak, and as strong; as silly and as wise; as bad and good. Let us, therefore, study the incidents of this, as philosophy to learn wisdom from, and none of them as wrongs to be avenged."[17]

Lincoln's basic nature was forgiving and conciliatory. "I am…not a vindictive man," he told John Hay. In the immediate aftermath of the election, his anger was not directed at the rebels, but at one of his generals, whose actions had been threatening the restored government of Virginia throughout the year.[18]

Benjamin Butler, who had been recalled from New Orleans in December 1862, was given command of the Department of Virginia and North Carolina in November 1863. Almost immediately, Butler made himself obnoxious to Governor Pierpont and the Restored Government of Virginia by imposing military authority over matters of civil governance in Norfolk and Portsmouth. He reestablished military courts and issued multiple orders that interfered with the collection of monies by municipal authorities, charged merchants a percentage of goods shipped to support the restored military courts, and threatened to take control of local banks. Pierpont wrote the general to explain that he had struggled to eliminate these military provost judge's courts that secessionists favored because they did not have to take an oath of allegiance to appear before them. Now, as of January 1864, "your officers had more fully than ever opened these courts, and were intermeddling with the civil authorities of the cities in a most licentious manner." Butler pleaded ignorance, but Pierpont submitted the written orders to Lincoln and told Edwin Stanton that Butler's actions "tend to the oppression of the people and [are] subversive of good government." A note signed by Stanton, but written by Lincoln, gently requested that Butler suspend the measures involving municipal officers and banks.[19]

Pierpont was displeased. "The Government I represent," he reminded Butler, "is the government of the state of Virginia, as recognized by the President of the United States and both Houses of

Congress." Technically, only one chamber, the Senate, recognized the Restored Government: those men who had been elected to the House of Representatives were not seated. In the Senate, Lemuel Bowden died of smallpox on January 2, 1864, and was not replaced. That left John S. Carlile, who had become a virulent opponent of emancipation, as Virginia's sole senator. Lincoln gave little attention to Pierpont's Restored Government, the size of which, Lincoln recognized, "gives a somewhat farcical air to his dominion."[20]

Lincoln could not have been happy with the publication in April 1864 of a long letter from Pierpont, addressed to him and every member of Congress, in which the governor aired his concerns about "the abuses of military power in Virginia." Radical Republicans were keenly sensitive to signs of executive and military despotism and Pierpont's charges could only inflame Congress as it considered its own response to Lincoln's Proclamation of Amnesty and Reconstruction. Moreover, Lincoln seemed indifferent to the actions of a state constitutional convention that met in February 1864 and, on March 10, approved a constitution that abolished slavery. (Pierpont sent Lincoln a telegram with the news.) While this made Virginia the first Confederate state to adopt emancipation, there were only a few delegates who had been chosen by a small number of voters. Moreover, it went into effect without being put to a vote of the people. This was hardly the kind of constitutional process Lincoln had in mind. At the precise moment in March that he was congratulating Michael Hahn in Louisiana and Isaac Murphy in Arkansas, he was silent on developments in Restored Virginia.[21]

Butler was not to be deterred, and in the summer authorized putting to a vote whether the people of Norfolk wanted to discontinue municipal government, and until such time as the election was held he abolished civil government. Lincoln began a letter to Butler on August 9, 1864, in which he said affairs in Norfolk have "caused considerable trouble, forcing me to give a good deal of time and reflection to it." He tried to sort through the points of disagreement between Butler and Pierpont, and then decided against sending the letter. At a cabinet meeting on July 20, he said, according to Edward Bates, that he was "much perplexed to know what to do." But Bates was "mortified that the President has not yet announced his determination on this important business. It ought not to have occupied an hour. The Genls proceedings are flat usurpation, and ought to have been put down instantly."[22]

Bates believed that Lincoln did not act because he feared Butler's political influence. Many radicals were favoring Butler to replace Lincoln as the party's nominee, and Lincoln did not want to empower them by revoking the general's orders. "My heart is sick," Bates wrote, "when I see the President shrink from the correction of gross and heinous wrong because he is afraid 'Genl Butler will raise a hubbub about it.'" As the election approached, Bates confided, "I wish the election was over. The President, I think, as soon as re-elected, will be a freer and bolder man."[23]

On this issue, at least, Bates was right. On December 21, Lincoln took the unusual step of sending Butler the letter he had drafted the previous August in which he admonished, "nothing justifies the suspending of the civil by the military authority, but military necessity," and that decision was not to be left to a vote. In the cover note, he ordered Butler to suspend yet another election, this one called to vote on replacing the Restored Government with military control. Finally, on January 7, acting at Grant's behest, he removed Butler from command, primarily because of his failure as a general (most recently during the first attempt to take Fort Fisher, near Wilmington, North Carolina, on December 23–25, when he blundered badly), but also because of his ongoing interference with the Restored Government. On April 11, following the fall of Richmond, Salmon Chase wrote Lincoln, "by the action of every branch of the Government we are committed to the recognition & maintenance of the State organization of which Governor Pierpont is the head." In June 1865, Pierpont would relocate the Restored Government from Alexandria back to Richmond, and the constitution adopted in 1864 remained in effect until a new one was adopted in 1870.[24]

Virginia was a restored state that in part because of Butler and the irregular way in which a new constitution was adopted seemed to stand outside the Union. Tennessee, by comparison, was not a restored state, but because of Andrew Johnson and the oddity of its participation in the presidential election, it acted as if it were. On September 11, 1863, Lincoln had written Johnson to praise him for embracing emancipation and encourage him to reinaugurate a loyal state government. "Not a moment should be lost," he advised. Even then, Lincoln was thinking about reelection and reminded Johnson, "it is something on the question of *time*, to remember that it can not be known who is next to occupy the position I now hold, nor what he will do."[25]

On January 21, 1864, in the aftermath of Lincoln's Proclamation of Amnesty and Reconstruction, Johnson offered a plan for emancipation and restoration in Tennessee. He called for elections for local officials to be held in March. Following that, he expected that there would be a call for a convention to pass a resolution that abolished slavery. "The question of slavery has been the disturbing element in this Government," Johnson declared, "and the time has now come to settle it." Johnson pronounced slavery dead in Tennessee, and gave his support to immediate emancipation. He also considered what the "new relation" of the freedmen would be to society and argued that "in less than five years after this question is settled upon the principle of hired labor, the negro's labor will be more productive than it ever was." Johnson made it clear, "I do not argue that the negro race is equal to the Anglo-Saxon," and announced "I am for a white man's government." He continued over the next several months to press for emancipation and, in April, assured Lincoln that a convention "will Settle the Slavery question definitely and finely."[26]

But such a convention was slow to be held. Part of the problem was Johnson's demand for a more stringent oath—one requiring those taking it not only to pledge support of the Constitution but also to affirm their desire for an end to the insurrection and "the success of its [the Union's] armies and the defeat of all those who oppose them."

Lincoln received complaints about the oath but backed Johnson, saying that "the oath prescribed in the proclamation of Governor Johnson...is entirely satisfactory to me as a test of loyalty" and did not conflict with the oath required by his Proclamation of Amnesty and Reconstruction.[27]

Despite Lincoln's endorsement, Johnson faced continued opposition from Tennessee conservatives who coalesced around opposition to emancipation as well as the governor's heavy-handed leadership. "Andy will let us vote," declared one conservative Unionist, "if we swear to vote for him—not otherwise." When Johnson wound up as Lincoln's running mate, these conservative Unionists organized to oppose the Republican ticket and gave their support to McClellan, though not before complaining to Lincoln that Johnson had ordered an election for president. Lincoln responded, "My conclusion is that I can have nothing to do with the matter, either to sustain the plan as the Convention and Governor Johnson have initiated it, or to revoke or modify it as you demand." On Election Day, some thirty-five thousand votes were cast in Tennessee, thirty thousand going for Lincoln, though Congress would not accept the legitimacy of the state's twelve electoral votes.[28]

Johnson's long-promised convention finally took place when five hundred delegates gathered in Nashville on January 9, 1865. By then, the battle of Nashville had decimated John Bell Hood's Army of Tennessee and driven it from the state. In its aftermath, General George H. Thomas, commander of the Army of the Cumberland, wired Johnson to "respectfully suggest that immediate measures be taken for the reorganization of the Civil Government of the state." In his convention speech, Johnson implored the delegates to send an emancipation amendment to the voters for approval: "we see the great slave monopoly is gone. The great principles of freedom, working onward, have destroyed it. It is a dead carcass. The sooner we abolish it by law, the better for the State, the better for the Nation." The convention adopted an amendment abolishing slavery and, on February 22, some twenty-five thousand voters ratified it, a number that exceeded Lincoln's 10 percent requirement.[29]

After the convention adopted the abolition amendment, Johnson wrote to Lincoln: "Thank God that the tyrants' rod has been broken...the state will be redeemed and the foul blot of Slavery erased from escutcheon." Lincoln's response was muted. He offered "thanks to the Convention & to you" and asked the vice president–elect "when do you expect to be here?" If Tennessee's action did not overly excite Lincoln, it was because he had waited a long time for military governor Johnson to restore the state, and by the time the deed was accomplished a constitutional amendment that abolished slavery had been approved by Congress and sent to the states for ratification. (On April 7, Tennessee became the twentieth state to ratify it.) Johnson himself knew it was coming and told the convention in January, "If you delay, there will be an amendment to the Federal Constitution which will do it for you. Let us take the credit of this work on ourselves."[30]

While Virginia and Tennessee drew some of Lincoln's attention during the fall, it was the restoration of Louisiana to the Union that preoccupied him. On August 9, he had written Nathaniel Banks to express eagerness that the newly adopted constitution be ratified and pledged his support. "Let me know at once," he wrote, which civil officers "openly declare for the constitution, and who of them, if any, decline to so declare." (This was on the same date that he wrote to Butler to express his concerns about events in Virginia.) In an election held on September 5, voters ratified the new state constitution and elected representatives to Congress. The total vote was a little over 8,400, with 6,836 in favor and 1,566 opposed. Banks wrote a long letter to Lincoln, trying to rationalize a vote that "was not so large as we expected." There was fear that those who voted would be forced into military service, and little help in the election was provided by Treasury Department agents. Coming in the heat of "the fever month," many prominent potential voters were not in residence. And Lincoln's political opponents in the North, Banks reported, persuaded opponents in Louisiana to suppress the vote. Nonetheless, it was "a good and honest vote." In late September, Banks returned to Washington where he remained to help lobby for recognition of Louisiana when the lame-duck session of the Thirty-eighth Congress assembled in December.[31]

General Stephen Hurlbut assumed Banks's duties, and almost immediately a clash erupted between military and civil authorities. Hurlbut expressed the opinion that "it would be far better for all concerned that military government prevail." In reply, commanding general Edward R. S. Canby agreed that any civilian government would be created by the military authorities and subject to it. Governor Hahn was outraged and reported to Lincoln that military officers seemed set on preventing the state government from forming and "extinguishing" what had been formed. He pleaded for Banks's return.[32]

Lincoln was furious. Less than a week after the joyous news of his reelection, which Michael Hahn thought should "put to rest all doubts on the question of the entire and early restoration of the Union," the president wrote to Hurlbut. "Few things," he began, "since I have been here, have impressed me more painfully than what, for four or five months past, has appeared as bitter military opposition to the new State Government of Louisiana." He had seen the correspondence between Hurlbut and Canby, and he provided an education and an admonishment:

> A very fair proportion of the people of Louisiana have inaugerated a new State Government, making an excellent new constitution— better for the poor black man than we have in Illinois. This was done under military protection, directed by me, in the belief, still sincerely entertained, that with such a nucleus around which to build, we could get the State into position again sooner than otherwise. In this belief a general promise of protection and support, applicable alike to Louisiana and other states, was given in the last annual message. During the formation of the new government

and Constitution, they were supported by nearly every loyal person
and opposed by every secessionist. And this support, and this opposition, from the respective stand points of the parties, was perfectly consistent and logical. Every Unionist ought to wish the new
government to succeed; and every disunionist must desire it to fail.
It's failure would gladden the heart ... of every enemy of the old flag
in the world. Every advocate of slavery naturally desires to see
blasted, and crushed, the liberty promised the black man by the
new Constitution. But why Gen. Canby and Gen. Hurlbut should
join on the same side is to me incomprehensible.

Both Hurlbut and Canby responded to their commander in chief.
Hurlbut expressed surprise at Lincoln's tone and offered reassur-
ances; Canby claimed to have "little official connection" to the goings-
on in New Orleans and pledged to "give whatever support and aid
I can, to the State Government." Lincoln told Canby, "it [is] a worthy
object to again get Louisiana into proper practical relations with the
nation; and we can never finish this, if we never begin it."[33]

Lincoln had the lame-duck session of Congress on his mind. He
was preparing his annual message, and he knew whatever chances he
would have to get Louisiana recognized might be jeopardized by any
hint of military dictatorship. As it stood, Lincoln knew that radicals
could not have been happy with the failure of the Louisiana legislature to pass legislation that extended the vote to some blacks. Hahn
wrote Lincoln on November 11 to ask if he could use Lincoln's
March 13, 1864, letter privately expressing support for limited black
suffrage. It "would prove of some service to the colored race and do
you no harm. Please read, and inform me whether it would be advis-
able to make it public?" Apparently, Lincoln did not respond; he was
not yet ready publicly to endorse black suffrage.[34]

Lincoln devoted the weeks following his reelection to his upcoming
annual message, which, according to Welles, "seemed to dwell heavy
on his mind." With the election over, and military success virtually

assured, only one question remained. "The subject of Reconstruction and how it should be effected is the most important theme," reported Welles after hearing a draft of the message on November 25. At the cabinet meeting, Welles suggested that Lincoln should invite back to the Union not only the people but the states as well. Stanton, whom Welles often criticized and could not resist noting was present for only the first time in six weeks, suggested that the president maintain his former policy and ask those in the Confederacy "whether it would not have been better for them and for all, had they a year since accepted his offer." A week later, Welles said the message was "much improved."[35]

In the message sent to Congress on December 6, 1864, Lincoln celebrated the strength and growth of the nation. After treating foreign affairs, the Treasury, and reports of the secretaries of war and navy, he noted, "the steady expansion of population, improvement and governmental institutions over the new and unoccupied portion of our country have scarcely been checked, much less impeded or destroyed, by our great civil war, which at first glance would seem to have absorbed almost the entire energies of the nation." The war was awful, and all-consuming, but it had not depleted the nation. He emphasized that "we have *more* men *now* than we had when the war *began*; that we are not exhausted, nor in the process of exhaustion; that we are *gaining* strength, and may, if need be, maintain the contest indefinitely. This is as to men. Material resources are now more complete and abundant than ever." He talked about reconstruction in terms of important steps taken "to the effect of moulding society for durability in the Union." He noted the newly organized state governments with free constitutions in Louisiana and Arkansas. He anticipated the same for Tennessee, and observed that the border states of Missouri and Kentucky were also moving toward emancipation. Abolition had taken effect in Maryland on November 1 and the state was "secure to Liberty and Union for all the future." Lincoln asked the House again to consider passing an amendment abolishing slavery, which the Senate had approved the previous April. He noted that the results of the November election meant the next Congress would no doubt do so, but why wait: "may we not agree that the sooner the better?" The election results were "the voice of the people now, for the first time, heard upon the question." He noted that a year had passed since his Proclamation of Amnesty and Reconstruction. Many white Southerners had taken advantage of the offer, and he affirmed that the door was still open. But, he warned, the time will come when "public duty shall demand that it be closed" and "more rigorous measures than heretofore shall be adopted." Lincoln did not specify what those measures might entail, but the sentiment no doubt pleased radicals who all along believed he had been too lenient toward the rebels. He closed by reasserting his commitment to emancipation in the strongest possible terms: "I retract nothing heretofore said as to slavery.... If the people should, by whatever mode or means, make it an Executive duty to re-enslave such persons, another, and not I, must be their instrument to perform it." In short, he would resign rather than restore slavery. As for peace, he asserted in his final sentence that there was only one condition: "the war will cease on the part of the government, whenever it shall have ceased on the part of those who began it."[36]

As the clerk, Edward McPherson, read the message silence "pervaded the vast hall and the breathless, crowded galleries." When the clerk reached the part about emancipation in Maryland, applause burst out. Noah Brooks observed "smiling faces and long sighs of satisfaction" when the clerk read the restatement of Lincoln's amnesty policy. At the close, there "was a long, loud, and continued burst of applause." Brooks reported that while the message had "all the dignity and polish of a first-rate state paper" it also exhibited "strong common sense and practical knowledge." Privately, he wrote to a friend that there was widespread "enthusiastic praise" for the message, and reported that Thaddeus Stevens, who was no great believer in Lincoln, had told him it was the best message sent by a president to Congress in sixty years. Indeed, Stevens would pronounce in Congress, "there never was a day since Abraham Lincoln was elected President that he stood so high, or deserved to stand so high in the estimation of the people as at this moment."[37]

Whitelaw Reid, whose dispatches under the byline "Agate" appeared in the *Cincinnati Gazette*, claimed the message has "united in approbation and admiration all wings and divisions of Unionists."[38] Both Brooks and Reid commented on how Lincoln had written the message. Brooks informed readers that the president's habit was to write out his ideas on "slips of pasteboard or boxboard." He then sat in his armchair and rewrote in pencil. Finally, following a proof with space for more corrections, the document was printed. "The complete collection of original scraps," thought Brooks, "would be a valuable prize for an autograph hunter." Reid, with more literary panache, reported that "if History wants any Boswellian particulars, it may be interesting to put in print the fact that the President wrote the Message on stiff sheets of a sort of cardboard, which he could lay upon his knee and write upon as he sat with his feet on the table and his chair tilted back in the 'American attitude.'"[39]

Republican editors exalted the man and the message. "God Bless Abraham Lincoln!," exclaimed the radical *Independent*. "A document more full of sound sense, high-toned patriotism, fidelity to moral principle, Christian courage in the Good Cause, has never come from his homely pen. Like gold cast upon the counter, it falls upon the country with a true and genuine ring." The final sentence was "pure wheat, winnowed of all chaff of compromise." The last sentence, proclaimed *Zion's Herald*, "will live in history, and be remembered and quoted as specimens of the heroic and morally sublime."[40]

"Mr. Lincoln tells his story in a blunt, business-like way," thought the *Albany Evening Journal*, "with the best possible expenditure of rhetoric and the least possible waste of words." And its message was as explicit as it was direct. The *New York Tribune* posited that "not even the most violent opponent of Mr. Lincoln can complain that his policy has an uncertainty about it, or that it is not as thoroughly radical as his warmest admirer would have it. Peace by the submission or conquest of Rebels, and the total abolition of Slavery, will be the determined purpose of the new Administration."[41]

There was little that opposition newspapers could say except to condemn a war that would end only with abolition, denounce the president's alleged abuse of executive authority, and lament his unwillingness to consider any peace proposals. The response of the *New York World* could have been penned before the message was delivered: "a more tame, jejune, commonplace state paper never emanated from a man clothed with high responsibilities." Lincoln's optimism was troubling to some. The *Daily Eastern Argus* found Lincoln's attitude offensive: "what must strike every one on reading this message is its cheerful tone. Everything appears to be going on finely— in sea, earth, and sky, all is serene." The message was not only "vague and superficial," it was pure radicalism, argued the *Boston Post*, a declaration that the war would go on for the destruction of slavery. In conclusion, the New York *Tribune* thought, "the Message seems to be about what everybody expected; satisfies the Unionists, and dissatisfies the other kind. Which we presume satisfies Mr. Lincoln."[42]

Much had changed since Congress had adjourned in July, five months earlier. The war had turned decidedly in the Union's favor; Lincoln had been decisively reelected; Louisiana had ratified its new state constitution. Lincoln had reason to hope that the imbroglio over the Wade-Davis bill had passed and that he and Congress would be able to work together. On the same day as the message, Lincoln had even nominated Chase to the Supreme Court, much to the delight of Sumner and other radicals who had been lobbying the president.

On December 13, Thomas D. Eliot of Massachusetts introduced a resolution to allow Louisiana to "resume its political relations with the Government of the United States." That the measure was proposed by Eliot, a radical who had supported the Wade-Davis bill and favored congressional reconstruction, and that Republicans tried to keep it out of Henry Winter Davis's Committee on Rebellious States, seemed to bode well for Lincoln's desire to see Louisiana restored.[43]

Two days later, James Ashley reported reconstruction legislation entitled "A Bill to Guarantee to Certain States Whose Governments Have Been Usurped or Overthrown a Republican Form of Government." The bill called for the appointment of a provisional governor to execute the laws, "but no law or usage whereby any person was heretofore held in involuntary servitude shall be recognized," and "all persons held to involuntary servitude or labor...are hereby emancipated and discharged therefrom, and they and their posterity shall be forever free." Like the Wade-Davis bill, Ashley's required a majority of eligible voters. Unlike it, the bill extended suffrage to blacks by specifying that those voters would consist of loyal male citizens of the United States twenty-one or older. The bill also stipulated that the laws for regulating trial and punishment of white persons would be extended to all persons—thus blacks would serve as jurors. One section of the bill explicitly stated that Congress "do hereby recognize the government of Louisiana."[44]

The bill was a compromise. Sumner explained to Francis Lieber, a jurist and author of a code summarizing the laws of war, "I have persuaded the Presdt. the duty of harmony between Congress & the Executive. He is agreed. It is proposed to admit La (which ought not to be done) & at the same time pass the Reconstruction Bill for all the other states, giving the electoral franchise to 'all citizens,' without distinction of color. If this arrangement is carried out it will be an immense political act."[45]

On December 18, the same day as Sumner's letter, Lincoln discussed Ashley's bill with Montgomery Blair and Nathaniel Banks. Having been forced out of the cabinet, Blair had little good to say and spent the time attacking the radicals. Lincoln no doubt expected this from his former postmaster general. Less than two weeks earlier he had received from Blair a lengthy screed on reconstruction in which he warned against radical attempts to deprive the states of their right to regulate suffrage and to "disfranchise the white race" and to throw state governments "into the hands of the African race."[46]

Lincoln did not need Blair to tell him that black male suffrage might be problematic. According to John Hay, Lincoln had been reading Ashley's bill "carefully & said that he liked it with the exception of one or two things which he thought rather calculated to conceal a feature which might be objectionable to some." One was the provision that would have made voters and jurors of the freedmen. Banks said, "'what you refer to would be a fatal objection to the Bill. It would simply throw the Government into the hands of the blacks, as the white people under that arrangement would refuse to vote.'" The other issue that troubled Lincoln was the provision whereby Congress declared slaves to be free. As he had declared in not signing the Wade-Davis bill, and as he had consistently held, he did not believe Congress had the authority to interfere with slavery in the states where it existed. Beyond these objections, according to Hay, "the President and General Banks spoke very favorably" about the bill. It settled the status of Louisiana without, Lincoln believed, "laying down any cast-iron policy" with regard to the organization and recognition of other states. Banks thought Congress was eager to pass a bill so as to claim "a hand in the reconstruction," and if those two areas of disagreement could be resolved, Lincoln would unquestionably sign it if it came to his desk.[47]

Banks communicated Lincoln's concerns to Ashley who, on December 20, reported back the bill with amendments. In the new version, voting was limited to "all *white* male citizens" and those "*in the military or naval service*," which would have enfranchised black soldiers and sailors. And instead of Congress freeing the slaves, the bill was amended to read that persons would be emancipated "*who have been declared free by any Proclamation of the President.*" Even Henry Winter Davis seemed to succumb to the pressure. The pressure from the president and all the Massachusetts representatives "was plainly a combination not to be resisted so I had to let La. in under Banks' govt in condition of it going in the *Bill* defeated by the Prest. last year." On January 1, Sumner wrote "the Presdt. is exerting every force to bring Congress to receive Louisiana under her Banks govt."[48]

In the revised bill, Lincoln had gotten what he wanted, but the compromise did not last long. On January 7, Ashley's bill, reported back from Davis's Committee on Rebellious States, included two revisions that would never be acceptable to Lincoln even if they could get through Congress. One amendment now called for the guarantee of *"equality of civil rights before the law…to all persons."* The second broke the compromise over admitting Louisiana by allowing Louisiana and Arkansas to be recognized provided they went through the new enrollment process, which meant a majority of voters and not the 10 percent under which the states had been reorganized, and included in their constitutions provisions for equal civil rights, exclusion of Confederate officeholders from political rights, and repudiation of all Confederate debts. Some Republicans clearly opposed these changes, and new amendments came forward. Most of this maneuvering occurred behind the scenes, but on January 16 House members began publicly to debate the bill.

Pennsylvania congressman William Darrah Kelley proposed an amendment that would provide the vote to all male citizens who could read the Constitution. In a lengthy speech, Kelley surveyed American history and asked, "Did God ordain our country for a single race of men? Is there reasons [*sic*] why the intelligent, wealthy, loyal man of color shall stand apart, abased, on election day while his ignorant, intemperate, vicious, and disloyal white neighbor participates in making laws for his government?" If "we ignore the rights of these four million people and their posterity," he predicted, "the demon of agitation will haunt us in the future fearfully as it has in the past."[49]

Kelley opposed the bill because it did not go far enough with respect to providing limited black suffrage. Thomas D. Eliot, by comparison, went through the bill section by section and opposed it for going too far—this despite his reputation as a radical. For example, he rejected the idea that anyone who held office in the rebel government is "hereby declared not to be a citizen of the United States." "That is applying the punishment before the offense is committed," thought Eliot. The heart of his criticism was the change in the provision for recognizing Louisiana that would require "applying the machinery of this bill" to the state. Eliot concluded that there was no need to pass a general bill because the situation would differ state by state and he thought it would be "more wise to take the States as they shall present themselves for admission."[50]

The Republicans, clearly, were deeply divided—some seeing the bill as too limited in its reach, others seeing it as objectionable for different reasons, chief among them that it repeated the error of the Wade-Davis bill and again repudiated the president on reconstruction. James F. Wilson of Iowa offered a motion to postpone, to which Davis replied that "a vote to postpone is equivalent to a vote to kill the bill."[51] The motion carried 103–34 with 45 not voting. Fifty-eight Republicans voted in favor of killing the measure.

The *Springfield Republican* thought the bill defective. The *New York Times* expressed relief that "the schemes of 'reconstruction' now before Congress are likely to be abandoned or fail. They are utterly needless, and may prove mischievous." Eventually, the editors thought, a Congress will be elected that will support the new state governments organized under Lincoln's plan.[52]

When Ashley again brought the bill before the House on February 20, it had been amended yet again. Now all male citizens age twenty-one or over would be enrolled to vote. Louisiana and Arkansas would not have to go through the process of enrolling a majority of their citizens, but all the rebel states would have to add to their constitutions provisions for equal civil and political rights and repudiation of their war debt. The latest version also incorporated changes suggested by Eliot, including elimination of the provision permanently excluding rebel officeholders from citizenship.

Ashley's untiring efforts to craft an acceptable bill were commendable, but he must have come to realize that it was hopeless. Repeatedly retailoring the bill in quest of the right formula to get it passed would not work. Everyone had their reasons for opposing it. A number of radicals refused to support a bill that did not include suffrage and equal rights. Some radicals and most moderates would not support a bill that repudiated progress made by Lincoln on reconstruction whereas others opposed recognizing Louisiana. The Democrats, of course, rejected any bill and found the entire spectacle amusing.

Henry L. Dawes of Massachusetts, for one, had had enough. This was the fourth draft of the bill to appear and he understood that a fifth was waiting in the wings. Dawes attacked a number of specific clauses of the legislation, such as the responsibilities of a provisional governor and methods of taxation, but the essence of his critique was that the bill dictated too much and ignored the "great element of American character"—let the people decide for themselves how they wanted to be governed. Dawes defended the process and result in Louisiana and rejected any attempt to "lay down an iron rule for all the other States in rebellion." He opposed the bill on those grounds. Conservative Democrat Fernando Wood took the floor and preened that "I have listened with pleasure to the gentleman," an accolade that led Dawes to inform his wife, "we killed the Bill dead—and Fernando Wood killed me dead by complimenting me."[53]

The radical *Independent* lamented that "the Thirty-Eighth Congress could not rise above the level of the word 'white.'" Most other assessments, however, expressed relief. The *New York Herald* reported that killing the bill "meets with general approval." The *Springfield Republican* wrote, "The president's reconstruction policy stands, and the readmission of the recovered states will be obstructed by no inflexible rule." The *Daily Evening Bulletin* in San Francisco claimed, "The refusal of Congress at the present session to pass a reconstruction bill is manifestly an admission that the President's policy is the wisest." The *New York Tribune* was also pleased and reminded readers, "this Congress is soon to disperse.... The country confides in the President, and would to-morrow decide unhesitatingly to leave the matter to his uncontrolled discretion."[54]

At about the same time efforts to pass a reconstruction bill collapsed, so did the last chance for recognition of Louisiana, when both houses of Congress decided not to seat any members from the state. The House of Representatives simply took no action on seating M. F. Bonzano, W. D. Mann, and Alexander P. Field, even though the Committee on Elections reported in their favor. It didn't help Field's case that, incensed over comments by William Darrah Kelley, he assaulted the congressman with a knife at a Washington hotel, an attack for which he was arrested and censured. In the Senate, Lyman Trumbull's Judiciary Committee reviewed the credentials of Charles Smith and R. King Cutler. On December 14, Trumbull asked Lincoln for any papers related to the establishment of civil government in Louisiana. Asked for his opinion on the facts submitted by Banks, Lincoln responded that they accorded with what he believed to be true and, careful not to argue or take sides, asked, "can Louisiana be brought into proper practical relations with the Union, sooner, by *admitting* or by *rejecting* the proposed Senators?" The Senate decided that joint congressional action recognizing the government of Louisiana would be necessary before it reached a decision about Smith and Cutler. But the resolution was doomed. One writer noted that "radicals of both parties . . . have united to defeat the resolution—the copperheads because they see danger that their set may be put down in States thus reorganized, and Mr. Sumner because negro suffrage is not made a fundamental condition of readmission." On February 27, Zachariah Chandler wrote his wife, "we killed the Louisiana Bill yesterday morning so dead that it will not pass this session."[55]

Despite this setback, Lincoln would not abandon Louisiana any more than he had abandoned Arkansas after Congress rejected its claimants to seats. Soon enough, Congress would be out of session, and the rebellion over, and Lincoln could take the case of Louisiana directly to the people.

Chapter 7

"A Righteous and Speedy Peace"

In an editorial on "The Question of Reconstruction in the Present Congress," the *New York Times* concluded, "this Thirty-eighth Congress...will do well to finish its dying without any further attempt to dictate to the future.... The real responsibilities connected with the work of reconstruction, rest with the next Congress." However much James Ashley was disappointed by his failure to get a reconstruction bill enacted, his place in history had been assured when he secured passage of the Thirteenth Amendment on January 31, 1865 (with two votes to spare). The amendment declared that "neither slavery nor involuntary servitude...shall exist within the United States." Carl Schurz was in the gallery for the vote and when the amendment passed "the ladies waved their handkerchiefs, the men threw their hats into the air, they embraced, they shook hands, and ten minutes passed before the hurrahing and the enthusiastic racket ceased." Schurz told his wife, "It is worthwhile to live in these days." On the following day, Illinois became the first state to ratify, as Lincoln proudly noted when speaking in response to a celebratory serenade. The Thirteenth Amendment resolved all the issues left dangling by the Emancipation Proclamation, which might have been ruled legally invalid or not applicable to the children of slaves. "This Amendment is a King's cure for all the evils," he told the serenaders. "It winds the whole thing up."[1]

The Thirteenth Amendment resolved the issue of slavery, but it did not address the issue of the formers slaves' rights and welfare. It was an old issue, not a new one, one that often appeared as some version of the question: "What is to be done with them?" Lincoln posed the issue in a speech at Peoria in 1854, long before the Civil War and the reality of emancipation. "If all earthly power were given me," he confessed on that occasion, "I should not know what to do, as to the existing institution." He thought he would free all the slaves and send them to Liberia. Although he would continue to promote colonization schemes in the first two years of the war, even in 1854 he realized "its sudden execution is impossible." "What then?" he continued. "Free them, and make them politically and socially, our equals?" He acknowledged, "My own feelings will not admit of this." And even if they did, "we well know that those of the great mass of white people will not."[2]

In 1862, in a letter to the editor of the *New York Times* titled "What Shall We Do with the Slaves," a writer observed, "this is the question everywhere asked by patriots and traitors." Frederick Douglass, for one, dismissed the question. In "What Shall Be Done with the Slaves if Emancipated?" an article in the January 1862 issue of *Douglass' Monthly* he wrote, "What shall be done with them? Our answer is, do nothing with them; mind your business, and let them mind theirs. Your *doing* with them is their greatest misfortune. They have been undone by your doings, and all they now ask, and really have need of at your hands, is just to let them alone." The problem was to convince millions of Americans who saw slaves either as brute savages or docile children that they were humans driven by the same capacities and desires as any person. "What shall be done with the Negro if emancipated?" Douglass asked. The answer: "Deal justly with him. He is a human being, capable of judging between good and evil, right and wrong, liberty and slavery, and is as much a subject of law as any other man; therefore, deal justly with him. He is, like other men, sensible of the motives of reward and punishment. Give him wages for his work, and let hunger pinch him if he don't work. He knows the difference between fullness and famine, plenty and scarcity."[3]

Consideration of the problem of freedom did not await the abolition of slavery and restoration of the union, but was an ongoing concern throughout the war and took concrete form in Secretary of War

Stanton's creation of the American Freedmen's Inquiry Commission in March 1863. The three commissioners reported in May 1864 that those who had been freed were "loyal men, putting faith in the Government, looking to it for guidance and protection, willing to work for moderate wages if promptly paid, docile and easily managed, not given to quarreling among themselves, of temperate habits, cheerful and uncomplaining under hard labor when treated with justice." The problem, according to a supplemental report issued in 1864 and subtitled *The Emancipated Slave Face to Face with His Old Master,* was that former slave owners "scoff at the idea of freedom for the negro." "The difficulty is not with the emancipated slave," wrote James McKaye, one of the commissioners, "but with the old master."[4]

Recognizing that the emancipated slaves would need some protection from their former owners, and that loyal white refugees would also require assistance, Congress passed the Freedmen's Bureau Act in March 1865, a measure introduced in 1863. The bill authorized the War Department, for up to one year after the war ended, to provide for the assignment to freedmen and refugees of up to forty acres of abandoned land or property to which the government had acquired title. Rent would be paid for three years during or after such time the occupants could purchase the plots. The bill also provided for distribution of food and clothing as well as emergency shelter. Additionally, the bureau played a role, in conjunction with privately funded freedmen's aid societies, in establishing schools.[5]

Land, shelter, clothing, supplies, and education were all important, but suffrage, an idea that a few years earlier was advocated only by abolitionists and radical Republicans, became increasingly central to conversations about the freedmen and reconstruction. Perhaps playing off Confederate vice president Alexander Stephens's March 1861 speech declaring that the Confederate government's "corner-stone rests, upon the great truth that the negro is not equal to the white man," Adam Gurowski noted, "the loyal Africo-American ought to be the corner-stone of reconstruction.... The time is past and gone to force the loyal Africo-American to be tutored otherwise than by laws of equality with the whites, and whoever legislates differently is a traitor to humanity and to his country."[6]

In April 1865, James Russell Lowell, antislavery poet, Harvard professor, and editor, published a piece on reconstruction in the *North American Review*. "The first question that arises in the mind of everybody in thinking of reconstruction is...What is to be done about the negro?...Our answer to the question, What are we to do with the negro? is short and simple. Give him a fair chance." Lowell argued that the war had been "carried on for the principles of democracy" and "the only way to fit men for freedom is to make them free, the only way to teach them how to use political power, is to give it to them."[7]

Sidney George Fisher, a Philadelphia aristocrat, read the article and disagreed with the rush to embrace suffrage: "this absurd plan gains supporters. The abolitionists cannot bear to lose so fruitful a theme of excitement as the position of the Negro race, so that now, having emancipated him, they propose going a step further by granting him political power."[8]

Lincoln's support for limited black suffrage no doubt grew out of his belief that men who fought to preserve the Union had earned the right to vote, and nearly 200,000 black soldiers and sailors had played a critical role in helping to win the war. The position he had expressed in his confidential letter to Michael Hahn became known within Republican political circles. B. Gratz Brown, senator from Missouri, quoted from it in a letter to his constituents on December 22, 1864. With respect to the Hahn letter, William Darrah Kelley asserted, "my recollection is that it was marked 'private.' But this restriction was long since removed by the exhibition by Mr. Lincoln of a copy of the letter to several persons." Nathaniel Banks, in a letter published in the *Liberator* on February 24, 1865, wrote that, in Louisiana, "the President...desired that measures should be taken to extend suffrage to colored citizens." In the weeks after the president's death, Kelley claimed that support for black suffrage "was not a mere sentiment with Mr. Lincoln. He regarded it as an act of justice to the citizens, and a measure of sound policy for the States."[9]

As suggested by Lincoln's comment to Hay, after reading a version of Ashley's reconstruction bill, that it contained a "feature which might be objectionable to some," the president would not suddenly force his beliefs on an unwilling public and, by doing so, jeopardize the return of the rebellious states to the Union. If he was willing to consider suffrage and endorse, through the Freedmen's Bureau, a role for the federal government in helping blacks make the transition from slavery to freedom, he was also more than willing simply to let matters take their course until circumstances arose favorable to a change in policy.[10]

On February 3, Lincoln met at Hampton Roads with three peace commissioners from the Confederacy—Alexander Stephens, R. M. T. Hunter, and John A. Campbell. Seward was also present. The men agreed not to take notes, but several accounts of the discussion were published afterward. At one point, the conversation turned to reconstruction. Lincoln restated the position he had articulated in his annual message—the war would end once rebels laid down their arms and returned to federal allegiance. Lincoln stood by emancipation, but did suggest compensation to slaveholders if they freed their slaves. According to Campbell, "Mr. Lincoln stated that he regarded the North to be as much responsible for slavery as the South, and that he would be rejoiced to be taxed on his property for indemnities to the masters of slaves." Upon his return, Lincoln even presented to the cabinet a draft of a joint congressional resolution authorizing the allocation of four hundred million dollars to the slave states if they ended all resistance and abandoned slavery. Welles, who tersely noted "it did not meet with the cabinet's favor, but was dropped," thought the idea demonstrated "the earnest desire of the President to conciliate and effect peace … but there may be such a thing as so overdoing as to cause a distrust or adverse feeling."[11]

Lincoln's willingness to try anything that promised to reunite the nation and move it past slavery was typical of him, much to the chagrin of many. Welles noted that Lincoln "has often strange and incomparable whims, takes sometimes singular and unaccountable freaks." No doubt he recalled the brouhaha over the proposal Lincoln made in his annual message in 1862 for a constitutional amendment that would have compensated states for gradually abolishing slavery by the year 1900. Upon reading the proposal, which came just weeks before issuance of the Emancipation Proclamation, Douglass called the president "demented."[12]

Now, in February 1865, it seemed as if Lincoln was acting in similar fashion. The Thirteenth Amendment had been passed and the war was winding to its conclusion. Why compensate slaveholders for relinquishing what by law and war they would soon be required to abandon? Lincoln did not say, but he may have been concerned about ratification of the abolition amendment, which required twenty-seven of the thirty-six states. No rebel state had yet been readmitted to the Union, and he could not be certain as to what the future would bring. If he could simultaneously eradicate slavery by another means, why not do it? As for compensation, the issue never troubled Lincoln in the way it did abolitionists, who believed one should not be paid for doing what "God, justice, humanity, and our Constitution require *him* to do." But as Campbell's comment suggested, Lincoln did not see slaveholding solely as a Southern sin. In his second inaugural, only weeks away, he would declare slavery an offense that God "now wills to remove, and that he gives to both North and South, this terrible war, as the woe due to those by whom the offence came."[13]

The conversation at Hampton Roads turned to what Alexander Stephens called "the evils of immediate emancipation," by which he had in mind the problems faced by women, children, and the infirm. According Campbell, "Mr. Lincoln replied with a story, of a man who had planted potatoes for his hogs, and left them in the ground to be rooted for; the ground froze, but the master said the hog must root nevertheless." Stephens said that Lincoln responded by "telling the anecdote, which has been published in the papers, about the Illinois farmer and his hogs."[14]

Stephens recounted a generic version of the story in a footnote. The most complete version came from Francis B. Carpenter, a painter who lived in the White House in 1864 and visited Lincoln in February 1865. While Carpenter's account cannot be taken literally, it captures something of Lincoln as storyteller and certainly conveys the meaning, if not the precise language, of the tale he told:

> It reminds me of a man out in Illinois, by the name of Case, who undertook, a few years ago, to raise a very large herd of hogs. It was a great trouble to *feed* them, and how to get around this was a puzzle to him. At length he hit on the plan of planting an immense field of potatoes, and, when they were sufficiently grown, he turned the whole herd into the field, and let them have full swing, thus saving not only the labor of feeding the hogs, but also of digging the potatoes.... A neighbor came along, "Well, well," said he, "Mr. Case, this is all very fine. Your hogs are doing very well just now, but you know out here in Illinois the frost comes early, and the ground freezes a foot deep. Then what are they going to do?" This was a view of the matter Mr. Case had not taken into account.... He scratched his head, and at length stammered, "Well, it may come pretty hard on their *snouts*, but I don't see but that it will be 'root, hog, or die!'"[15]

It was a harsh judgment. Even Stephens later thought the tale "was far from entitled to a place on a list of his best and most felicitous hits of this character."[16] But it revealed an essential truth. The war would soon be over and slavery abolished. The rebellious states would return. The freedmen would not be the only ones trying to cope with a new set of conditions. Lincoln knew there was only so much he could do to help the newly liberated slaves. He favored limited suffrage, but most white Americans, North as well as South, were not ready to take that step. He endorsed federal efforts to administer the transition from slavery to freedom, but such efforts cut against the widespread preference for limited government and the American self-help ideology. He could seek ways to keep Confederate leaders

from regaining political power, but for Lincoln mercy trumped retribution, and throngs of Southern Unionists eligible for amnesty
seemed as equally determined as Confederate politicians to subju-
gate the blacks. Lincoln was aware of all these difficulties; soon he
would have a second term to deal with them.

Everyone expected a brief address. Prior to Lincoln's inauguration
on March 4, 1865, newspapers informed the public, "it is the briefest
inaugural ever written, [Lincoln] says, and he hopes that it will not
be announced the worst." One journalist reported, "A gentleman to
whom it has been read says it will not occupy more than six or seven
minutes in its delivery, and that it will be very generally indorsed
[sic] as the best inaugural address ever made. He was strikingly
reminded of the President's brief but famous Gettysburg speech
while listening to it."[17]

As many as forty thousand people, according to some police es-
timates, waited in ankle-deep mud for the ceremonies to begin.
Heavy rains the previous day and through the morning had drenched
the Capitol grounds, and the sky remained dark and threatening.
At noon, the vice-presidential swearing in took place in the Senate
chamber. After a brief speech by Hannibal Hamlin, in which the
departing vice president thanked the members of the Senate,
Andrew Johnson spoke before taking the oath of office. The kindest
report called his speech "ridiculous." Others labeled it incoherent,
undignified, insulting. Noah Brooks wrote simply: "the Vice President
of the United States, was in a state of manifest intoxication." The
Independent declared, "It is the plain duty of Mr. Johnson either to
apologize for his conduct, or resign his office." At the moment,
many of those present must have wished that Hamlin had remained
vice president.[18]

The dignitaries moved to the East Portico for Lincoln's inauguration. The president delivered his address in "clear, light tones" that
"rang out over the vast throng." Lincoln's second inaugural address
offered no policy proposals and no summary of the previous four

years. His explanation for what had transpired in 1861 sounded prophetic: "both parties deprecated war; but one of them would *make* war rather than let the nation survive; and the other would *accept* war rather than let it perish. And the war came."[19]

Lincoln turned to slavery. If the war had begun only to save the Union, it was ending with slavery vanquished from the land. Slavery, Lincoln said, was "somehow, the cause of the war." In precisely what way, no one could say. A substantial part of the story was the battle over the extension of slavery into the territories. But it was more than that; it had to be. There was a moral battle being waged as well, and Lincoln contemplated the conundrum that both sides "read the same Bible, and pray to the same God, and each invokes His aid against the other." He added, "The prayers of both could not be answered; that of neither has been answered fully. The Almighty has His own purposes." God willed "this terrible war" for the sin of slavery. And the war will continue until "this mighty scourge" is ended; it will continue "until every drop of blood drawn with the lash, shall be paid by another drawn with the sword." It was an astonishing judgment: retributive, vengeful, unforgiving. Lincoln quoted from Psalm 19: "the judgments of the Lord, are true and righteous altogether."

But if the inaugural struck an Old Testament note, its tune was New Testament. The singular final sentence expresses Lincoln's essence, the phrases "with malice toward none; with charity for all" as much an articulation of how he would treat the rebels once they laid down their arms and returned to the Union as a philosophy of life. He paraphrased Matthew 7: "judge not that we be not judged." Magnanimity, generosity, forgiveness would guide Lincoln's approach to reconstruction. As he spoke, the sun burst through the darkened skies. Noah Brooks recalled Lincoln saying that he took it as "a happy omen." David Homer Bates, War Department telegraph operator, also noticed the sunshine and recorded in his diary, "the omen was favorable, every man noticed it & it is hoped that it pictures the history of our country. We have been under dark clouds for 4 years & now the signs of peace brighten."[20]

Lincoln's sermon, homily, sacred speech—commentators used these words in describing the inaugural—thrilled most listeners who marveled at its wisdom and simplicity. One writer thought the final paragraph "should be printed in gold." Of course, the opposition press, such as the Democratic *New York World*, condemned Lincoln's "devotional fervor" and "substitution of religion for statesmanship," but few others complained. The private reaction of one soldier, Private David Lane of the Seventeenth Michigan, no doubt spoke for many: "I have just read the President's Inaugural. I consider it the most remarkable state paper of modern times. Beautiful in its simplicity; grand and majestic in its expressions of lofty faith in the 'Great Ruler of Nations'; it resembles more the production of one of Israel's ancient rulers than the Inaugural Address of a modern politician. I gathered strength and courage from its perusal."[21]

Charles Francis Adams Jr. also marveled at the speech. A colonel with the Fifth Massachusetts Cavalry, a black regiment, he was the grandson and great-grandson of presidents. In a letter to his father, Adams proclaimed, "That rail-splitter lawyer is one of the wonders of the day. Once at Gettysburg and now again on a greater occasion he has shown a capacity for rising to the demands of the hour.... The inaugural strikes me in its grand simplicity and directness as being for all times the historical keynote of this war."[22]

If that keynote placed mercy ahead of justice, not everyone felt the same way. A month earlier, Adams described the retributive feelings among many New England radicals. "The old Puritan vindictiveness is beginning to stick out strongly," he observed. The leader of a growing pack of avengers seemed to be Charles Sumner. Marquis Adolphe de Chambrun, a French journalist visiting Washington, described Sumner in a letter home written on February 27, 1865: "his opinions are so radical that they are far in advance of actual possibility; revolution, confiscation, violent means of every sort, forced expropriation of slave-holders, everything appears to him legitimate and necessary in order to arrive at his objective.... Any opposition to his principles constitutes 'moral turpitude' and he hates turpitude as God detests sin." At that moment, Sumner was orchestrating the defeat of the motion to recognize Louisiana; a week later, he dismissed the inaugural as an "augur [of] confusion & uncertainty in the future." Adams could not fathom the extremists who seemed intent on making "an aggravated Vendee, Hungary or Poland of the South and will ruin us as sure as shooting.... People seem to me as ugly and vindictive as possible. They really don't want peace, unless with it comes the hangman."[23]

While Adams overstated the public's desire to treat rebels as traitors, Lincoln's relatively benign reconstruction policy was increasingly anathema to those who demanded that the rebels be made to pay a steeper price and that the freedmen be protected. Lincoln must have been relieved that Congress would now be out of session until December and he would have time to advance his plans without interference by the lawmakers. He believed that his inaugural address would "wear as well as—perhaps better than—any thing I have produced; but I believe it is not immediately popular. Men are not flattered by being shown that there has been a difference of purpose between the Almighty and them."[24]

The inaugural called on the Union to "finish the work we are in." By March, the work of war was nearly over: in December, Sherman had taken Savannah ("I beg to present you as a Christmas gift the city of Savannah," the general wired to Lincoln); in January, Fort Fisher, on the Cape Fear River leading to the port of Wilmington, North Carolina, had surrendered; in February, Union forces had occupied an evacuated Charleston. George Templeton Strong rejoiced that from the spot where the war began nearly four years earlier, "the national flag floats over the ruins of Sumter."[25]

The inauguration and planning for a second term had left Lincoln exhausted. Noah Brooks reported that "the President's health has been worn down by the constant pressure of office seekers and legitimate business." The *Chicago Tribune* noted that "many who saw him at his inauguration ... were painfully impressed with his gaunt, skeleton-like appearance." In an editorial titled "The President's Health," the *New York Tribune* observed that "all who knew him in 1860 and have met him in 1865, must have observed his air of fatigue, exhaustion and languor—so different from his old hearty, careless, jovial manner." Lincoln's "death or permanent disability now would be a calamity—very generally and justly deplored. We cannot forecast the future which that bereavement would open: yet we think few Americans, even disloyal, can wish to confront its realization."[26]

For several days after the inauguration, he received no visitors. On March 20, a telegram arrived from Grant: "Can you not visit City Point for a day or two? I would very much like to see you and the rest would do you good." Lincoln responded instantly: "had already thought of going immediately after the next rain."[27]

Lincoln enjoyed visiting the front to meet with his generals and to review the troops. It offered an escape from the pressures of Washington and an opportunity to greet the soldiers, tour the battlefield, and comfort the wounded in field hospitals. During the war, he visited the Army of the Potomac eleven times for a total of forty-two days. After one trip, in June 1864, Welles recorded that Lincoln's journey "has done him good, physically, and strengthened him mentally." Lincoln wasted no time and left for Grant's headquarters at City Point, overlooking the James and Appomattox Rivers, on March 23 with a party that included Mary Todd and his son Tad. An additional incentive was to see his son Robert who, upon graduation from Harvard, was appointed to Grant's staff. On the day of departure, Mary Todd Lincoln wrote, "I cannot but devoutly hope, that change of air & rest may have a beneficial effect on my good Husband's health." She later recalled, "Down the Potomac, he was almost boyish, in his mirth."[28]

On March 28, Lincoln met with Grant, Sherman, and Rear Admiral David Dixon Porter aboard the *River Queen*. Porter published an account twenty years later based on notes he jotted down that evening. The end of the war was near and the conversation turned to terms of surrender. According to Porter, Lincoln said, "Let them once surrender and reach their homes, they won't take up arms again. Let them all go, officers and all. I want submission, and no more bloodshed. Let them have their horses to plow with, and, if you like, their guns to shoot crows with. I want no one punished; treat them liberally all round."[29]

General Godfrey Weitzel, who commanded Union forces in Richmond after the city fell on April 3, also recalled a conversation about how to treat the conquered rebels. "The pith of his answers," wrote Weitzel, "was that he did not wish to give me any orders on that subject, but as he expressed it: 'If I were in your place, I'd let 'em up easy—let 'em up easy.'"[30]

Porter and Weitzel were not the only ones to record Lincoln's generosity of spirit. Marquis Chambrun was among the travel party with Lincoln for part of the time at City Point. The day after arriving back in Washington he reported, "it was impossible to discover in Lincoln any thought of revenge or feeling of bitterness toward the vanquished." Whenever anyone spoke of reprisal, he became impatient. Pardon "appeared to him an absolute necessity. Never did clemency suggest itself more naturally to a victorious chief." Someone said that Davis's capture was possible and that he should be hanged. Lincoln "replied very calmly by repeating the phrase he had used in his Inaugural Address: 'Let us judge not that we be not judged.' Assailed anew by the remark that the sight of Libby prison [where Union prisoners suffered] rendered mercy impossible, he twice repeated the same biblical sentence."[31]

Sumner, who had come to City Point with Chambrun, Senator James Harlan of Iowa (whom Lincoln had named secretary of the interior effective May 16), and Attorney General James Speed on April 6, found Lincoln's sentiments objectionable. He reported to Chase, "The Presdt. Is full of tenderness to all & several times repeated 'Judge not that ye be not judged.' This he said—even when Jeff. Davis was named as one who should not be pardoned."[32]

While Lincoln was at City Point, Petersburg and Richmond fell and he visited the cities on April 3 and 4 with Tad in tow. Stanton was anxious about the president's safety, but Lincoln assured the secretary of war, "I will take care of myself." In Richmond, he walked hand in hand with his son, guarded only by a small group of sailors. Crowds gathered and blacks converged on the president. "The joy of the negro knew no bounds," reported Charles Page of the *New York Tribune*. "It found expression in whoops, in contortions, in tears, and incessantly in prayerful ejaculations of thanks."[33]

Lincoln entered Jefferson Davis's residence, the Confederate "White House." Tired from the long walk on a warm day, Lincoln sat down in Davis's desk chair. The room fell silent. More than forty years later a navy captain recalled: "it was a supreme moment—the home of the fleeing President of the Confederacy invaded by his opponents after years of bloody contests for its possession, and now occupied by the President of the United States, Abraham Lincoln, seated in a chair almost warm from the pressure of the body of Jefferson Davis! What thoughts were coursing through the mind of this great man no one can tell." All Lincoln said was, "I wonder if I could get a glass of water."[34]

Weitzel soon appeared. His notice of Lincoln's arrival had been delayed and he was embarrassed not to have greeted the president at the landing point. Rather than wait, Lincoln had walked. At Davis's mansion, now Weitzel's headquarters, Lincoln met with several Richmond residents, including John A. Campbell, whom he had seen two months earlier at Hampton Roads. Campbell, assistant secretary of war, was in all likelihood the highest-ranking Confederate official remaining in Richmond. A brilliant jurist, he was appointed to the Supreme Court in 1853 and joined with the majority in the *Dred Scott* decision. With secession, Campbell resigned, but he was never a Confederate war hawk and at Hampton Roads had been concerned primarily with the question of reconstruction. Campbell made it clear that he had no commission from the Confederate government to negotiate, but neither was he prohibited from doing so.[35]

Amid the smoldering ruins of Richmond, Lincoln and Campbell discussed peace. The president invited him to meet again in the morning on his gunboat, the *Malvern*, and suggested he bring along some leading citizens, but only the attorney Gustavus Myers accompanied him. Lincoln laid out three indispensable conditions for peace: the restoration of national authority in all the states, no retraction on the slavery question, and the disbanding of all enemy forces. If those conditions were met, he would consider "all propositions coming from those now in hostility to the government." The men discussed ways to accelerate peace. Campbell asked for amnesty, which Lincoln said he could not promise but told him "he had the pardoning power, and would save any repentant sinner from hanging." According to Campbell, Lincoln then said "he had been thinking of a plan for calling the Virginia Legislature, that had been sitting in Richmond, together, and to get them [to] vote for the restoration of Virginia to the Union." The legislature would repeal the ordinance of secession and recall Virginia's troops, thus putting an end to Lee's army. Lincoln said he had not yet decided, but clearly the idea appealed to him that "the 'very legislature' that had been sitting in Richmond should vote upon the question," perhaps in the belief that it would leave no doubt about the war's end. Writing several months after the event, Campbell claimed Lincoln said "that the Virginia Legislature was in the condition of a tenant between two contending landlords and that it should attorn [a formal acknowledgment of transfer] to the party that had established the better claim."[36]

The next day, April 6, Lincoln wrote to Weitzel and told him to give "permission and protection" to the gentlemen of the Virginia legislature to assemble and take measures to end the resistance to national authority. He asked Weitzel to show the letter only to Campbell and otherwise "do not make it public." In taking these steps, Lincoln was subverting Pierpont's restored government and giving the appearance of doing what he had refused to do for four years: recognizing the legitimacy of a rebel government. At the same time, he was a pragmatist, not an ideologue, and if this plan worked, lives would be saved and the uncertainty of how the war would end lifted.[37]

News of Lincoln's meeting with Campbell quickly leaked. On April 7, the *New York Herald* speculated that the two were engaged in peace negotiations. The editors were unaware of the Virginia legislature proposal and concluded, "we know nothing of the purposes or views of President Lincoln in connection with his visit to Richmond; but we do know something of his humane disposition, and shall be somewhat disappointed if we do not receive before his departure from Richmond the announcement of a proclamation which will finish the disarming of the rebellion, and win back the masses of the Southern people to the blessings of Union and of peace."[38]

Lincoln asked Welles his opinion of calling together the Virginia legislature. According to Welles, the president thought it best for prominent Virginians to "undo their own work" and quickly reestablish civil government to prevent disbanded armies from becoming "robber bands and guerillas," something he feared. But whatever the merits of Lincoln's idea, politically it was not sustainable. The cabinet opposed the idea. Stanton especially was livid, and the ire of the radicals was raised. Sumner wrote to Chase that Stanton was "much disconcerted & feeling that we might lose the fruits of our victories." When Weitzel issued a public notice, calling for the rebel legislature to meet, there was no containing the news that Lincoln had wanted to keep private. George Julian, radical congressman from Illinois, read the announcement and was "thunder-struck.... This fake magnanimity is to be our ruin after all, I fear."[39]

Lincoln told Welles that "he had perhaps made a mistake, and was ready to correct it if he had." James Speed believed that the president thought he had "made a mistake at Richmond in sanctioning the assembling of the Virginia Legislature and had perhaps been too fast in his desires for early reconstruction." On April 10, Lincoln had a long meeting with Pierpont and tried to reassure him that he had no intention of compromising his authority. Although on the morning of April 12, Lincoln wired Weitzel and asked whether there were any signs of the rebel legislature coming together, that evening he instructed the general to withdraw and countermand his earlier instructions and to inform Campbell of his decision. "Do not allow them to assemble," ordered Lincoln. The president was perturbed by a letter that Campbell had written to Weitzel in which the Confederate official "assumes as appears to me that I have called the insurgent Legislature of Virginia together, as the rightful Legislature of the State, to settle all differences with the United States. I have done no such thing. I spoke of them not as a Legislature, but as 'the gentlemen who have *acted* as the Legislature of Virginia in support of the rebellion.' I did this on purpose to exclude the assumption that I was recognizing them as a *rightful* body." He had dealt with them, he said, only as men with the de facto power to remove Virginia's troops from the field.[40]

Campbell, writing in August from a prison cell in Georgia, having been arrested for suspected involvement in Lincoln's death and misconduct with respect to General Weitzel, defended his actions: "I neither misunderstood nor misrepresented Mr. Lincoln....It never entered my imagination to conceive that he used the word 'Legislature' to express a convention of individuals having no public significance or relations." Campbell was soon released and moved to New Orleans where he reestablished a law practice.[41]

Whether Lincoln or Campbell was correct is of little significance. Whatever Lincoln intended, his willingness to consider dealing with rebel legislators in any capacity again displayed that when it came to trying any measure to end the war and restore peace, he was initially tone-deaf to its political consequences. Perhaps even more alarming, it won the support of the *New Work World*, an antagonistic Democratic paper that the administration had shut down for several days in 1864 for printing a spurious proclamation from Lincoln calling for a draft. Hearing of developments with the Virginia legislature, the *World* cooed that "Lincoln will pursue a wise and statesmanlike course in restoring the states." Lee's surrender at Appomattox on April 9 provided the best of all distractions from the misstep with the Virginia legislature. It also rendered whatever he was thinking in terms of the Virginia legislature moot; Pierpont recalled that Lincoln told him, "If I had known that General Lee would surrender so soon I would not have issued the proclamation."[42]

"The nation seems delirious with joy," recorded Gideon Welles as the news of Appomattox spread. Grant's terms were generous: the Confederate soldiers would be paroled; officers would be permitted to keep sidearms and their mounts; any soldier who owned a horse or mule could take the animal with him; rations were provided for Lee's starving men. There would be no imprisonment, trials, or executions. George Templeton Strong believed, at first, "that Grant had been too liberal." "But I was wrong," he confessed later. Under these terms, Southerners would understand that "the surrender was unavoidable; that the Confederacy was overmatched; that fighting was a useless waste of life; that the rebel cause was hopeless." These conditions also jibed with what Lincoln wanted. Indeed, newspapers reported "these terms were doubtless approved of in advance by President Lincoln." The *Daily National Intelligencer* observed that "General Grant, in his magnanimous terms of surrender to General Lee, disarming his veteran legions of their physical and moral weapons of resistance, has indicated the true policy for the Administration."[43]

Ralph Waldo Emerson, for one, was concerned with Grant's terms and feared that "the high tragic historic justice which the nation with severest consideration should execute, will be softened & dissipated & toasted away at dinner-tables." The war had turned the Concord idealist into a saber-rattling realist. The philosopher understood that "the problems that now remain to be solved are very intricate & perplexing, & men are very much at a loss as to the right action." The terms of surrender had been made clear; now it was time to define the terms of reunion.[44]

On the day of Lee's surrender, Lincoln and his party were steaming up the Potomac aboard the *River Queen* on their return from City Point. Chambrun recorded that "Mr. Lincoln read aloud to us for several hours. Most of the passages he selected were from Shakespeare, especially Macbeth. The lines after the murder of Duncan, when the new king falls a prey to moral torment, were dramatically dwelt. Now and then he paused to expatiate on how exact a picture Shakespeare here gives of murderer's mind when, the dark deed achieved, its perpetrator already envies the victim's calm sleep. He read the scene over twice." No doubt Lincoln recited Macbeth's speech in act 3, scene 2, which includes the lines:

> Duncan is in his grave;
> After life's fitful fever he sleeps well.
> Treason has done his worst; nor steel, nor poison,
> Malice domestic, foreign levy, nothing
> Can touch him further.

The words "malice" and "treason" in the speech must have registered with the group; the idea of a sound, untroubled sleep must have appealed to Lincoln. On passing Mt. Vernon, Chambrun remarked that one day Springfield would also carry special meaning for Americans. The president answered, "How happy I shall be four years hence to return there in peace and tranquility."[45]

Arriving back at the capital, Lincoln rushed to visit Seward, who had been in a terrible carriage accident days earlier and lay recovering from a broken jaw and arm. "I think we are near the end at last," Lincoln told him. That night, he received word of the surrender. By morning, much of the nation knew.[46]

Chapter 8

"The Egg Is to the Fowl"

In Washington, people awoke to the sound of jubilation, to cannon exploding at dawn to mark the occasion. "Guns are firing, bells ringing, flags flying, men laughing, children cheering," reported Welles. "The merchants have closed their places of business and the workmen and mechanics have left their shops and are marching through the streets with bands of music, banners and cannon. The town is a perfect Babel of excitement, such as has never been witnessed here before," noted one correspondent. Twice on April 10 crowds assembled at the White House to try and coax a speech from Lincoln, and twice he demurred. He needed time to prepare, he said. He took advantage of the presence of multiple bands to request "Dixie." Mary Todd noted that "the crowds around the house have been immense, in the midst of the bands playing, they break forth into singing. If the close of that terrible war, has left some of our hearthstones, very, very desolate, God, has been as ever kind & merciful, in the midst of our heavy afflictions as nations, & as individuals."[1]

In the early evening on April 11, Lincoln appeared on the balcony at the North Portico and read his speech. Noah Brooks recalled that he stood behind the drapery and held a candle to illuminate the sheets as Lincoln read them. After finishing each page, the president allowed it to fall to the floor where Tad scampered about picking them up.[2]

The manuscript is divided in two. The first numbered page begins with Lincoln commenting, "as a general rule, I abstain from reading reports of attacks upon myself." Two pages, marked "A" and "B" come before. These begin "we meet this evening, not in sorrow, but in gladness of heart," and conclude "nor is it a small additional embarrassment that we, the loyal people, differ among ourselves as to the mode, manner, and means of reconstruction." It would seem that part of Lincoln's speech was prepared earlier and intended as a rejoinder to accusations that Louisiana should not be readmitted because only a minority of potential voters had held elections and ratified a new constitution. Those accusations came in January and February; Lincoln's statement "I am much censured for supposed agency in setting up and seeking to sustain, the new State Government of Louisiana" certainly would have applied weeks or months earlier, but it is a peculiar note to sound in a speech expected to celebrate the end of the war. Thus the addition of pages A and B, written the evening before or that day, where Lincoln gives thanks to God, calls for a day of national thanksgiving, and praises Grant and the navy.[3]

He then transitioned to reconstruction, the topic of his speech, a subject "fraught with great difficulty" because "unlike the case of a war between independent nations, there is no authorized organ for us to treat with." He devoted the remainder of his remarks to his wartime reconstruction plans and the case of Louisiana. He reminded listeners that his Proclamation of Amnesty and Reconstruction issued in December 1863 was only "*a* plan of re-construction (as the phrase goes)" and restated the necessity of flexibility and his awareness that different plans may be appropriate for different states. His cabinet unanimously approved the plan, even the one member (Chase, alluded to but unnamed in the speech) who opposed various elements.

Lincoln pointed out that not a single "professed emancipationist" opposed his plan, and that his only involvement was corresponding with General Banks to offer support for Louisiana's plan of reconstruction. Lincoln was responding to the accusation that Louisiana's loyal government was the product of executive and military interference, not an authentic expression of a majority of the people. Lincoln said that nothing he had heard or read convinced him that he should not sustain his promise to support the loyal government of Louisiana: "as bad promises are better broken than kept, I shall treat this as a bad promise, and break it, whenever I shall be convinced that keeping it is adverse to the public interest. But I have not yet been so convinced."

As to the theoretical question of whether the seceded states were in or out of the Union, Lincoln had no patience for it. "I have *purposely* forborne any public expression upon" the issue, he claimed. While perhaps literally true, he had repeatedly refused to acknowledge the legitimacy of secession, which meant the states were never out of the Union. The only effect of the question, he thought, was "the mischievous one of dividing our friends," though the scope of reconstruction might be predicated on at least a tacit answer to the question (conceivably, more could be imposed upon a state out of the union as a condition of its return than on one that had never left). Lincoln had no tolerance for the issue: "the question is bad, as the basis of a controversy, and good for nothing at all—a merely pernicious abstraction."

If Lincoln had a theory it fell under the rubric of "proper practical relation." In January, he had asked Trumbull, as noted, "can Louisiana be brought into proper practical relations with the Union, sooner, by *admitting* or by *rejecting* the proposed Senators?" Now, he asked the American public, "Can Louisiana be brought into proper practical relation with the Union *sooner* by *sustaining*, or by *discarding* her new State Government?" It was a matter of common sense. Twelve thousand voters had done the work of organizing a loyal state government, adopting a constitution that abolished slavery, and empowering the legislature to bestow the vote on black men, a measure that Lincoln now publicly endorsed for "the very intelligent, and on those who serve our cause as soldiers." In addition, the legislature had already ratified the Thirteenth Amendment.

Repudiating Louisiana would be "discouraging and paralyzing [to] both white and black." But by sustaining and recognizing the state government, "we encourage the hearts, and nerve the arms of the twelve thousand to adhere to their work.... The colored man too, in seeing all united for him, is inspired with vigilance and energy." Lincoln returned to suffrage for the freedman: "will he not attain it sooner by saving the already advanced steps toward it, than by running backward over them?" The analogy of the egg to the fowl applied: "we shall sooner have the fowl by hatching the egg than by smashing it." He again asked the question, "Can Louisiana be brought into proper practical relation with the Union *sooner* by *sustaining*, or by *discarding* her new State Government?" He ended by insisting on the importance of flexibility with regard to plans and acknowledging the fluidity of "the present '*situation*,'" which might require him to make "some new announcement to the people of the South." He would act "when satisfied that action will be proper."[4]

In this last speech, Lincoln had taken his case for reconstruction directly to the people. The tone was temperate, yet firm, in challenging the radicals who had prevented the readmission of Louisiana. At the same time, he nodded in their direction by supporting limited black suffrage. He knew a struggle lay ahead. But Congress was not scheduled to meet until December, and he had no inclination to call it back for a special session. Perhaps by December, his approach to reconstruction would have been so far advanced that Congress would not have dared fail to ratify it. Charles Sumner, no doubt, would continue to be an obstacle. Mary Todd Lincoln invited him to the White House to hear Lincoln's speech and celebrate, but he declined. He told Chase, "I . . . was unwilling to put myself in the position of opposing him on his own balcony or assenting by silence."[5]

The first lady also invited Marquis Chambrun. After the speech, she took him through the White House and when "we came opposite the President's door, she threw it open without knocking. There was Mr. Lincoln, stretched at full length, resting on a large sofa from his oratorical efforts. . . . We exchanged several words on the subject of his address and the extremely moderate ideas which he had expressed therein. He spoke at length of the many struggles he foresaw in the future and declared his firm resolution to stand for clemency against all opposition."[6]

The speech received extensive commentary. Noah Brooks reported in the *Sacramento Daily Union*, "the views of the President concerning reconstruction, as enunciated in his speech of the 11th April, are very animatedly discussed and meet with widely different comments from different people." Except for brief remarks to an Indiana regiment that were not widely reported (a speech in which he offered a cogent rebuttal to slavery's defenders: "whenever [I] hear any one, arguing for slavery I feel a strong impulse to see it tried on him personally"), it was Lincoln's first address since the inaugural. People might have expected something as memorable and, if they did, they were disappointed.[7]

Still, there was ample praise. Privately, Lincoln heard from a writer in Hartford who reported that the speech "is the subject of universal approbation.... Public opinion here is almost unanimous in its praise." The *Philadelphia Press* reported that the speech "gives universal satisfaction," and believed "Radicals and Conservatives, Republicans and Democrats, and in some cases even original Secessionists, are eulogizing it." The *Cincinnati Commercial* found "real statesmanship in it—that is, the application of common sense to public affairs." The *Milwaukee Daily Sentinel* noted, "A peculiarly gratifying and encouraging document." The *Daily National Intelligencer* predicted, "The speech is from a lofty stand-point; it soars away above party; it is paternal as well as fraternal; it is Christian, and its spirit will be hailed with delight and responded to by almost the unanimous voice of the masses of the people, South as well as North." The *Washington Chronicle* declared, "His views are almost irresistible."[8]

Others were less generous. Even the *New York Times*, a proadministration newspaper, reported that "those who expected from the President the statement of a settled reconstruction policy have been disappointed. His speech disclosed nothing new on that subject." The editors tried to turn vice into virtue by asserting that the "special characteristic of the speech was its reserve" and calling it "wisdom." The rival *Tribune* disagreed: "It is no criticism of the speech to say that it fell dead, wholly without effect, upon the audience." The Democratic *Daily Argus* in Portland, Maine, claimed, "The speech itself is little more than a repetition of his characteristic style of discussing important questions—a considerable one way and about as much the other—non-committal, utterly wanting in direct, frank avowals of policy, and but little calculated to strengthen the hope that the great issues of the hour are to be grasped and adjusted by bold decisive statesmanship, instead of being allowed to drift hither and thither as events and circumstances may determine." The *New York World* called it "vague and vacillating.... Mr. Lincoln gropes in his speech like a traveler in an unknown country without a map."[9]

Many observers recognized that Lincoln's speech challenged the radicals. Noah Brooks claimed that the radicals "are as virulent and bitter as ever, and they have gladly seized upon this occasion to attempt to reorganize the faction which fought against Lincoln's nomination." Brooks, at this point, had been tapped by Lincoln to take over as one of his secretaries to replace John Nicolay, who was given a diplomatic post, and was responding accordingly. The *New York World* noted that the speech has "stirred up the ire of the radicals" and if Lincoln "allows himself to be cowed by the radicals, he will drift like a hull without a helm." The *New York Herald* reported, "A very active minority of the more radical of the republicans...will try to make difficulty and complicate matters as much as possible." The *Baltimore Sun* claimed, "the signs are unmistakable of an impending disagreement between what are called extremists and the administration, relative to the reconstruction policy. The breach is said to be widening, but the policy of the President seems most likely to win, and be accepted by the people as the most practicable one."[10]

The *Commonwealth*, an abolitionist newspaper published in Boston, hoped that eventually Lincoln would realize that his promise to Louisiana was indeed a bad one that should be broken. His opinion "will be turned," they predicted, because "the absurdity, the impossibility of administering a State government, based upon the support of one-tenth of the voters, will become apparent, and the only alternative will be either keeping the rebel States under military government, until the white population is loyal—and that means for a generation—or enfranchising the blacks." Sarah Browne, a New England abolitionist, wrote about the speech in her diary: "I am much disappointed at finding it unmistakably conservative. Why can't he cut down the whole tree, instead of lopping off the branches."[11]

Voicing the concerns of radical Republicans, Salmon Chase was not about to accept the president's policy. Coincidentally, on the day of Lincoln's speech, the chief justice wrote the president a letter about "the principles which are to govern reconstruction." Chase called for extending the right of suffrage to "loyal citizens, without regard to complexion." Unless this was done, "the colored loyalists of the rebel states shall be left to the control of restored rebels." After reading Lincoln's April 11 speech, in which the president alluded to Chase, the chief justice wrote again. He revisited the subject of Louisiana and argued that Banks's mistake was in ignoring the Free State Committee, an action that unsettled the radical Republicans at the time. The only way to have Congress extend to Louisiana her right to representation as a loyal state in the Union would be by the Louisiana legislature "passing an act extending suffrage to colored citizens." In response to Lincoln's expression of support for black suffrage, Chase said, "once I should have been, if not satisfied, reasonably contented by suffrage for the more intelligent & for those who have been soldiers; now I am convinced that universal suffrage is demanded by sound policy and impartial justice alike." In his journal, Chase confessed he was happy to see Lincoln openly avow support for limited suffrage, but "sorry that he is not yet ready for universal or at least equal suffrage."[12]

Chase heard from Sumner that "so far as I can see, his speech has fallen very dead," but that was desire rather than reality. The speech prompted discussion of several topics, including black suffrage. Lincoln's comment on the issue did not go unnoticed. "Mark...the significant and well considered passage on the delicate issue of extending the right of suffrage to the colored people of the South," observed the *Philadelphia Press*. The president "briefly alluded to the question of negro suffrage at the South, which is soon to become one of the most important issues of reconstruction," reported the *Albany Evening*

Journal, which went on to argue that the elective franchise should be based on "patriotism and intelligence, and not upon birth, caste, or color." The editor pointed out, "We propose to permit the Confederate soldier, who has been an armed foe of the flag, and of the principles it represents, to return to his forfeited allegiance and resume its immunities," and asked, "shall we be less generous to the black who has stood for our banner upon the bloody field?"[13]

In what may have been a case of wishful thinking, the Democratic press saw Lincoln's comment on suffrage as little more than a "temporizing concession" to the radicals. Lincoln should have told them, advised the *New York World,* that "the qualifications of voters in the states is a subject in which the federal government cannot intermeddle without a plain violation of the Constitution." However much Lincoln abjured the "pernicious abstraction" of theories about the status of the states, reconstruction policies were contingent on them:

> if they are states in the Union, neither he nor Congress, have any voice in prescribing the qualification of their voters, any more than they have in determining whether negroes shall, or shall not, vote in the State of New York. If they are not states in the Union, but mere dependents, like our territories, Congress can regulate the elective franchise while they remain in the territorial condition. On this single point the radical leaders, like Mr. Sumner, are logical and consistent: but Mr. Lincoln's notions are a muddle.

For conservatives, the rebel states remained in the Union and still maintained their rights as states. "Because States' Rights run mad have brought on this war," observed the *New York Herald,* "is no reason States' Rights should be ignored."[14]

Lincoln's lengthy defense of Louisiana seemed to resolve itself into the egg-fowl analogy, and opponents of recognizing the state government, whether radical Republicans or Democrats, found ways to turn the metaphor to their advantage. "This figure of speech in behalf of the Louisiana scheme of reconstruction," reported the *New York Tribune*, "provoked great laughter from a portion of the crowd. It had its comment from an invalid soldier. He said: 'Bad eggs can't be hatched, and ought to be smashed.'" A writer to the *Milwaukee Sentinel* wondered, "But what if the egg is illegitimate? Then the fowl will be a bastard I suppose!" The *New York Evening Post* asked, "But if it should happen that these eggs are cockatrices eggs, what then? . . . No egg is better than a rotten one or ones filled with the germs of snakes and monsters."[15]

The *New York Sun* called the president "facetious" and asked, "What would Mr. Lincoln say if a young hawk or buzzard emerged from the egg he so carefully watched over?" In Louisiana, "the few . . . are imposed upon the many, by the military authorities, and when their representatives are sent to Washington, the President believes he has secured an egg from which will be hatched the fowl of a sound and loyal State Government in Louisiana. Artificial incubation is seldom as profitable as Dame Nature's better process, and although the latter may be more tedious, a more reliable fowl would be produced."[16]

While it was easy to mock the egg-fowl analogy, Lincoln's audience was not newspaper editors or even politicians but the public, to whom he was directly taking the case for reconstruction. The *New York Tribune* observed that "one sentiment in the whole of it [the speech] was applauded—that which favored getting of chickens by hatching eggs instead of smashing them." Lincoln, according to the *New York Commercial Advertiser*, "places the question before them in language as homely yet as expressive as his own countenance. . . . The war-worn people, depend upon it, will say *hatch* rather than *smash*, and will rally around the Executive, rather than follow what Mr. Lincoln last night called 'some vague and undefined when, where and how.'" The alternative would be to follow "an 'opposition party' crystalizing around such radical men as Chase, Sumner, Wade, Butler, Winter Davis, Stanton and others who may insist upon the rejection of the application of any once rebellious State for re-admission into the

Union, until its Constitution recognizes all men, no matter what may be their color, as *equal before the law.*"[17]

Radicals knew that equality before the law for blacks would require intervention on the part of the government and that generosity toward the defeated Confederacy, what they derided as "unconditional forgiveness," might interfere with gaining such a result. The day before Lincoln spoke, Benjamin Butler delivered a speech from the balcony at Willard's Hotel. He called for punishment and asked, "shall we not by example teach every officer who deserts his flag that he shall suffer the same penalty for desertion which the government and the law has enforced upon so many of our soldiers for the same crime?" The crowd cheered and some cried out "hang every one of them." As for those in the ranks of the army, they should be disfranchised and kept from exercising political power. Only Southern unionists and the black man, Butler argued, were entitled to "liberty and equality of right under the laws forever."[18]

Many moderates and conservatives condemned Butler's speech, "a covert and malignant onslaught upon General Grant and the Administration." A headline in the Democratic *Daily Eastern Argus* read, "They Thirst for Blood." In the immediate aftermath of Appomattox, however, radicals were not the only ones who may have sought vengeance. "Are not the leaders of the rebellion worse thieves than any inmates in our State Prison, and murderers on a more stupendous scale than all the imitators of Cain's crime who have yet swung from a scaffold?" asked one writer. George Templeton Strong recorded that "a rather lively theoretical controversy has arisen" over whether to hang Jefferson Davis when he was caught. "Justice requires his solemn pubic execution," thought Strong, whereas "sound policy would probably let him live." "I should vote to hang him," he added. Even the moderate *New York Times* believed that "if he is caught, he should be hung."[19]

Others disagreed with imposing retributive justice on any of the rebel leaders, and the question of what was to be done with them momentarily shifted from the freedmen to the fugitives. "What shall be done with these" traitors? asked the *New York Herald*. "Against these the radicals would pursue the bitter policy followed by governments from time immemorial, and mete out slaughter and confiscation to the utmost limit. We do not believe that the dignity and power of our government require to be asserted in that way." John Forney wrote in the *Philadelphia Press*, "We have no time to give to vengeance, now that we have vindicated our Government, defeated the rebellion, and consolidated a great party around our faithful Chief Magistrate." The *Tribune* proclaimed that "we are most anxious to secure the assent of the South to emancipation: not that assent which the condemned gives to being hung when he shakes hands with the jailer and thanks him for past acts of kindness; but that hearty assent which can only be won by magnanimity.... Our triumph is complete—it only remains that we take care not to sully it by virtually degrading a great conflict of ideas and principles into a paltry matter of detected felony and legal retribution." If Lincoln "is firm in his mercy, strong in conscious magnanimity, resolute 'to hatch and not to smash,' determined not to soil the materials of his reconstructed Union with blood, there may be a genial, gentle tint in the troubled dawn which is breaking, and his second administration may win a higher triumph than that of successful war—peaceful, thorough reconciliation."[20]

Lincoln needed no encouragement to be merciful, and he no doubt agreed with the sentiments expressed in a letter he received the day after his speech: "the people want no manifestations of a vengeful spirit. They are willing to let the unhappy rebels live, knowing that at the best, their punishment, like that of Caine [*sic*], will be greater than they can bear." While at City Point, he had explained to Grant and Sherman what his preferences were as far as the capture of Jefferson Davis. According to a reporter, who heard it from Sherman, the president answered by telling a story:

"I'll tell you, General," Mr. Lincoln was said to have begun; "I'll tell you what I think about taking Jeff. Davis. Out in Sangamon County there was an old temperance lecturer, who was very strict in the doctrine and practice of total abstinence. One day, after a long ride in the hot sun, he stopped at the house of a friend who proposed making him a lemonade. As the mild beverage was being mixed, the friend insinuatingly asked if he wouldn't like just the least drop of something stronger, to brace up his nerves after the exhausting heat and exercise. 'No,' replied the lecturer, 'I couldn't think of it; I'm opposed to it on principle. But,' he added, with a longing glance at the black bottle that stood conveniently at hand, 'If you could manage to put in a drop unbeknownst to me, I guess it wouldn't hurt me much.'"[21]

Lincoln's message was clear enough: if Davis escaped, he would not object. He hoped for peace to be restored quickly. On April 13, he told Welles, "there must be courts, and law, and order, or society would be broken up, the disbanded armies would turn into robber bands and guerillas." Trials and executions would only hinder reconciliation and reconstruction. Welles recalled that Lincoln "hoped there would be no persecution, no bloody work, after the war was over. None need expect he would take any part in hanging or killing those men, even the worst of them.... Enough lives have been sacrificed. We must extinguish our resentments if we expect harmony and union." On the last day of his life, Lincoln wrote that he desired "a Union of hearts and hands as well as of States."[22]

The cabinet met at 11 a.m. on April 14 and one of the topics discussed was reconstruction. General Grant appeared at the meeting, and Frederick Seward attended on behalf of his still-ailing father. Stanton presented a plan for asserting federal authority and establishing state governments by appointing military governors and imposing martial law. Frederick Seward later recalled that, under the plan, different departments would assume various functions: Treasury would collect revenue; War would garrison forts; Navy control harbors; Interior put land and pension agents to work; the postmaster general reestablish mail routes; the attorney general get the courts running.

In sum, "the machinery of the United States Government should be set in motion."[23]

One of Stanton's proposals was for a single military governor for Virginia and North Carolina. No doubt he was still fuming over Lincoln's flirtation with authorizing the rebel state legislature in Virginia to reconvene. Welles objected that Virginia already had a government that had been recognized throughout the war and that the administration was obligated to continue to support. In North Carolina, by contrast, a loyal state government had first to be organized and "the State reestablished in her proper relations to the Union." Lincoln, who had met with Pierpont and reassured him of his status as governor, agreed with the point. He asked the cabinet "to deliberate and carefully consider" Stanton's general proposal for military rule, and expressed satisfaction that Congress was not in session. Lincoln remarked, "this was the great question now before us, and we must soon begin to act."[24]

That Good Friday afternoon he took a carriage ride with his wife. He told her, "I consider *this day*, the war, has come to a close." Through it all, he had never renounced the areas in rebellion. Twice in his last speech he referred to the seceded states as "so-called." There were no seceded states, never were. He held fast to the doctrines he proclaimed in his first inaugural: "the central idea of secession, is the essence of anarchy" and "in contemplation of universal law, and of the Constitution, the Union of these States is perpetual." From the start of the war he sought to restore proper, practical relations with those states, both as a means of helping to terminate the rebellion and with an eye toward the ultimate end of reunifying the nation. Guided by principles of mercy and practicality, he was prepared to advance his plans for reunion, restoration, and reconstruction— interchangeable words for his purposes. Soon, perhaps, in the unsettled "present *'situation,'*" he would have another announcement to make. He would not be given that chance.[25]

"The Present 'Situation'"

It was easy to portray Lincoln in death as more radical than he had been in life. On April 15, Attorney General Speed spoke to Chief Justice Chase about the previous day's cabinet meeting at which reconstruction was discussed. Speed said he had never seen Lincoln in better spirits and "he [never] seemed so near our views." Speed also told Chase that Lincoln had shared with him the justice's letter on reconstruction and called it "a clear & compact statement of the case." At the meeting, according to Speed, the president admitted that his actions with respect to the Virginia legislature were in error, and that "he had perhaps been too fast in his desires for early reconstruction."[1]

In his shock and grief it is understandable that Speed would want to remember Lincoln as moving in the radicals' direction and had forgotten that the president's last speech had displayed little evidence of a change of heart. It is more likely that most radical Republicans concerned with the future of reconstruction silently agreed with George Julian, who candidly acknowledged that "the universal feeling among radical men here is that his death is a godsend." Julian explained that "hostility toward Lincoln's policy of conciliation and contempt for his weakness were undisguised.... The dastardly attack upon Lincoln and Seward, the great leaders in this policy of mercy, put to flight utterly any vestige of humanitarian weakness." Twenty-two-year-old David Homer Bates, a telegraph operator in the War Department, expressed similar thoughts, if more diplomatically: "I have seen him and conversed with him nearly every day and have learned to love him for his many virtues & his few faults. If he did err it was in being too lenient with the vile traitors seething the life of the nation, and perhaps in this we can see the hand of Providence. If he had lived his leniency may have given the rebels courage & power & at some future time caused another rebellion and more bloodshed. This however is avoided."[2]

In the immediate aftermath of Lincoln's assassination, many Americans believed that Andrew Johnson would demand more rigorous terms for reconstruction than Lincoln was willing to consider. "He is as radical as I am and as fully up to the work," Zachariah Chandler told his wife. It was not only politicians who thought this way. On April 17, Andrew Evans, an Ohio farmer, wrote his son Sam, who was serving as an officer with the Fifty-ninth United States Colored Troops, that "the Rebs will not profit by the operation for old Andy Johnson will hold them flatter and give less leniency than Lincoln did. He has been among them enough to know their ways & what they deserve, and I am of opinion they cannot get as good a bargain of him [as] they could of Lincoln." The *New York Evangelist* went so far as to suggest that the hand of God was at work in order to spare Lincoln from "a work of judgment for which a sterner temper was needed.... It will be found that the little figure of Andrew Johnson is thicker than the loins of his predecessor."[3]

The belief that Johnson would be sympathetic to radical desires was not just wishful thinking in April 1865. During the war Johnson had declared that "treason must be made odious," a line so identified with him that on April 21 he acknowledged "it is not promulgating anything I have not heretofore said to say that traitors must be made odious, that treason must be made odious, that traitors must be punished and impoverished. They must not only be punished, but their social power must be destroyed." But while he threatened the leaders, he also, in the same speech, offered "leniency, conciliation, and amnesty to the thousands" who had been misled. And while he had converted to immediate emancipation and told blacks that he would be their Moses, he also affirmed during the war his belief that "this is a white man's government." On taking the oath of office he said, "the only assurance that I can now give of the future, is by reference to the past." For radicals, that statement could be both comforting and unsettling.[4]

William Robinson, an antislavery activist in Massachusetts, recognized the dangers. "Lincoln had no adequate idea of what ought to be done," he wrote, "but I fear Johnson has still less. Lincoln was, at least, master of himself, and master of the situation: Johnson *may* be the tool of anybody and everybody. Lincoln we have summered and wintered for four years, and knew exactly what he was; Johnson is wholly untried." Marquis Chambrun also had his doubts: "I am trying to discover in Johnson a governing thought but have as yet not succeeded. To punish traitors may be the order of the day, but afterwards what? He is a radical to be sure, no one denies that, but what sort of radical is he?"[5]

In the assassination's immediate aftermath, Chambrun observed that "vengeance on the rebel leaders is the universal cry heard from one end of the country to the other. Lincoln's recommendations are forgotten." Sidney George Fisher thought that Lincoln's death was "perhaps even a greater loss to the South than to the North, for Mr. Lincoln's humanity & kindness of heart stood between them and the party of the North who urge measures of vengeance & severity."[6]

"Public opinion insists upon executions," wrote Charles Sumner on April 24. While a sanguinary spirit ruled in the weeks immediately following the assassination ("we hold that the leaders of this rebellion deserve to be executed"), no one really had an appetite for "a reign of blood and terror." "My anxious hope has been that the war might be closed without a capital punishment," wrote Sumner.[7]

Lincoln's compassion, mentioned in countless editorials and eulogies, no doubt helped moderate the desire for retribution. "Could his frozen lips speak," noted one writer, "he would say Deal mercifully with my assassin." George S. Boutwell, lecturing in Lowell, Massachusetts, reminded listeners that Lincoln "desired to close the war, and restore the Union, without exacting the forfeit of a single life as a punishment for the great crime of which the leaders in this rebellion are guilty." In a eulogy delivered at Springfield, Massachusetts,

J. G. Holland observed, "I do not believe the ruler ever lived who loved his enemies so well as he....I dare not speak the thoughts of vengeance that burn within me when I recall this shameless deed. I feel the presence of that kindly spirit, the magnetism of those kindly eyes, appealing to me to forbear."[8]

Rather than advocating revenge, radicals focused on winning support for black suffrage. Sumner even included a plea for suffrage in his eulogy of Lincoln delivered in June. "The argument for colored suffrage is overwhelming," he said. "It springs from the necessity of the case, as well as from the rights of man." By then, the radicals realized that they had probably misjudged Johnson, whom Sumner described in April as a "sincere friend of the negro, & ready to act for him decisively," and reported in May that the president told him, "'there is no difference between us.'"[9]

Just days after Lincoln's assassination, questions of leniency and reconstruction arose when news circulated of the terms of surrender between William T. Sherman and Joseph E. Johnston, commander of Confederate forces in North Carolina. In a memorandum of agreement dated April 18, the Confederates were not only offered general amnesty but the restoration of all political rights as well as the recognition of state governments upon their taking an oath. Northerners were "thunderstruck." "You can hardly guess whether Johnston was to surrender to Sherman or Sherman to Johnston," marveled the *New York Tribune*. Sherman has "surrendered the whole cause for which he has rendered brilliant service" and granted terms that, in effect, "recognize the extreme Calhoun doctrine of States Rights," asserted the *Ohio Farmer*. The public and press viewed Sherman as insubordinate, even treasonous, in his actions.[10]

Upon hearing of the details, the administration, at a hastily called cabinet meeting held at 8 p.m. on Friday, April 21, immediately rejected Sherman's agreement. Stanton was especially outspoken in his condemnation of Sherman's actions. The general, Stanton thundered, had no authority to enter into negotiations that encroached on civil as opposed to military matters; he threatened the outcome of the war by authorizing the reestablishment of rebel state governments; he left the rebel debt intact for the federal government to pay; he put in dispute the status of loyal state governments and even West Virginia; and he violated Lincoln's express instructions to Grant a month prior to negotiations with Lee that "you are not to decide, discuss or confer upon any political questions." Grant personally left Washington for North Carolina to inform Sherman that the agreement had been rejected.[11]

Coming so soon after Lincoln's death, as Northerners struggled with feelings of mercy and revenge, and as reconstruction policy remained undefined, the response to Sherman's actions is understandable, though Sherman held he was only acting on what he believed had been Lincoln's wishes. In a letter to Grant he explained that he had never seen Lincoln's order from March. Indeed, "on the contrary, I had seen General Weitzel's invitation to the Virginia Legislature made in Mr. Lincoln's very presence, and failed to discover any other official hint of a plan of reconstruction." Welles believed that Sherman's error "had its origins I apprehend with President Lincoln, who was for prompt and easy terms with the Rebels. Sherman's terms were based on a liberal construction of President Lincoln's benevolent wishes and the order to Weitzel concerning the Virginia legislature, the revocation of which S. had not heard." Sherman never forgave Stanton for leaking his virulent condemnation of the general's action to the press. Ten years later, with the publication of his *Memoirs*, Sherman continued to defend his actions. In 1891, at Sherman's funeral, one of the pallbearers was Joseph E. Johnston.[12]

Although Andrew Johnson, along with everyone else, rejected Sherman's actions, regardless of the extent to which they conformed to Lincoln's intentions, it seemed initially that the president would follow the path to reconstruction outlined by his predecessor. On May 8, he recognized Pierpont's government as the official government of Virginia. (In June, the administration moved from Alexandria to Richmond.) On May 29, Johnson issued two proclamations. The first offered amnesty with restitution of property except for slaves to those who took an oath of allegiance. There were multiple exceptions, including Confederate officials, military officers above the rank of colonel in the army and lieutenant in the navy, anyone who had resigned a federal office to join the rebellion, and those who owned taxable property with a value of more than $20,000. This last provision, which was not included in the Lincoln proclamation of December 8, 1863, reflected Johnson's continued antipathy to the Southern gentry. "The wealthy men of the South who dragooned the people into Secession" should be made to pay, he believed.[13]

The second proclamation issued on May 29 named a provisional governor of North Carolina and authorized him, once a majority of qualified white voters had taken a loyalty oath, to call an election of delegates to frame a new state constitution. The plan was essentially the one Stanton had presented on April 14. Several cabinet members, including Stanton, now supported adding a provision for black suffrage, but Johnson did not include such a measure in the proclamation. Welles, who remained in Johnson's cabinet, did not support black suffrage and said he "was for adhering to the rule prescribed in Lincoln's proclamation." Johnson believed the question of suffrage was a matter of state, not federal, jurisdiction. He did express support for limited black suffrage and recommended as much to Mississippi's provisional governor William L. Sharkey in August. Johnson suggested that enfranchising literate blacks and those who owned property worth $250 would "completely disarm the adversary.... [T]he radicals, who are wild upon negro franchise, will be completely foiled." Clearly, Johnson saw black suffrage as a political stratagem, not a political right. The defeat of referendums for black suffrage in Connecticut, Minnesota, and Wisconsin in the fall elections could be interpreted as general national opposition to extending the franchise, and Johnson was happy to leave matters where they stood.[14]

During the summer, Johnson continued to appoint provisional governors, except in Louisiana, Arkansas, and Tennessee, where he recognized the governments established under Lincoln's wartime reconstruction plan. (Johnson appointed Andrew Jackson Hamilton provisional governor in Texas.) Through the fall, state constitutional conventions met, drafted constitutions, and elected representatives. But reports from the South dismayed Republicans—and not just the radicals. South Carolina, North Carolina, Georgia, Alabama, and Florida elected conservative governors who appointed secessionists rather than union men to state and local offices. Mississippi rejected the Thirteenth Amendment and elected former Confederate general Benjamin G. Humphreys, who had not yet been pardoned, as governor. The conventions in South Carolina, North Carolina, and Georgia refused to repudiate the Confederate war debt. South Carolina, Georgia, and Florida only repealed rather than nullified secession. State legislatures began to pass black codes designed to circumscribe black freedom and rights by such measures as excluding blacks from juries, prohibiting intermarriage, segregating public accommodations, and limiting freedom of movement. Some codes contained provisions that included apprenticeship laws for minors and requirements that adult males sign year-long labor contracts that were enforceable under the criminal law, not the civil law usually used to enforce contracts. These aspects particularly rankled Northerners who saw the codes as seeking to relegate the freed people to a kind of quasi-slavery. Equally disturbing, voters elected former Confederate congressmen, generals, and colonels to seats in Congress. Perhaps most galling of all, in 1866, the Georgia legislature selected Alexander H. Stephens, former vice president of the Confederacy, to a seat in the Senate.[15]

In Louisiana, as well, conservatives gained power. In March, Michael Hahn had resigned as governor to enter the United States Senate and Lieutenant Governor James Madison Wells took over. Wells moved to replace the incumbents from Hahn's moderate regime with conservative planters and former rebels loyal to him. Moderates and radicals joined forces and placed their hopes with General Banks, still in command of the Department of the Gulf, who promptly revoked the governor's removals and new appointments. Wells protested to Andrew Johnson that Banks's actions represented an overthrow of civil authority. Banks countered that Wells had removed Unionists and "put in their place the worst of Rebels and secessionists." Johnson sided with Wells. He reorganized the military department in the southwest and Banks lost his command. He also supported Wells's actions as well as entreaties: in response to complaints from the governor, Johnson removed the Freedmen's Bureau Commissioner and replaced him with someone who closed bureau courts, suspended a tax to support schools, and restored buildings and land to former Confederates. In the fall election, Wells and the Democrats were overwhelmingly victorious. Lincoln's fragile egg had turned rotten.[16]

William Lloyd Garrison spoke for many radicals and reformers when he observed in October 1865, "the aspect of things at the South is somewhat portentous. If the rebel States, 'reconstructed' so as to leave the colored people at the mercy of the savage whites, are suddenly admitted into the Union, there will assuredly be a terrible state of affairs, perhaps leading to a war of extermination. I begin to feel more and more uneasy about the President."[17]

After nine months' absence, Congress returned to session in December. By prearrangement, Edward McPherson, clerk of the House of Representatives, did not include the names of those newly elected representatives from formerly rebellious states. The Southerners would not be seated. Congress then formed a Joint Committee on Reconstruction to formulate policy. The committee itself was balanced, with as many moderates, such as William Pitt Fessenden, as radicals, such as Thaddeus Stevens. While Johnson no doubt had enjoyed the freedom to act independently of Congress, he acknowledged in his annual message, as Lincoln had previously, that the legislative body alone could judge the qualifications of its members.

Johnson directed his speech to moderates and conservatives. He reasserted the perpetuity of the Union while also defending limited government and emphasizing the federal government's limited authority. He explained his actions "to restore the rightful energy of the General Government and of the States." Johnson considered the ratification of the Thirteenth Amendment as the measure that would, in effect, "complete the work of restoration.... The adoption of the amendment reunites us beyond all power of disruption; it heals the wound that is still imperfectly closed: it removes slavery, the element which has so long perplexed and divided the country; it makes of us once more a united people, renewed and strengthened, bound more than ever to mutual affection and support." Johnson argued that the question of suffrage was exclusively a state issue and not in the purview of executive or congressional power. He suggested that

> the freedmen, if they show patience and manly virtues, will sooner obtain a participation in the elective franchise through the States than through the General Government, even if it had power to intervene. When the tumult of emotions that have been raised by the suddenness of the social change shall have subsided, it may prove that they will receive the kindest usage from some of those on whom they have heretofore most closely depended. Good faith requires the security of the freedmen in their liberty and their property, their right to labor, and their right to claim the just return of their labor.[18]

Two weeks later, Johnson sent a sanguine message to Congress to accompany the reports of Carl Schurz and Ulysses S. Grant, who had toured the South to survey conditions. Johnson called the situation "promising" and claimed "the people throughout the entire South evince a laudable desire to renew their allegiance to the Government and to repair the devastation of war by a prompt and cheerful return to peaceful pursuits." What disorders existed were "local in character," and "systems are gradually developing themselves under which the freedman will receive the protection to which he is justly deserved."[19]

Sumner, for one, could not believe what he had heard. He knew that Schurz's report was anything but positive. Schurz told Sumner in October that the views expressed in his letters to Johnson "were radically at variance with his policy." Indeed, Schurz wrote to Johnson in September of "outrages committed upon Union people and negroes," and informed his wife, "the proslavery element is gaining the upper hand everywhere and the policy of the government is such to encourage this outcome." In his report, Schurz wrote, "As to what is commonly termed 'reconstruction,' it is not only the political Machinery of the States and their constitutional relations to the general government, but the whole organism of southern society that must be reconstructed, or rather constructed anew, so as to bring it in harmony with the rest of American society."[20]

Given the call for a social revolution in the South, it is little wonder Johnson ignored what the report actually said. (Schurz claimed that Johnson told a senator, "the only great mistake I have made yet was to send Schurz to the South.") Sumner was so outraged that he denounced Johnson as attempting "to whitewash the unhappy condition of the Rebel States, and to throw the mantle of official oblivion over sickening and heartrending outrages." By then Sumner had abandoned any hope for Johnson who, during a nearly three-hour meeting with the senator on December 2, had "unconsciously" used Sumner's hat as a spittoon. Sumner summarized the essential problem with Johnson: "he has no sentiment or heart for the poor freedmen;—& he forgets also the white unionist who has kept his faith to the flag." It may have occurred to Sumner at that moment just how badly Lincoln would be missed.[21]

Despite radical animus toward Johnson, moderates and conservatives praised Johnson's annual message and the measures that he had taken. Editors called it "straightforward and clear," "able and high-toned," a state paper of "signal ability and universal frankness." The *Maine Farmer* went further and predicted that any concern that Johnson's position would "bring him in immediate and hostile collision with Congress" was misplaced. "The tone and tenor of the message," thought the editor, "has dissipated such apprehensions."[22]

Few would have prophesied in December 1865 warfare between Congress and the president, as the entire Republican Party became radicalized and Johnson returned to his Democratic roots. Few would have foreseen the extent of racial hatred and violence as riots convulsed Memphis and New Orleans and the Ku Klux Klan terrorized blacks and Northerners who had come south. Few could have imagined the passage of two constitutional amendments, the Fourteenth and Fifteenth, designed to protect the equal rights of all citizens and give black men the vote. Few could have anticipated that the president would be impeached and narrowly escape conviction.

Congress assumed control over reconstruction and divided the former Confederacy into military districts, authorized state constitutional conventions, and required ratification of the Fourteenth Amendment for readmission. In June 1868, Congress readmitted representatives from seven states, including Louisiana. (Tennessee escaped military reconstruction because it had ratified the proposed Fourteenth Amendment on July 18, 1866.) Virginia, Mississippi, Texas, and Georgia followed in 1870. It had taken longer after the war to reconstruct the Union than it had during the war to save it. By 1874, in seven of the eleven states that had constituted the Confederacy, the Democratic Party had reestablished control.

In his message to Congress in 1865, after thanking God, Johnson said, "Our thoughts next revert to the death of the late President." Less than a year later, in September 1866, his "swing around the circle," in which he sought to bolster support for his policies in the upcoming elections, and during which he denounced radicals as traitors, brought him to Springfield, Illinois, where he visited Lincoln's grave. Mary Todd Lincoln made it a point to be out of town. The presence of Johnson and his travel party tortured her, and she believed that their visit "*desecrated* my beloved husband's resting place." She wrote, "Our Country is in a fearful state, & another civil war appears inevitable."[23]

It can never be known what new announcement Lincoln would have made after April 11 or whether and how reconstruction might have turned out differently had he lived. In all likelihood, he would have revisited his amnesty proclamation and revised it once all Confederate armies had surrendered. All that can be said with certainty concerns character, not policy, and Lincoln's character did not allow politics to become personal. During the war, his disagreements with the radicals never turned malicious—he was not given to personal resentments. Neither was he doctrinaire. He recognized there were plans other than his worth considering, and said so repeatedly. Time and again he changed his mind and altered his position. There is every reason to believe that after the war he would have moved the nation toward a political reconstruction that did not forsake Southern loyalists, and a social reconstruction that may not have provided the freedmen with all that the radicals envisioned, but would have afforded more by way of government support and protection than Southern blacks ended up receiving.

Frederick Douglass certainly thought so. In a speech written in December 1865 he observed, "had Mr. Lincoln lived, we might have looked for still greater progress. Learning wisdom by war, he would have learned more from peace." Referring to Lincoln's last speech, Douglass noted that

> already he had expressed himself in favor of extending the right of suffrage to two classes of colored men, first to the brave colored soldiers who had fought under our flag—and second to the very intelligent part of the colored population south. This declaration on his part, though it seemed to mean but little meant a great deal. It was like Abraham Lincoln. He never shocked prejudices unnecessarily. Having learned statesmanship while splitting rails, he always used the thin edge of the wedge first and the fact that he used this at all meant that he would if need be, use the thick as well as the thin.

Douglass believed that "had Abraham Lincoln been spared to see this day the negro of the south would have more than the hope of enfranchisement and no rebels could hold the reins of government in any one of the late rebellious states." But now one could only lament for what might have been: "Whoever else have cause to mourn the loss of Abraham Lincoln, to the colored people of the country his death is an unspeakable calamity."[24]

Despite dark days, Lincoln never surrendered hope that the Union would be saved, because what was the Union itself but hope incarnate, "the last best hope of earth" for democracy and freedom? With the war over, he sought to unify the nation, to rebuild it on principles of justice and mercy. He knew there would be significant obstacles to reunion, but there had been obstacles to winning the war and those had been overcome. So, too, would the problems of reconstruction. For all the sadness he had endured ("there is a soft shade of melancholy in his smile & in his eyes," observed a diarist after meeting him), Lincoln was at heart an optimist. His final speech sought to define—and redefine—terms. During the war he had offered "*a* plan of re-construction (as the phrase goes)," but he understood that in fundamental ways the phrase was inadequate for the rebirth that he desired. He would not allow a return to the status quo, and had he lived his humanity might have led the nation toward the righteous peace that he envisioned for all Americans.[25]

Text of Lincoln's Last Speech, April 11, 1865

We meet this evening, not in sorrow, but in gladness of heart. The evacuation of Petersburg and Richmond, and the surrender of the principal insurgent army, give hope of a righteous and speedy peace whose joyous expression can not be restrained. In the midst of this, however, He from whom all blessings flow, must not be forgotten. A call for a national thanksgiving is being prepared, and will be duly promulgated. Nor must those whose harder part gives us the cause of rejoicing, be overlooked. Their honors must not be parcelled out with others. I myself was near the front, and had the high pleasure of transmitting much of the good news to you; but no part of the honor, for plan or execution, is mine. To Gen. Grant, his skilful officers, and brave men, all belongs. The gallant Navy stood ready, but was not in reach to take active part.

By these recent successes the re-inauguration of the national authority—reconstruction—which has had a large share of thought from the first, is pressed much more closely upon our attention. It is fraught with great difficulty. Unlike a case of a war between independent nations, there is no authorized organ for us to treat with. No one man has authority to give up the rebellion for any other man. We simply must begin with, and mould from, disorganized and discordant elements. Nor is it a small additional embarrassment that we, the loyal people, differ among ourselves as to the mode, manner, and means of reconstruction.

As a general rule, I abstain from reading the reports of attacks upon myself, wishing not to be provoked by that to which I can not properly

offer an answer. In spite of this precaution, however, it comes to my knowledge that I am much censured for some supposed agency in setting up, and
seeking to sustain, the new State government of Louisiana. In this I have
done just so much as, and no more than, the public knows. In the Annual
Message of Dec. 1863 and accompanying Proclamation, I presented a plan
of re-construction (as the phrase goes) which, I promised, if adopted by
any State, should be acceptable to, and sustained by, the Executive government of the nation. I distinctly stated that this was not the only plan which
might possibly be acceptable; and I also distinctly protested that the Executive claimed no right to say when, or whether members should be admitted
to seats in Congress from such States. This plan was, in advance, submitted
to the then Cabinet, and distinctly approved by every member of it. One of
them suggested that I should then, and in that connection, apply the Emancipation Proclamation to the theretofore excepted parts of Virginia and
Louisiana; that I should drop the suggestion about apprenticeship for
freed-people, and that I should omit the protest against my own power, in
regard to the admission of members to Congress; but even he approved
every part and parcel of the plan which has since been employed or touched
by the action of Louisiana. The new constitution of Louisiana, declaring
emancipation for the whole State, practically applies the Proclamation to
the part previously excepted. It does not adopt apprenticeship for freed-
people; and it is silent, as it could not well be otherwise, about the admission of members to Congress. So that, as it applies to Louisiana, every
member of the Cabinet fully approved the plan. The message went to Congress, and I received many commendations of the plan, written and verbal;
and not a single objection to it, from any professed emancipationist, came
to my knowledge, until after the news reached Washington that the people
of Louisiana had begun to move in accordance with it. From about July
1862, I had corresponded with different persons, supposed to be interested,
seeking a reconstruction of a State government for Louisiana. When the
message of 1863, with the plan before mentioned, reached New-Orleans,
Gen. Banks wrote me that he was confident the people, with his military
co-operation, would reconstruct, substantially on that plan. I wrote him,
and some of them to try it; they tried it, and the result is known. Such only
has been my agency in getting up the Louisiana government. As to sustaining it, my promise is out, as before stated. But, as bad promises are better

broken than kept, I shall treat this as a bad promise, and break it, whenever I shall be convinced that keeping it is adverse to the public interest. But I have not yet been so convinced.

I have been shown a letter on this subject, supposed to be an able one, in which the writer expresses regret that my mind has not seemed to be definitely fixed on the question whether the seceding States, so called, are in the Union or out of it. It would perhaps, add astonishment to his regret, were he to learn that since I have found professed Union men endeavoring to make that question, I have *purposely* forborne any public expression upon it. As appears to me that question has not been, nor yet is, a practically material one, and that any discussion of it, while it thus remains practically immaterial, could have no effect other than the mischievous one of dividing our friends. As yet, whatever it may hereafter become, that question is bad, as the basis of a controversy, and good for nothing at all—a merely pernicious abstraction.

We all agree that the seceded States, so called, are out of their proper relation with the Union; and that the sole object of the government, civil and military, in regard to those States is to again get them into that proper practical relation. I believe it is not only possible, but in fact, easier to do this, without deciding, or even considering, whether these States have ever been out of the Union, than with it. Finding themselves safely at home, it would be utterly immaterial whether they had ever been abroad. Let us all join in doing the acts necessary to restoring the proper practical relations between these States and the Union; and each forever after, innocently indulge his own opinion whether, in doing the acts, he brought the States from without, into the Union, or only gave them proper assistance, they never having been out of it.

The amount of constituency, so to speak, on which the new Louisiana government rests, would be more satisfactory to all, if it contained fifty, thirty, or even twenty thousand, instead of only about twelve thousand, as it does. It is also unsatisfactory to some that the elective franchise is not given to the colored man. I would myself prefer that it were now conferred on the very intelligent, and on those who serve our cause as soldiers. Still the question is not whether the Louisiana government, as it stands, is quite all that is desirable. The question is, "Will it be wiser to take it as it is, and help to improve it; or to reject, and disperse it?" "Can Louisiana be brought into proper practical relation with the Union *sooner* by *sustaining*, or by *discarding* her new State government?"

Some twelve thousand voters in the heretofore slave-state of Louisiana have sworn allegiance to the Union, assumed to be the rightful political power of the State, held elections, organized a State government, adopted a free-state constitution, giving the benefit of public schools equally to black and white, and empowering the Legislature to confer the elective franchise upon the colored man. Their Legislature has already voted to ratify the constitutional amendment recently passed by Congress, abolishing slavery throughout the nation. These twelve thousand persons are thus fully committed to the Union, and to perpetual freedom in the state— committed to the very things, and nearly all the things the nation wants— and they ask the nations recognition and its assistance to make good their committal. Now, if we reject, and spurn them, we do our utmost to disorganize and disperse them. We in effect say to the white men "You are worthless, or worse—we will neither help you, nor be helped by you." To the blacks we say "This cup of liberty which these, your old masters, hold to your lips, we will dash from you, and leave you to the chances of gathering the spilled and scattered contents in some vague and undefined when, where, and how." If this course, discouraging and paralyzing both white and black, has any tendency to bring Louisiana into proper practical relations with the Union, I have, so far, been unable to perceive it. If, on the contrary, we recognize, and sustain the new government of Louisiana the converse of all this is made true. We encourage the hearts, and nerve the arms of the twelve thousand to adhere to their work, and argue for it, and proselyte for it, and fight for it, and feed it, and grow it, and ripen it to a complete success. The colored man too, in seeing all united for him, is inspired with vigilance, and energy, and daring, to the same end. Grant that he desires the elective franchise, will he not attain it sooner by saving the already advanced steps toward it, than by running backward over them? Concede that the new government of Louisiana is only to what it should be as the egg is to the fowl, we shall sooner have the fowl by hatching the egg than by smashing it? Again, if we reject Louisiana, we also reject one vote in favor of the proposed amendment to the national Constitution. To meet this proposition, it has been argued that no more than three fourths of those States which have not attempted secession are necessary to validly ratify the amendment. I do not commit myself against this, further than to say that such a ratification would be questionable, and sure to be persistently questioned; while a ratification by three-fourths of all the States would be unquestioned and unquestionable.

I repeat the question, "Can Louisiana be brought into proper practical relation with the Union *sooner* by *sustaining* or by *discarding* her new State Government?"

What has been said of Louisiana will apply generally to other States. And yet so great peculiarities pertain to each state, and such important and sudden changes occur in the same state; and withal, so new and unprecedented is the whole case, that no exclusive, and inflexible plan can be safely prescribed as to details and colatterals [*sic*]. Such exclusive, and inflexible plan, would surely become a new entanglement. Important principles may, and must, be inflexible.

In the present "*situation*" as the phrase goes, it may be my duty to make some new announcement to the people of the South. I am considering, and shall not fail to act, when satisfied that action will be proper.

ACKNOWLEDGMENTS

The idea for this book emerged from an invitation by Steven Schragis of One Day University to lecture on Lincoln and Reconstruction. I am grateful to Steve, Kevin Brennan, Blair Erich, and James Klingensmith for their support and to One Day University for giving me an opportunity to lecture around the country.

I am delighted to be published again by Oxford University Press and to be part of Pivotal Moments in American History, which is coedited by James McPherson, David Hackett Fischer, and David Greenberg. Jim supported this project from the start, and his suggestions have made this a better book and saved me from numerous errors. It is an honor to publish a book on Lincoln in a series that he coedits. There is not a page that Timothy Bent has not improved; he is one of the finest editors with whom I have ever worked. I am grateful as well to Gwen Colvin, Keely Latcham, and Robert Milks for guiding the manuscript through the press. Zoe Pagnamenta continues to find good homes for my work.

At Rutgers University, Allan Isaac, chair of American Studies, and Mark Wasserman, chair of the History Department, have provided unconditional support. I am grateful to my colleagues in both departments. I offer thanks as well to Christopher Rzigalinski, and to my students Kevin Oller, Mikhail Relushchin, and Sarah Schwartz. I am especially grateful to Jonathan and William Freedman for a memorable morning of research at the New-York Historical Society, and to Dale Gregory and Alexander Kassl who have invited me to participate in the remarkable public programs that are offered there.

As always, I have been able to count on Dave Masur, Bruce Rossky, Mark Richman, Bob Allison, Jim Goodman, Doug Greenberg, Peter Mancall, Jeff Roderman, Aaron Sachs, and Tom Slaughter (who also offered valuable comments on an earlier draft of the manuscript).

For the past decade, Ron Spencer has been a constant source of insight and inspiration and has provided keen editorial suggestions on nearly everything that I have published. Dedicating this book to him does not begin to express what his friendship means to me, but it is a start.

I never need to look further than my personal life to appreciate the contingency and unpredictability of history. Had I been told when I was younger that Jani and I would one day celebrate the fortieth anniversary of our first date, or that our children, Ben and Sophie, would attend graduate school, I would have marveled at the prophecy. But here we are. Nothing means more to me than the everlasting wild, real love that we share.

NOTES

Prologue

1 *Evening Star*, April 12, 1865.

2 *Sacramento Daily Union*, May 8, 1865.

3 *Daily National Intelligencer*, April 11, 1865; *Boston Daily Advertiser*, April 11, 1865.

4 *Eastern Argus*, April 11, 1865; *Albany Journal*, April 11, 1865.

5 *Daily Age*, April 12, 1865; *Daily National Republican*, April 11, 1865.

6 *Evening Star*, April 12, 1865.

7 Noah Brooks, *Sacramento Daily Union*, May 8, 1865; Elizabeth Keckley, *Behind the Scenes; or, Thirty Years a Slave, and Four Years in the White House* (New York: G. W. Carleton, 1868), p. 176; *Evening Star*, April 12, 1864.

8 *The Collected Works of Abraham Lincoln*, ed. Roy P. Basler, 9 vols. (New Brunswick, NJ: Rutgers University Press, 1953–1955), 8:399 (hereafter cited as *CW*).

9 *CW*, 3:550.

10 *CW*, 6:39–40.

11 *CW*, 8:333.

12 *CW*, 8:400.

13 *CW*, 7:52, 6:440.

14 *CW*, 8:404; Allen Thorndike Rice, ed., *Reminiscences of Abraham Lincoln by Distinguished Men of His Time* (New York: North American, 1886), pp. 427–428. See James McPherson, "How Lincoln Won the War with

Metaphors," *Abraham Lincoln and the Second American Revolution* (New York: Oxford University Press, 1990), pp. 93–112.

15 Henry Ward Beecher to Abraham Lincoln (hereafter AL), February 4, 1865, in Abraham Lincoln Papers, Library of Congress (hereafter cited as ALP). On wartime reconstruction see especially William C. Harris, *With Charity for All: Lincoln and the Restoration of the Union* (Lexington: University Press of Kentucky, 1997), and Herman Belz, *Reconstructing the Union: Theory and Policy during the Civil War* (Ithaca, NY: Cornell University Press, 1969). Also see William B. Hesseltine, *Lincoln's Plan of Reconstruction* (Gloucester, MA: Peter Smith, 1963), and John C. Rodrique, *Lincoln and Reconstruction* (Carbondale: Southern Illinois University Press, 2013). For reconstruction generally see Eric Foner, *Reconstruction: America's Unfinished Revolution, 1863–1877* (New York: Harper & Row, 1988), and on the politics of reconstruction see Eric L. McKitrick, *Andrew Johnson and Reconstruction* (Chicago: University of Chicago Press, 1960), and Michael Les Benedict, *A Compromise of Principle: Congressional Republicans and Reconstruction, 1863–1869* (New York: Norton, 1974).

16 Brooks, *Sacramento Daily Union*, May 5, 1865.

17 *Impeachment Investigation: Testimony Taken before the Judiciary Committee of the House of Representatives in the Investigation of the Charges against Andrew Johnson, Second Session Thirty-Ninth Congress, and First Session Fortieth Congress, 1867* (Washington, DC: Government Printing Office, 1867), p. 674; *Intimate Letters of Carl Schurz*, ed. Joseph Schafer (Madison: State Historical Society of Wisconsin, 1928), p. 340.

Chapter 1

1 "Reconstruction," *Louisville Journal*, February 5, 1861.

2 *New York Tribune*, February 7, 1861; Dwight Lowell Dumond, *Southern Editorials on Secession* (New York: Century, 1931), p. 489.

3 Dumond, *Southern Editorials on Secession*, p. 490; *Charleston Mercury*, February 8, 1861.

4 "Secession and Reconstruction," *New York Times*, January 21, 1861; letter, *Richmond Whig*, February 1, 1861; "Reconstruction Not Practicable," *Chicago Tribune*, January 9, 1861.

5 "Reconstruction the New Danger," *Douglass's Monthly*, March 1861; "Let There Be No Deception," *Liberator*, March 21, 1862; *Baltimore American* quoted in *Fayetteville Observer*, January 31, 1861.

6 *Chicago Tribune*, December 11, 1863; *The Collected Works of Abraham Lincoln*, ed. Roy P. Basler, 9 vols. (New Brunswick, NJ: Rutgers University Press, 1953–1955), 4:138, 142–143 (hereafter cited as *CW*).

7 *CW*, 4:170.

8 For a discussion of the various peace proposals, see William J. Cooper, *We Have the War upon Us: The Onset of the Civil War, November 1860–April 1861* (New York: Random House, 2012); Russell McClintock, *Lincoln and the Decision for War: The Northern Response to Secession* (Chapel Hill: University of North Carolina Press, 2008); Kenneth Stampp, *And the War Came: The North and the Secession Crisis* (Baton Rouge: Louisiana State University Press, 1950).

9 *CW*, 4:149–150; 183.

10 *CW*, 4:183.

11 *CW*, 4:162.

12 Duff Green to Abraham Lincoln (hereafter AL), January 7, 1861, Abraham Lincoln Papers, Library of Congress (hereafter ALP).

13 *Intimate Letters of Carl Schurz, 1841–1869*, ed. Joseph Schafer (Madison: State Historical Society of Wisconsin, 1928), p. 237.

14 See Robert Gray Gunderson, *Old Gentlemen's Convention: The Washington Peace Conference of 1861* (Madison: University of Wisconsin Press, 1961).

15 *Mr. Lincoln's Washington: The Civil War Dispatches of Noah Brooks*, ed. P. J. Staudenraus (South Brunswick, NJ: Thomas Yoseloff, 1967), p. 175; *The Union: Speech of William H. Seward, in the Senate of the United States, January 12, 1861* (Washington, DC: Government Printing Office, 1861), p. 2.

16 *The Selected Letters of Charles Sumner*, ed. Beverly Wilson Palmer, 2 vols. (Boston: Northeastern University Press, 1990), 2:44, 43.

17 *Intimate Letters of Schurz*, pp. 242–243.

18 *Speech of Hon. Jas. H. Campbell, of Pa., on the State of the Union, Delivered in the House of Representatives, February 14, 1861* (Washington, DC: Government Printing Office, 1861), p. 2; *State of the Union: Speech of Hon. Sidney Edgerton, of Ohio, Delivered in the House of Representatives January 31, 1861* (Washington, DC: Government Printing Office, 1861), p. 2.

19 *Mr. Lincoln's Washington: Dispatches of Brooks*, pp. 103–104.

20 *State of the Union: Speech of the Hon. Thaddeus Stevens, of Pennsylvania, Delivered in the House of Representatives, January 29, 1861* (Washington, DC: Government Printing Office, 1861), p. 8.

21	*The Cause and Cure of Our National Troubles: Speech of Hon. Geo. W. Julian, of Indiana, Delivered in the House of Representatives, January 14, 1862* (Washington, DC: Scammell, 1862), p. 7.

22	*New York Herald*, January 28, 1861, quoted in David Donald, *Lincoln* (New York: Simon & Schuster, 1995), p. 268; Oliver P. Morton to AL, January 29, 1861, in ALP; *Intimate Letters of Schurz*, p. 246; Kenneth M. Stampp, ed., "Letters from the Washington Peace Conference of 1861," *Journal of Southern History* 9 (August 1943), p. 402.

23	Inauguration eyewitness quoted in Donald, *Lincoln*, p. 283: CW, 4: 262–271.

24	*CW*, 4:270–271.

25	CW, 4:423, 426, 438. See as well Lincoln's comments of February 12, 1861, with respect to lifting burdens: "It is not my nature, when I see a people borne down by the weight of their shackles—the oppression of tyranny—to make their life more bitter by heaping upon them greater burdens." *CW*, 4:202.

26	CW, 4:437–439.

27	Carlile quoted in William C. Harris, *With Charity for All: Lincoln and the Restoration of the Union* (Lexington: University Press of Kentucky, 1997), p. 20.

28	See "A State of Convenience: The Creation of West Virginia," *West Virginia Archives and History*, http://www.wvculture.org/history/statehood/declaration .html. Also see Richard O. Curry, *A House Divided: A Study of Statehood Politics and the Copperhead Movement in West Virginia* (Pittsburgh: University of Pittsburgh Press, 1964). Most historians spell Pierpoint's name as Pierpont; Pierpoint himself changed the spelling of his name at one point. So as not to confuse readers, I have chosen to follow the established convention.

29	*Congressional Globe*, 37th Congress, 1st Session, pp. 103–109 (hereafter *CG*).

30	On Foster, see Donald E. Collins, "Charles Henry Foster: A Unionist Confederate in North Carolina," in Steven E. Woodworth, ed., *The Human Tradition in the Civil War and Reconstruction* (Wilmington: Scholarly Resources, 2000), pp. 61–78. Also see William C. Harris, "Lincoln and Wartime Reconstruction in North Carolina, 1861–1863," *North Carolina Historical Review* 63 (April 1986), 153–154; *Hinds' Precedents of the House of Representatives*, 5 vols. (Washington, DC: Government Printing Office, 1907), 1:290.

31 "Virginia: The Restored Government of Virginia—History of the New State of Things," *New York Times*, June 26, 1864. On military strategy see Curry, *House Divided*, p. 67.

32 Simon Cameron to Francis Pierpont quoted in "Virginia: The Restored Government."

33 *CW*, 4:428.

34 *CG*, 37th Congress, 3rd Session, pp. 50–51; *CG*, 37th Congress, 2nd Session, p. 2942.

35 *The Diary of Orville Hickman Browning*, ed. Theodore Calvin Pease and James G. Randall, 2 vols. (Springfield: Illinois State Historical Library, 1925), 1:596.

36 Edward Bates to AL, December 27, 1862; Montgomery Blair to AL, December 26, 1861; Gideon Welles to AL, December 29, 1862, in ALP.

37 William H. Seward to AL, December 26, 1862; Edwin M. Stanton to AL, December 26, 1862; Salmon P. Chase to AL, December 29, 1861, in ALP.

38 *CW*, 6:27–28.

Chapter 2

1 Edwin M. Stanton to Col. George F. Shepley, June 10, 1862, in *War of the Rebellion: A Compilation of the Official Records of the Union and Confederate Armies*, 70 vols. in 128 serials (Washington, DC: Government Printing Office, 1880–1901), ser. 3, 2:141 (hereafter *OR*).

2 See Paul H. Bergeron, *Andrew Johnson's Civil War and Reconstruction* (Knoxville: University of Tennessee Press, 2011), Clifton R. Hall, *Andrew Johnson, Military Governor of Tennessee* (Princeton: Princeton University Press, 1916), and Eric L. McKitrick, *Andrew Johnson and Reconstruction* (Chicago: University of Chicago Press, 1960). The most complete biography is Hans L. Trefousse, *Andrew Johnson: A Biography* (New York: Norton, 1989).

3 *The Collected Works of Abraham Lincoln*, ed. Roy P. Basler, 9 vols. (New Brunswick, NJ: Rutgers University Press, 1953–1955), 5:91 (hereafter *CW*).

4 *CW*, 5:313.

5 *CW*, 5:302–303; Stephen A. Hurlbut to Abraham Lincoln (hereafter AL), August 11, 1863, in Abraham Lincoln Papers, Library of Congress (hereafter ALP).

6   "Appeal to the People of Tennessee," March 18, 1862, in *The Papers of Andrew Johnson*, ed. Leroy P. Graf, Ralph W. Haskins, and Paul H. Bergeron, 16 vols. (Knoxville: University of Tennessee Press, 1967–2000), 5:209–212 (hereafter *PAJ*).

7   "Speech at Nashville," July 4, 1862, *PAJ*, 5:534–540.

8   *New York Times*, April 1, 1862.

9   David Herbert Donald, *Charles Sumner and the Rights of Man* (New York: Random House, 1970), p. 52; Frederick Douglass, "The War and How to End It: An Address Delivered in Rochester, New York, on March 25, 1862," in *The Frederick Douglass Papers*, ser. 1: *Speeches, Debates and Interviews*, ed. John W. Blassingame, 5 vols. (New Haven, CT: Yale University Press, 1985), 3:518.

10   See Louis P. Masur, *Lincoln's Hundred Days: The Emancipation Proclamation and the War for the Union* (Cambridge, MA: Harvard University Press, 2012).

11   "Petition to the President," December 4, 1862, *PAJ*, 6:85–86.

12   "The Moses of the Colored Men" speech, October 24, 1864, *PAJ*, 7:252–253.

13   *CW*, 6:440.

14   See Judkin Browning, *Shifting Loyalties: The Union Occupation in Eastern North Carolina* (Chapel Hill: University of North Carolina Press, 2011).

15   *OR*, ser. 1, 9:400. On Stanly, see Norman D. Brown, *Edward Stanly: Whiggery's Tarheel "Conqueror"* (University: University of Alabama Press, 1974), and "Closing Schools for Contrabands in North Carolina," *Douglass's Monthly*, July 1862.

16   *Congressional Globe*, 37th Congress, 2nd Session, p. 2596 (hereafter *CG*).

17   Edward Stanly to AL, July 7, 1862, in ALP; *CW*, 5:445.

18   *Hinds' Precedents of the House of Representatives*, 5 vols. (Washington, DC: Government Printing Office, 1907), 1:395.

19   *Letter from the Hon. Edward Stanly: His Reasons for Supporting Gen. Geo. H. McClellan* (n.p., 1864), p. 2; *A Military Governor among Abolitionists: A Letter to Charles Sumner* (New York, 1865), pp. 20, 45; *CW*, 7:158.

20   *OR*, ser. 3, 2:233; John S. Phelps Scrapbook, State Historical Society of Missouri, online at http://statehistoricalsocietyofmissouri.org/cdm/compoundobject/collection/GovColl/id/132.

21   John S. Phelps to AL, November 18, 1861, in ALP.

22   *OR*, ser. 1, 13:751–753.

23 *CW*, 5:500.

24 William M. McPherson to AL, November 28, 1862; McPherson to Montgomery Blair, December 10, 1863; McPherson to AL, December 25, 1862, in ALP.

25 McPherson to AL, December 25, 1862, in ALP.

26 Benjamin Gratz Brown to AL, December 3, 1862, in ALP.

27 *CW*, 6:359.

28 *CW*, 6:358.

29 *CW*, 6:358; Stephen A. Hurlbut to AL, November 8, 1863, in ALP.

30 Stephen A. Hurlbut to AL, December 8, 1863, in ALP.

31 *Speech of Hon. Andrew J. Hamilton of Texas on the State of the Union Delivered in the House of Representatives of the United States, February 1, 1861* (Washington, DC: Lemuel Towers, 1861), p. 5. On Hamilton see John L. Waller, *Colossal Hamilton of Texas: A Biography of Andrew Jackson Hamilton* (El Paso: Texas Western Press, 1968).

32 Waller, *Colossal Hamilton*, p. 16; *Speech of Hon. Andrew Jackson Hamilton of Texas on the Condition of the South under Rebel Rule* (Washington, DC, 1862), pp. 6, 9.

33 *Wheeling Daily Intelligencer*, October 8, 1862; *New York Tribune*, October 4, 1862; *New York Times*, October 4, 1862.

34 *OR*, ser. 3, 2:782.

35 For report of expedition see *OR*, ser. 1, 19:457–459.

36 Andrew Jackson Hamilton to AL, February 16, 1863, in ALP; *Speech of Gen. A. J. Hamilton of Texas at the War Meeting at Faneuil Hall* (Boston: T. E. Marvin, 1863), p. 11.

37 *Speech of Hamilton* , pp. 43–46.

38 *Letter of Gen. A. J. Hamilton of Texas, to the President of the United States* (Washington, DC, 1863), p. 11; *CW*, 6:408; *Columbian Register*, September 12, 1863.

39 *Letter of Gen. A. J. Hamilton of Texas*, pp. 16–17.

40 *CW*, 6:354, 356.

41 *Inside Lincoln's White House: The Complete Civil War Diary of John Hay*, ed. Michael Burlingame and John R. Turner Ettlinger (Carbondale: Southern Illinois University Press, 1997), p. 71; *CW*, 6:364, 374.

42 *CW*, 6:465–466.

43　*Private and Official Correspondence of Gen. Benjamin F. Butler during the Period of the Civil War*. 5 vols. (n.p.: privately printed, 1917), 2:317.

44　*OR*, ser. 3, 2:141.

45　Chester G. Hearn, *When the Devil Came to Town: Ben Butler in New Orleans* (Baton Rouge: Louisiana State University Press, 1997), p. 103. On Louisiana and reconstruction see Peyton McCrary, *Abraham Lincoln and Reconstruction: The Louisiana Experiment* (Princeton, NJ: Princeton University Press, 1978), and Ted Tunnell, *Crucible of Reconstruction: War, Radicalism, and Race in Louisiana, 1862–1877* (Baton Rouge: Louisiana State University Press, 1992).

46　*Mr. Lincoln's Washington: The Civil War Dispatches of Noah Brooks*, ed. P. J. Staudenraus (South Brunswick, NJ: Thomas Yoseloff, 1967), p. 136; Reverdy Johnson to AL, July 16, 1862, in ALP. Also see Jacob Barker to AL, July 6, 1862, in ALP.

47　*CW*, 5:342–344. Also see *The Diary of Orville Hickman Browning*, ed. Theodore Calvin Pease and James G. Randall, 2 vols. (Springfield: Illinois State Historical Library, 1925), 1:564.

48　*CW*, 5:344–346.

49　*CW*, 5:350–351; Masur, *Lincoln's Hundred Days*, p. 54.

50　*CW*, 5:350.

51　*CW*, 5:504–505.

52　George Shepley to AL, December 9, 1862; Benjamin Butler to AL, December 4, 1862, in ALP. Also see John Wilson Shaffer to Ward H. Lamon, December 3, 1862, in ALP.

53　*CG*, 37th Congress, 2nd Session, pp. 831, 832, 836, 834.

54　*CW*, 6:287–288.

55　*CW*, 6:364–365.

56　*CW*, 7:1; Thomas Durant to AL, October 1, 1863, in ALP.

57　*CW*, 7:1–2.

58　Nathaniel P. Banks to AL, December 6, 1863, in ALP. Also see *Inside Lincoln's White House*, pp. 129–130.

Chapter 3

1　"The 'Reconstruction' Discussions," *Harrisburg (PA) Patriot and Union*, September 3, 1863.

2 *Wisconsin Patriot,* October 3, 1863; William Rosecrans to Abraham Lincoln (hereafter AL), October 3, 1863, in Abraham Lincoln Papers, Library of Congress (hereafter ALP); *The Collected Works of Abraham Lincoln,* ed. Roy P. Basler, 9 vols. (New Brunswick, NJ: Rutgers University Press, 1953–1955), 6:498 (hereafter *CW*).

3 For example, *New York Herald,* September 8, 1863; *New York Tribune,* September 8, 1863; *New York Times,* September 8, 1863; *Boston Daily Advertiser,* September 9, 1863; *Daily National Intelligencer,* September 9, 1863.

4 *CW,* 5:553–554.

5 *New York Tribune,* September 8, 1863.

6 *Return of the Rebellious States to the Union: A Letter from Honorable Wm. Whiting to the Union League of Philadelphia* (Philadelphia: Sherman & Son, 1864), pp. 4, 6, 8, 15.

7 *Springfield (MA) Weekly Republican,* August 15, 1863; *New York World* quoted in *Wisconsin Patriot,* August 29, 1863.

8 *New York Times,* August 14, 1863; *Louisville Journal* quoted in *Wisconsin Daily Patriot,* August 22, 1863. Also see *Boston Post,* August 13, August 17, 1863, and *Daily National Intelligencer,* August 14, 1863.

9 *Diary of Gideon Welles,* ed. Howard K. Beale, 3 vols. (New York: Norton, 1960), 1:381, 400.

10 *Diary of Gideon Welles,* 1:407–408.

11 *Diary of Gideon Welles,* 1:410; *Mr. Lincoln's Washington: The Civil War Dispatches of Noah Brooks,* ed. P. J. Staudenraus (South Brunswick, NJ: Thomas Yoseloff, 1967), p. 177.

12 *Diary of Gideon Welles,* 1:410–415, 403, 429.

13 *The Conditions of Reconstruction; in a Letter from Robert Dale Owen to the Secretary of State* (New York: Wm. C. Bryant, 1863), p. 4.

14 *Conditions of Reconstruction,* pp. 6, 9, 19.

15 Robert Dale Owen to AL, September 30, 1863, in ALP.

16 *Milwaukee Daily Sentinel,* May 13, 1864; Noah Brooks, "Recollections of Abraham Lincoln," *Harper's New Monthly Magazine* 31 (July 1865), p. 225.

17 *Speech of Hon. Henry Winter Davis at Concert Hall, Philadelphia, September 24, 1863* (n.p., n.d.), pp. 4, 9, 11, 12.

18 *Speech of Davis,* p. 26.

19 *Speech of Hon. Montgomery Blair (Postmaster General,) on the Revolutionary Schemes of the Ultra Abolitionists and in Defence of the Policy of the President. Delivered at the Unconditional Union Meeting Held at Rockville, Montgomery Co., Maryland on Saturday October 3, 1863* (n.p., n.d.), pp. 5, 8.

20 *Speech of Blair*, p. 16.

21 *The Selected Papers of Thaddeus Stevens*, ed. Beverly Wilson Palmer and Holly Byers Ochoa, 2 vols., vol. 1: *January 1814–March 1865* (Pittsburgh: University of Pittsburgh Press, 1997), 1:413; Henry Wilson to AL, October 25, 1863, in ALP; *Mr. Lincoln's Washington*, p. 247; Adam Gurowski, *Diary from November 18, 1862, to October 18, 1863*, 2 vols. (New York: Carleton, 1864), 2:380; *New York Herald*, October 6, 1863.

22 *Mr. Lincoln's Washington*, pp. 178, 249; *Lincoln Observed: Civil War Dispatches of Noah Brooks*, ed. Michael Burlingame (Baltimore: Johns Hopkins University Press, 1998), p. 97; *Boston Daily Advertiser*, October 8, 1863.

23 *Congressional Globe*, 37th Congress, 2nd Session, pp. 736–737 (hereafter *CG*).

24 *New York Tribune*, February 25, 1862; "Political Metaphysics," *Daily National Intelligencer*, March 18, 1862; *New York Evening Post*, March 13, 1862; *The Selected Letters of Charles Sumner*, ed. Beverly Wilson Palmer, 2 vols. (Boston: Northeastern University Press), 2:105; *The Works of Charles Sumner*, 20 vols. (Boston: Lea and Shepard, 1874), 7:14. Also see Orestes Brownson, "State Rebellion, State Suicide," in *The Works of Orestes A. Brownson*, collected and arranged by Henry F. Brownson, 20 vols. (Detroit: Thorndike House, 1884), 17:228–253.

25 "Our Domestic Relations: Power of Congress over the Rebel States," *Atlantic Monthly* 71 (September 1863), pp. 507–529; *Works of Sumner*, 7:493.

26 "Our Domestic Relations," pp. 507, 509, 521, 527.

27 *Letters of Sumner*, 2:204–205.

28 Letter, *New York Times*, November 8, 1863.

29 *Inside Lincoln's White House: The Complete Civil War Diary of John Hay*, ed. Michael Burlingame and John R. Turner Ettlinger (Carbondale: Southern Illinois University Press, 1997), pp. 105–106.

30 Andrew Johnson to Montgomery Blair, November 24, 1862, in ALP.

31 "Reconstruction," *Continental Monthly* 4 (December 1863), p. 684.

32 "Reconstruction," pp. 685, 688.

33 "Reconstruction," p. 689.

34 *CW*, 8:402–403. For a discussion of the various approaches see Herman Belz, *Reconstructing the Union: Theory and Policy during the Civil War* (Ithaca, NY: Cornell University Press, 1969).

35 On Lincoln's belief, see *CW*, 6:410. Zachariah Chandler to AL, November 15, 1863, in ALP; *CW*, 7:23–24. John Hay thought Chandler a "lunatic." See entry for November 20, 1863, in *Diary of Hay*, p. 114.

Chapter 4

1 *New York World* quoted in *Chicago Tribune*, December 9, 1863.

2 *Inside Lincoln's White House: The Complete Civil War Diary of John Hay*, ed. Michael Burlingame and John R. Turner Ettlinger (Carbondale: Southern Illinois University Press, 1997), pp. 327–328n.

3 *Inside Lincoln's White House*, p. 121.

4 *The Collected Works of Abraham Lincoln*, ed. Roy P. Basler, 9 vols. (New Brunswick, NJ: Rutgers University Press, 1953–1955), 7:49 (hereafter *CW*).

5 *CW*, 7:50.

6 *CW*, 7:53–56.

7 *CW*, 7:50.

8 *CW*, 7:51.

9 *CW*, 7:52.

10 *CW*, 7:52n; *Inside Lincoln's White House*, pp. 124–125.

11 *New York Tribune*, November 23, 1863.

12 Isaac Arnold to Abraham Lincoln (hereafter AL), December 4, 1863, in Abraham Lincoln Papers, Library of Congress (hereafter ALP). See Michael Vorenberg, *Final Freedom: The Civil War, the Abolition of Slavery, and the Thirteenth Amendment* (Cambridge: Cambridge University Press, 2001), pp. 47–48.

13 *CW*, 7:149–150.

14 Nathaniel Banks to AL, January 22, 1864; Jacob Bowker to AL, January 22, 1864; Horace Maynard to AL, February 2, 1864, in ALP. Also see Herman Belz, *Reconstructing the Union: Theory and Policy during the Civil War* (Ithaca, NY: Cornell University Press, 1969), pp. 163–164.

15 *CW*, 7:162, 66.

16 *CW*, 7:169.

17 *CW*: 7:269.

18 *Inside Lincoln's White House*, pp. 121–122.

19 *Inside Lincoln's White House*, p. 125; Salmon Chase to AL, November 5, 1863, in ALP.

20 *CW*, 6:428–429.

21 *The Salmon P. Chase Papers*, vol. 4: *Correspondence, April 1863–1864*, ed. John Niven (Kent, OH: Kent State University Press, 1997), pp. 225–226, 231.

22 *Letter of Charles Eliot Norton*, ed. Sara Norton and Mark DeWolfe Howe, 2 vols. (Boston: Houghton Mifflin, 1913), 1:266; Edward Everett Hale, "Northern Invasions," *Atlantic Monthly* 13 (February 1864), p. 246; *Diary of the Civil War, 1860–1865: George Templeton Strong*, ed. Allan Nevins (New York: Macmillan, 1962), p. 379; *"I Hope to Do My Country Service": The Civil War Letters of John Bennitt, M.D., Surgeon, 19th Michigan Infantry*, ed. Robert Beasecker (Detroit: Wayne State University Press, 2005), p. 213.

23 *Baltimore Sun*, December 11, 1863.

24 *Lincoln Observed: Civil War Dispatches of Noah Brooks*, ed. Michael Burlingame (Baltimore: Johns Hopkins University Press, 1998), pp. 93–94; *New York World*, December 10, 1863.

25 *New York Times*, December 10, 1863; *New York Times*, January 28, 1864.

26 *New York Tribune*, December 10, 1863; *Chicago Tribune*, December 16, 1863.

27 *Daily National Intelligencer*, December 10, 1863; *Massachusetts Spy*, December 16, 1863.

28 *Jackson (MI) Weekly Citizen*, January 13, 1864; *New York Herald*, December 10, 1863.

29 "The Two Messages," *Christian Examiner* 76 (January 1864), p. 135; *Independent*, December 12, 1863; *New York Evangelist*, December 31, 1863.

30 *Daily News* quoted in *New York Tribune*, December 11, 1863; *New York World*, December 10, 1863; *New York Journal of Commerce* quoted in *New York Sun*, December 11, 1863; *Daily Age*, December 12, 1863, December 10, 1863.

31 "The Infamous Message and Proclamation," *Old Guard* 2 (January 1864), p. 15; *The World*, December 12, 1863; *Republican Farmer*, December 18, 1863.

32 *New York Journal of Commerce* quoted in *Boston Post*, December 14, 1863; *New Haven (CT) Daily Register* quoted in *Daily Age*, December 12, 1863; *Springfield (MA) Republican*, December 12, 1863.

33 *Mr. Lincoln's Washington: The Civil War Dispatches of Noah Brooks*. Edited by P. J. Staudenraus (South Brunswick, NJ: Thomas Yoseloff, 1967), p. 273; *The Selected Letters of Charles Sumner*, ed. Beverly Wilson Palmer, 2 vols. (Boston: Northeastern University Press, 1990), 2:214.

34 Adam Gurowski, *Diary, 1863–'64–'65* (Washington, DC: W. H. Morrison, 1866), pp. 41–42, 44.

35 *Letters of Sumner*, 2:196.

36 Orestes Brownson, "The President's Message and Proclamation," in *The Works of Orestes A. Brownson*, collected and arranged by Henry F. Brownson, 20 vols. (Detroit: Thorndike House, 1884), 17:516, 512–513.

37 Brownson, "President's Message and Proclamation," pp. 518, 522.

38 *Letters of Sumner*, 2:214; Brownson, "President's Message and Proclamation," pp. 519–520.

39 Brownson, "President's Message and Proclamation," p. 510; *Columbian Register*, December 19, 1863; *New York World*, December 10, 1863; *Albany Atlas and Argus* quoted in *Pittsfield (MA) Sun*, January 14, 1864; *New York Tribune*, December 11, 1863.

40 Brownson, "The American Republic," in *Works*, 18:181; "The President Falters," *Liberator*, December 18, 1863. Also see Henry Clarke Wright, "The President and the Reconstruction Policy: Lincoln the Next President," *Liberator*, January 29, 1864.

41 James Brewer Stewart, *Wendell Phillips: Liberty's Hero* (Baton Rouge: Louisiana State University Press, 1986), p. 186.

42 *"Speech of Wendell Phillips, ESQ, at the Cooper Institute, New York," Liberator*, January 1, 1864.

43 *Richmond Examiner*, January 20, 1864.

44 *Richmond Enquirer*, December 14, 1863; *Augusta (GA) Daily Constitutionalist*, December 18, 1863; *Richmond Examiner*, December 10, 1863; *Richmond Sentinel* quoted in *New York Herald*, December 18, 1863; *New York Times*, December 26, 1863.

45 *St. Louis Republican* quoted in *Boston Daily Advertiser*, December 15, 1863.

46 Stephen Hurlbut to AL, June 24, 1863; Edward W. Gantt to AL, July 15, 1863, in ALP.

47 *New York Times*, November 11, 1863; *Address of Brig-Gen. E.W. Gantt, C.S.A.: First Published October 7, 1863 at Little Rock, Arkansas* (np: nd), pp. 13–14, 25–26. Also see his speech at the Cooper Union, *New York Times*, February 2, 1864.

48 *New York Times*, December 30, 1863. On pardons see Jonathan Truman Dorris, *Pardon and Amnesty under Lincoln and Johnson* (Chapel Hill: University of North Carolina Press, 1953).

49 Russell Alger to John G. Nicolay, February 9, 1864, in ALP.

50 *War of the Rebellion: A Compilation of the Official Records of the Union and Confederate Armies*, 70 vols. in 128 serials (Washington, DC: Government Printing Office, 1880–1901), ser. 1, 33:170–171.

51 *CW*, 7:153–154. See *New York Tribune*, January 25, 1864, and *New York Times*, January 28, 1864.

52 *Inside Lincoln's White House*, p. 133; John Hay to AL, February 8, 1864, in ALP; *New York Herald*, February 23, 1864. On reconstruction in Florida see John E. Johns, *Florida during the Civil War* (Gainesville: University of Florida Press, 1963), and Jerrell H. Shofner, *Nor Is It Over Yet: Florida in the Era of Reconstruction, 1863–1877* (Gainesville: University of Florida Press, 1974).

Chapter 5

1 Noah Brooks, *Sacramento Daily Union*, February 4, 1864.

2 *Congressional Globe*, 38th Congress, 1st Session, p. 33 (hereafter *CG*).

3 *CG*, 38th Congress, 1st Session, p. 33.

4 Dawes quoted in Herman Belz, *Reconstructing the Union: Theory and Policy during the Civil War* (Ithaca, NY: Cornell University Press, 1969), p. 173.

5 *CG*, 38th Congress, 1st Session, pp. 70, 97.

6 *Milwaukee Daily Sentinel*, February 5, 1864.

7 *New York Tribune*, December 28, 1863.

8 *The Collected Works of Abraham Lincoln*, ed. Roy P. Basler, 9 vols. (New Brunswick, NJ: Rutgers University Press, 1953–1955), 7:144, 89–90 (hereafter *CW*); Belz, *Reconstructing the Union*, pp. 80–81; *Journal of the House of Representatives of the United States, Being the First Session of the Thirty-Eighth Congress, Begun and Held at the City of Washington, December 3, 1863* (Washington, DC: Government Printing Office, 1863), p. 85.

9   *New York Times,* January 19, 1864, January 21, 1864; *New York Tribune,* December 28, 1864; *Harrisburg (PA) Weekly Patriot and Union,* January 14, 1864.

10 38th Congress, 1st Session, H.R. 118, January 11, 1864.

11 *CG,* 38th Congress, 1st Session, p. 316; Orestes Brownson, "Stevens on Reconstruction," *Brownson's Quarterly Review, National Series* 1 (April 1864), p. 166; *New York Herald,* February 7, 1864.

12 *Statutes at Large,* 37th Congress, 2nd Session, p. 502.

13 38th Congress, 1st Session, H.R. 244, February 15, 1864, pp. 1–9.

14 *New York Evening Post,* February 17, 1864; Adam Gurowski, *Diary, 1863– '64–'65* (Washington, DC: W. H. Morrison, 1866), pp. 68–69; *New York Independent,* February 6, 1864.

15 *Cases of Contested Elections in Congress from 1835–1865 Inclusive,* compiled by D. W. Bartlett (Washington, DC: Government Printing Office, 1866), p. 581; *CW,* 7:89–90.

16 Nathaniel P. Banks to Abraham Lincoln (hereafter AL), January 11, 1864, in Abraham Lincoln Papers, Library of Congress (hereafter ALP); *CW,* 7:124; Benjamin Flanders to AL, January 11, 1864, in ALP.

17 Banks to AL, January 22, 1864, in ALP.

18 *CW,* 7:162.

19 *Springfield (MA) Weekly Republican,* January 30, 1864.

20 Thomas J. Durant to AL, February 26, 1864, in ALP; *New York World* quoted in *Weekly Patriot and Union,* February 4, 1864; *CG,* 38th Congress, 1st Session, p. 682; *Independent,* February 18, 1864.

21 Banks to AL, February 25, 1864, in ALP.

22 Thomas J. Durant to AL, February 28, 1864; Thomas Bacon to AL, March 4, 1864; Cuthbert Bullitt to AL, February 25, 1864, in ALP; Banks to AL, February 25, 1864, in ALP.

23 Banks to John Hay, March 28, 1864, in ALP.

24 *CW,* 7:243.

25 "Speech of Wendell Phillips, ESQ," *Liberator,* May 29, 1863; *The Salmon P. Chase Papers,* vol. 4: *Correspondence, April 1863–1864,* ed. John Niven (Kent, OH: Kent State University Press, 1997), pp. 32, 147, 230.

26 *Liberator,* April 15, 1864; *New York Times,* March 5, 1864; *Chase Papers: Correspondence,* p. 365. Sumner presented the petition in the Senate on March 15; *CG,* 38th Congress, 1st Session, p. 1107.

27 *Official Journal of the Proceedings of the Convention for the Revision and Amendment of the Constitution of the State of Louisiana* (New Orleans: W. H. Fish, 1864) p. 71; *Debates on the Convention for the Revision and Amendment of the Constitution of the State of Louisiana* (New Orleans: W. H. Fish, 1864), p. 226. Also see Michael Hahn to AL, May 11, 1864, and May 14, 1864, in ALP.

28 Banks to AL, July 25, 1864, in ALP.

29 *CW*, 7:486; Banks to AL, September 6, 1864, in ALP.

30 *New York Times*, January 11, 1864; *CW*, 7:108.

31 *CW*, 7:144, 155, 161, 189.

32 Steele and Sherman quoted in William C. Harris, *With Charity for All: Lincoln and the Restoration of the Union* (Lexington: University Press of Kentucky, 1997), pp. 202–203.

33 *CW*, 7:253, 318; *New York Times*, March 21, 1864.

34 *The Constitution of the State of Arkansas* (Little Rock: Printing Company, 1891), p. 271.

35 *CG*, 38th Congress, 1st Session, pp. 680–681, 684.

36 *CG*, 38th Congress, 1st Session, p. 686; *Hinds' Precedents of the House of Representatives*, 5 vols. (Washington, DC: Government Printing Office, 1907), 1:326.

37 *New York Evening Post*, May 24, 1864.

38 *St. Louis Republican* quoted in *New York Times*, May 17, 1864; *New York Evening Post*, May 24, 1864; *Springfield (MA) Republican*, May 28, 1864.

39 *CG*, 1st Session, pp. 2897–2898; Bartlett, *Cases of Contested Elections*, pp. 641–643.

40 *New York Times*, June 3, 1864.

41 *CW*, 7:418.

42 *CW*, 7:226.

43 *CW*, 7:281; *New York Tribune*, April 29, 1864. Also see *Daily National Intelligencer*, April 29, 1864, and *Wisconsin Daily Patriot*, May 4 and 5, 1864.

44 *CW*, 7:302; *Richmond Whig*, April 24, 1864.

45 *CG*, 38th Congress, 1st Session, p. 521; *CW*, 7:380.

46 CG, 38th Congress, 1st Session, p. 2080, appendix, p. 83.

47 *CG*, 38th Congress, 1st Session, appendix, pp. 83–84.

48 *Chase Papers*, vol. 1: *Journals, 1829–1872*, ed. Niven (Kent, OH: Kent State University Press, 1993), p. 475.

49 *Chase Papers: Journals*, p. 477.

50 *Inside Lincoln's White House: The Complete Civil War Diary of John Hay*, ed. Michael Burlingame and John R. Turner Ettlinger (Carbondale: Southern Illinois University Press, 1997), pp. 217–219.

51 *CW*, 7:433–434.

52 *Daily National Intelligencer*, July 21, 1864.

53 *The Selected Papers of Thaddeus Stevens*, vol. 1: *January 1814–March 1865*, ed. Beverly Wilson Palmer and Holly Byers Ochoa, 2 vols. (Pittsburgh: University of Pittsburgh Press, 1997), p. 500.

54 *New York Tribune*, August 9, 1864.

55 *New York Tribune*, August 9, 1864.

56 *The Reconstruction of States: Letter of Major-General Banks to Senator Lane* (New York: Harper & Brothers, 1865), pp. 5, 8.

57 *New York Herald*, August 6, 1864; *Chicago Tribune*, August 11, 1864; *Albany Journal*, August 5, 1864; *Washington Star* quoted in *New London Daily Chronicle*, August 10, 1864; *New York Times*, August 11, 1864; *Albany Journal*, August 6, 1864.

58 *Diary of Gideon Welles*, ed. Howard K. Beale, 3 vols. (New York: Norton, 1960), 2:98; *Private and Official Correspondence of Gen. Benjamin F. Butler during the Period of the Civil War*, 5 vols. (n.p.: privately printed, 1917), 5:8; Benjamin Plumly quoted in Michael Burlingame, *Abraham Lincoln: A Life*, 2 vols. (Baltimore: Johns Hopkins University Press, 2008), 2:662; Solomon Pettis to AL, November 10, 1864, in ALP.

59 Weed quoted in David Donald, *Lincoln* (New York: Simon & Schuster, 1995), p. 528; Henry J. Raymond to AL, August 22, 1864, in ALP; *Diary of the Civil War, 1860–1865: George Templeton Strong*, ed. Allan Nevins (New York: Macmillan, 1962), p. 478; *Private and Official Correspondence*, 5:35.

60 Visitor quoted in Donald, *Lincoln*, p. 516; Brooks, *Sacramento Daily Union*, August 10, 1864; U. S. Grant quoted in William S. McFeely, *Grant: A Biography* (New York: Norton, 2002), p. 179; *CW*, 7:394.

61 *Diary of Gideon Welles*, 2:102–103; Horace Greeley to AL, July 7, 1864, in ALP; *CW*, 7:451.

62 *The Diary of Edward Bates, 1859–1866*, ed. Howard K. Beale (Washington, DC: Government Printing Office, 1933), p. 388; *CW*, 7:499–501.

63 Frederick Douglass to Theodore Tilton, October 15, 1864, in *Frederick Douglass: Selected Speeches and Writings*, ed. Philip Foner (Chicago: Lawrence Hill Books, 1999), p. 571.

64 *CW*, 7:514.

Chapter 6

1 *Lowell (MA) Daily Citizen*, September 5, 1864; *Diary of the Civil War, 1860–1865: George Templeton Strong*, ed. Allan Nevins (New York: Macmillan, 1962), pp. 480–481; *New York Times*, September 7, 1864.

2 *The Collected Works of Abraham Lincoln*, ed. Roy P. Basler, 9 vols. (New Brunswick, NJ: Rutgers University Press, 1953–1955), 7:533, 535 (hereafter *CW*).

3 Stephen W. Sears, *George B. McClellan: The Young Napoleon* (New York: Ticknor & Fields, 1988), p. 132.

4 Adam Gurowski, *Diary, 1863–'64–'65* (Washington, DC: W. H. Morrison, 1866), pp. 327–328.

5 "The Next General Election," *North American Review* 99 (October 1864), p. 560. See also "The Two Platforms," *Continental Monthly* 6 (November 1864), pp. 588, 599.

6 *New York Evening Post*, September 3, 1864.

7 *CW*, 8:73–74.

8 *The Selected Letters of Charles Sumner*, ed. Beverly Wilson Palmer, 2 vols. (Boston: Northeastern University Press), 2:252; *New York Times*, May 11, 1863; *CW*, 7:11; C. C. Hazewell, "The Twentieth Presidential Election," *Atlantic Monthly* 14 (November 1864), p. 641.

9 Worthington Chauncey Ford, ed., *A Cycle of Adams Letters, 1861–65*, 2 vols. (Boston: Houghton, Mifflin, 1920), 2:204; *New York Times*, October 13, 1864; *San Francisco Daily Evening Bulletin*, October 13, 1864.

10 Anonymous to Abraham Lincoln (hereafter AL), September 21, 1864, in Abraham Lincoln Papers, Library of Congress (hereafter ALP); Seymour Ketchum to AL, November 2, 1864, in ALP; John W. Forney, *Anecdotes of Public Men*, 2 vols. (New York: Harper & Brothers, 1881), 2:425. See David Donald, *Lincoln* (New York: Simon & Schuster, 1995), p. 549.

11 *The Lincoln Catechism, Wherein the Eccentricities & Beauties of Despotism Are Fully Set Forth* (New York: J. F. Feeks, 1864), pp. 3, 38.

12 Gurowski, *Diary, 1863–'64–'65*, p. 341.

13 *Intimate Letters of Carl Schurz, 1841–1869*, ed. Joseph Schafer (Madison: State Historical Society of Wisconsin, 1928), pp. 308–309.

14 *Mr. Lincoln's Washington: The Civil War Dispatches of Noah Brooks*, ed. P. J. Staudenraus (South Brunswick, NJ: Thomas Yoseloff, 1967), pp. 385–387; Ida M. Tarbell, *A Reporter for Lincoln: Story of Henry E. Wing, Solider and Newspaperman* (New York: Book League, 1929), p. 71; *Inside Lincoln's White House: The Complete Civil War Diary of John Hay*, ed. Michael Burlingame and John R. Turner Ettlinger (Carbondale: Southern Illinois University Press, 1997), p. 245.

15 *Mr. Lincoln's Washington*, p. 387; *Inside Lincoln's White House*, p. 246.

16 *Diary of Strong*, p. 511; Gurowski, *Diary, 1863–'64–'65*, pp. 392–393, 396.

17 *CW*, 8:96, 101.

18 *Inside Lincoln's White House*, p. 243.

19 *Private and Official Correspondence of Gen. Benjamin F. Butler*, 5 vols. (n.p.: privately printed, 1917), 3:282–383, 321; *CW*, 7:135–136.

20 *Private and Official Correspondence* , 3:282; *CW*, 7:487.

21 *Letter of Governor Pierpont to His Excellency the President and the Honorable Congress of the United States on the Subject of Abuse of Military Power in the Command of General Butler in Virginia and North Carolina* (Washington, DC: McGill & Witherow, 1864), p. 3.

22 *CW*, 7:487; *The Diary of Edward Bates, 1859–1866*, ed. Howard K. Beale (Washington, DC: Government Printing Office, 1933), p. 387.

23 *Diary of Edward Bates*, pp. 394, 422. Also see Edward Bates to AL, July 11, 1864, in ALP.

24 *CW*, 8:174; Salmon Chase to AL, April 11, 1865, in ALP.

25 *CW*, 6:440.

26 *The Papers of Andrew Johnson*, ed. Leroy P. Graf and Ralph W. Haskins, 16 vols. (Knoxville: University of Tennessee Press, 1983), 6:580, 582, 577, 659 (hereafter *PAJ*).

27 *CW*, 6:595, 7:209.

28 Paul H. Bergeron, *Andrew Johnson's Civil War and Reconstruction* (Knoxville: University of Tennessee Press, 2011), p. 62; *CW*, 8:71.

29 *PAJ*, 7:369, 395.

30 *PAJ*, 7:404; *CW*, 8:216; *PAJ*, 7:395, 408.

31 *CW*, 7:486; Nathaniel Banks to AL, September 6, 1864, in ALP.

32 *War of the Rebellion: A Compilation of the Official Records of the Union and Confederate Armies*, 70 vols. in 128 serials (Washington, DC: Government Printing Office, 1880–1901), ser. 1, vol. 41, pt. 4, p. 413 (hereafter *OR*); Michael Hahn to AL, October 29, 1864, in ALP.

33 *CW*, 8:106–108, 163–165.

34 Hahn to AL, November 11, 1864, in ALP.

35 *Diary of Gideon Welles*, ed. Howard K. Beale, 3 vols. (New York: Norton, 1960), 2:179, 190.

36 *CW*, 8:145–152.

37 *Lincoln Observed: Civil War Dispatches of Noah Brooks*, ed. Michael Burlingame (Baltimore: Johns Hopkins University Press, 1998), pp. 149–151, 155; *Congressional Globe*, 38th Congress, 2nd Session, p. 124 (hereafter *CG*).

38 *A Radical View: The "Agate" Dispatches of Whitelaw Reid, 1861–1865*, ed. James G. Smart, 2 vols. (Memphis: Memphis State University Press, 1976), 2:188.

39 *Lincoln Observed*, p. 397; *Dispatches of Reid*, 2:188–189.

40 *Independent*, December 8, 1864; *New York Times*, December 7, 1864; *Zion's Herald and Wesleyan Journal*, December 14, 1864.

41 *Albany Evening Journal*, December 7, 1864; *New York Tribune*, December 7, 1864.

42 *New York World* quoted in *New York Tribune*, December 8, 1864; *Daily Eastern Argus*, December 8, 1864; *Boston Post* quoted in *Daily Eastern Argus*, December 9, 1864; *New York Tribune*, December 8, 1864.

43 *CG*, 38th Congress, 2nd Session, p. 26. Also see Herman Belz, *Reconstructing the Union: Theory and Policy during the Civil War* (Ithaca, NY: Cornell University Press, 1968), pp. 244–276.

44 *CG*, 38th Congress, 2nd Session, p. 53; 38th Congress, 2nd Session, H.R. 602, December 15, 1864.

45 *Letters of Sumner*, 2:258.

46 Montgomery Blair to AL, December 6, 1864, in ALP.

47 *Inside Lincoln's White House*, pp. 253–254.

48 Davis quoted in Belz, *Reconstructing the Union*, p. 256; *Letters of Sumner*, 2:262.

49 *CG*, 38th Congress, 2nd Session, pp. 286–287.

50 *CG*, 38th Congress, 2nd Session, pp. 299–300.

51 *CG*, 38th Congress, 2nd Session, p. 301.

52 *Springfield (MA) Republican*, January 28, 1865; *New York Times*, January 19, 1865.

53 *CG*, 38th Congress, 2nd Session, pp. 935–936; Dawes quoted in Belz, *Reconstructing the Union*, p. 265.

54 *Independent*, March 16, 1865; *New York Herald*, February 22, 1865; *Springfield Republican*, February 25, 1865; *San Francisco Daily Evening Bulletin*, March 20, 1865; *New York Tribune*, February 23, 1865.

55 *Cases of Contested Elections in Congress from 1835–1865 Inclusive*, compiled by D. W. Bartlett (Washington, DC: Government Printing Office, 1866), pp. 583–597; *Hinds' Precedents of the House of Representatives*, 5 vols. (Washington, DC: Government Printing Office, 1907), 1:1097; *CW*, 8:206–207; Bartlett, *Cases of Contested Elections*, pp. 643–645; *New Haven (CT) Daily Palladium*, March 2, 1865; Chandler quoted in Hans Trefousse, *The Radical Republicans* (Baton Rouge: Louisiana State University Press, 1968), pp. 303–304. On Sumner's machinations see Michael Les Benedict, *A Compromise of Principle* (New York: Norton, 1974), pp. 95–96.

Chapter 7

1 *New York Times*, February 28, 1865; *Intimate Letters of Carl Schurz, 1841–1869*, ed. Joseph Schafer (Madison: State Historical Society of Wisconsin, 1928), p. 315; *The Collected Works of Abraham Lincoln*, ed. Roy P. Basler, 9 vols. (New Brunswick, NJ: Rutgers University Press, 1953–1955), 8:254 (hereafter *CW*).

2 *CW*, 2:255–256.

3 Letter, *New York Times*, March 20, 1862; Frederick Douglass, "What Shall Be Done with the Slaves if Emancipated?," *Douglass's Monthly*, January 1862. Also see *New York Times*, May 16, 1863.

4 *War of the Rebellion: A Compilation of the Official Records of the Union and Confederate Armies*, 70 vols. in 128 serials (Washington, DC: Government Printing Office, 1880–1901), ser. 3, vol. 3, pp. 430–454 (hereafter *OR*); James McKaye, *The Emancipated Slave Face to Face with His Old Master* (New York: W. C. Bryant, 1864), p. 24. Also see Robert Dale Owen, *Wrong of Slavery, the Right of Emancipation, and the Future of the African Race in the United States* (Philadelphia: Lippincott, 1864).

5 James M. McPherson, *The Struggle for Equality* (Princeton, NJ: Princeton University Press, 1964), pp. 178–191.

6 Henry Cleveland, *Alexander Stephens in Public and Private with Letters and Speeches* (Philadelphia: National Publishing, 1866), p. 721; Adam Gurowski, *Diary, 1863–'64–'65* (Washington, DC: W. H. Morrison, 1866), p. 342.

7 [James Russell Lowell,] "Reconstruction," *North American Review* 100 (April 1865), pp. 553–554.

8 *A Philadelphia Perspective: The Civil War Diary of Sidney George Fisher*, ed. Jonathan W. White (New York: Fordham University Press, 2007), pp. 250–251.

9 William Darrah Kelley quoted in LaWanda Cox, *Lincoln and Black Freedom* (Columbia: University of South Carolina Press, 1994), pp. 117–118, 129; letter, *Liberator*, February 24, 1865.

10 *Inside Lincoln's White House: The Complete Civil War Diary of John Hay*, ed. Michael Burlingame and John R. Turner Ettlinger (Carbondale: Southern Illinois University Press, 1997), p. 253.

11 "Memorandum of the Conversation at the Conference in Hampton Roads," in John A. Campbell, *Reminiscences and Documents Relating to the Civil War during the Year 1865* (Baltimore: John Murphy, 1877), p. 17; Alexander H. Stephens, *A Constitutional View of the Late War between the States*, 2 vols. (Philadelphia: National, 1870), 2:617; *CW*, 8:260–261; *Diary of Gideon Welles*, ed. Howard K. Beale, 3 vols. (New York: Norton, 1960), 2:237. On Hampton Roads see William C. Harris, "The Hampton Roads Peace Conference: A Final Test of Lincoln's Presidential Leadership," *Journal of the Abraham Lincoln Association* 21 (Winter 2000), pp. 30–61.

12 *Diary of Gideon Welles*, 2:232; "The President's Message," *Douglass's Monthly*, January 1863.

13 George Barrell Cheever quoted in McPherson, *Struggle for Equality*, p. 97.

14 Campbell, *Reminiscences and Documents*, p. 14; Stephens, *Constitutional View of the Late War*, p. 615.

15 Francis Bicknell Carpenter, *Six Months at the White House with Abraham Lincoln* (New York: Hurd and Houghton, 1866), pp. 210–211. One commentator noted, "'root hog or die' is full of meaning, and is a vigorous rendering of the judgment 'in the sweat of thy brow shall thou eat bread.'" George Wakeman, "Live Metaphors," *Galaxy* 2 (October 1, 1866) p. 277.

16 Stephens, *Constitutional View of the Late War*, p. 615n.

17 *Providence Evening Press*, March 4, 1865; *Boston Daily Advertiser*, March 4, 1865.

18 *New York Evangelist*, March 9, 1865; *Mr. Lincoln's Washington: The Civil War Dispatches of Noah Brooks*, ed. P. J. Staudenraus (South Brunswick, NJ: Thomas Yoseloff, 1967), p. 422; *Independent*, March 9, 1865.

19 *Mr. Lincoln's Washington*, pp. 425–426; *CW*, 8:332.

20 *CW*, 8:332–333; Noah Brooks, *Washington in Lincoln's Time* (New York: Century, 1896), p. 74; *The Telegraph Goes to War: The Personal Diary of David Homer Bates, Lincoln's Telegraph Operator*, ed. Donald E. Markle (Hamilton, NY: Edmonston, 2003), p. 193. On the second inaugural see Ronald C. White Jr., *Lincoln's Greatest Speech: The Second Inaugural* (New York: Simon & Schuster, 2002), and Douglas L. Wilson, *Lincoln's Sword: The Presidency and the Power of Words* (New York: Random House, 2006), pp. 238–278.

21 *Daily National Intelligencer*, March 6, 1865; *New York World* quoted in *Daily Cleveland Herald*, March 8, 1865; David Lane, *A Soldier's Diary: The Story of a Volunteer* (n.p.: 1905), p. 256.

22 Worthington Chauncey Ford, ed., *A Cycle of Adams Letters, 1861–1865*, 2 vols. (Boston: Houghton, Mifflin, 1920), 2:257.

23 Ford, *Cycle of Adams Letters*, 2:252; Marquis Adolphe de Chambrun, *Impressions of Lincoln and the Civil War* (New York: Random House, 1952), pp. 28–29; *The Selected Letters of Charles Sumner*, ed. Beverly Wilson Palmer, 2 vols. (Boston: Northeastern University Press, 1990), 2:275; Ford, *Cycle of Adams Letters*, 2:253.

24 *CW*, 8:356.

25 *CW*, 8:182; *Diary of the Civil War, 1860–1865: George Templeton Strong*, ed. Allan Nevins (New York: Macmillan, 1962), p. 556.

26 *Mr. Lincoln's Washington*, p. 420; *Chicago Tribune*, March 22, 1865; *New York Tribune*, March 17, 1865.

27 *CW*, 8:367.

28 On Lincoln's visits see James M. McPherson, *Tried by War: Abraham Lincoln as Commander in Chief* (New York: Penguin Press, 2008). *Diary of Gideon Welles*, 2:58; *Mary Todd Lincoln: Her Life and Letters*, ed. Justin G. Turner and Linda Levitt Turner (New York: Fromm International, 1987), pp. 209, 284.

29 Admiral [David] Porter, *Incidents and Anecdotes of the Civil War* (New York: Appleton, 1885), p. 314.

30 Godfrey Weitzel, *Richmond Occupied*, ed. Louis H. Manarin (Richmond: Civil War Centennial Committee, 1965), p. 58. Thomas Thatcher Graves

also recalled Lincoln saying "let 'em up easy." Don E. Fehrenbacher and Virginia Fehrenbacher, compilers and eds., *The Recollected Words of Abraham Lincoln* (Stanford, CA: Stanford University Press, 1996), p. 182.

31 Chambrun, *Impressions of Lincoln*, pp. 84–85.

32 *Letters of Sumner*, 2:282. Sumner repeated the story to the Duchess of Argyll in a letter written after Lincoln's death. *Letters of Sumner*, 2:295.

33 *CW*, 8:385; Charles A. Page, *Letters of a War Correspondent*, ed. J. R. Gilmore (Boston: L. C. Page, 1899), p. 325.

34 John S. Barnes, "With Lincoln from Washington to Richmond in 1865," *Appleton's Magazine* 9 (January–June 1907), pp. 748–749. See Richard Wightman Fox, "A Death-shock to Chivalry and a Mortal Wound to Caste: The Story of Tad and Abraham Lincoln in Richmond," *Journal of the Abraham Lincoln Association* 33 (Summer 2012), pp. 1–19, and "Lincoln's Practice of Republicanism: Striding through Richmond, April 4, 1865," in Thomas A. Horrocks, Harold Holzer, and Frank J. Williams, eds., *The Living Lincoln* (Carbondale: Southern Illinois University Press, 2011), pp. 131–151.

35 "Papers of Hon. John A. Campbell, 1861–1865," *Southern Historical Society Papers*, new ser. 4 (September 1917), pp. 66–74.

36 *CW*, 8:386–387; "Papers of Campbell," p. 69. Also see the memorandum by Gustavus Myers, which confirms Campbell's account. C. G. Chamberlayne, ed., "Abraham Lincoln in Richmond," *Virginia Magazine of History and Biography* 41 (October 1933), pp. 319–322.

37 *CW*, 8:389.

38 *New York Herald*, April 7, 1865.

39 *Diary of Gideon Welles*, 2:279–280; *Letters of Sumner*, 2:283; "George W. Julian's Journal—Assassination of Lincoln," *Indiana Magazine of History* 11 (December 1915), p. 333. Also see George W. Julian, *Political Recollections, 1840–1872* (Chicago: Jansen, McClurg, 1884), p. 254.

40 *Diary of Gideon Welles*, 2:280; Speed quoted in Richard N. Current, *The Lincoln Nobody Knows* (New York: Hill & Wang, 1963), p. 257; *CW*, 8:406–407.

41 "Papers of Campbell," pp. 66–74.

42 *New York World*, April 14, 1865; Pierpont quoted in William C. Harris, *With Charity for All: Lincoln and the Restoration of the Union* (Lexington: University Press of Kentucky, 1997), p. 252.

43 *Diary of Gideon Welles*, 2:278; *Diary of Strong*, pp. 578–579; *Centinel of Freedom*, April 11, 1865; *Daily National Intelligencer*, April 13, 1865. On the contested meanings of Appomattox see Elizabeth R. Varon, *Appomattox: Victory, Defeat, and Freedom at the End of the Civil War* (New York: Oxford University Press, 2013).

44 *The Journals and Miscellaneous Notebooks of Ralph Waldo Emerson*, ed. Ralph H. Orth, 16 vols. (Cambridge, MA: Harvard University Press, 1982), 15:459.

45 Chambrun, *Impressions of Lincoln*, pp. 83–84.

46 Frederick W. Seward, *Reminiscences of a War-Time Statesman and Diplomat, 1830–1915* (New York: Putnam's, 1916), p. 253.

Chapter 8

1 *Diary of Gideon Welles*, ed. Howard K. Beale. 3 vols. (New York: Norton, 1960), 2:278; *Chicago Tribune*, April 11, 1865; *Mary Todd Lincoln: Her Life and Letters*, ed. Justin G. Turner and Linda Levitt Turner (New York: Fromm International, 1987), p. 216.

2 Noah Brooks, *Washington in Lincoln's Time* (New York: Century, 1896), pp. 253–254.

3 A photocopy of the manuscript is in the collection of the Abraham Lincoln Presidential Library in Springfield, Illinois. The original manuscript is owned privately. I am grateful to James Cornelius, curator at the Lincoln library and museum.

4 *The Collected Works of Abraham Lincoln*, ed. Roy P. Basler, 9 vols. (New Brunswick, NJ: Rutgers University Press, 1953–1955), 8:399–405 (hereafter *CW*).

5 *The Selected Letters of Charles Sumner*, ed. Beverly Wilson Palmer, 2 vols. (Boston: Northeastern University Press, 1990), 2:284.

6 Marquis Adolphe de Chambrun, *Impressions of Lincoln and the Civil War* (New York: Random House, 1952), p. 93.

7 Noah Brooks, *Sacramento Daily Union*, May 5, 1865; *Lincoln Observed: Civil War Dispatches of Noah Brooks*, ed. Michael Burlingame (Baltimore: Johns Hopkins University Press, 1998), p. 183; *CW*, 8:361.

8 James Dixon to Abraham Lincoln (hereafter AL), April 12, 1865, in Abraham Lincoln Papers, Library of Congress (hereafter ALP); *Philadelphia Press*, April 13, 1865; *Cincinnati Commercial* quoted in *Milwaukee Daily*

Sentinel, April 19, 1865; *Milwaukee Daily Sentinel*, April 14, 1865; *Daily National Intelligencer*, April 13, 1865; *Washington Chronicle* quoted in *Philadelphia Press*, April 13, 1865.

9   *New York Times*, April 13, 1865; *New York Tribune*, April 11, 1865; *Portland (ME) Daily Argus*, April 14, 1865; *New York World*, April 13, 1865.

10   *Lincoln Observed: Civil War Dispatches of Noah Brooks*, ed. Michael Burlingame (Baltimore: Johns Hopkins University Press, 1998), p. 185; *New York World*, April 13, 1865; *New York Herald*, April 13, 1865; *Baltimore Sun*, April 13, 1865.

11   *Boston Commonwealth*, April 15, 1865; Sarah Browne quoted in Martha Hodes, *Mourning Lincoln* (New Haven, CT: Yale University Press, forthcoming).

12   Salmon P. Chase to AL, April 11, 1865, and April 12, 1865, in ALP; *The Salmon P. Chase Papers*, vol. 1: *Journals, 1829–1872*, ed. John Nevin (Kent, OH: Kent State University Press, 1993), p. 527.

13   *Letters of Sumner*, 2:284; *Philadelphia Press*, April 13, 1865; *Albany Evening Journal*, April 12, 1865.

14   *New York World*, April 13, 1865; *New York Herald*, April 13, 1865.

15   *New York Tribune*, April 11, 1865; letter, *Milwaukee Daily Sentinel*, April 18, 1865; *New York Evening Post*, April 12, 1865.

16   *New York Sun*, April 13, 1865.

17   *New York Tribune*, April 11, 1865; *New York Commercial Advertiser*, April 13, 1865.

18   *Albany Evening Journal*, April 12, 1865; *New York Tribune*, April 11, 1865.

19   *Albany Evening Journal*, April 12, 1865; *Daily Eastern Argus*, April 13, 1865; *Oswego Times* quoted in *Atlas and Argus*, April 13, 1865; *Diary of the Civil War, 1860–1865: George Templeton Strong*, ed. Allan Nevins (New York: Macmillan, 1962), p. 581; *New York Times*, April 12, 1865.

20   *New York Herald*, April 13, 1865; *Philadelphia Press*, April 14, 1865; *New York Tribune*, April 13, 1865.

21   James Dixon to AL, April 12, 1865, in ALP; *New York Times*, July 4, 1865.

22   *Diary of Gideon Welles*, 2:279; Gideon Welles, "Lincoln and Johnson," *Galaxy* 13 (April 1872), p. 526; *CW*, 8:413.

23   Frederick W. Seward, *Reminiscences of a War-Time Statesman and Diplomat, 1830–1915* (New York: Putnam's, 1916), pp. 256–257.

24 *Diary of Gideon Welles*, 2:280–281.

25 Mary Todd Lincoln, *Letters*, pp. 284–285; *CW*, 4:268.

Epilogue

1 *The Salmon P. Chase Papers*, vol. 1: *Journals, 1829–1872*, ed. John Niven (Kent, OH: Kent State University Press, 1993), p. 530.

2 "George W. Julian's Journal—Assassination of Lincoln," *Indiana Magazine of History* 11 (December 1915), p. 335; *The Telegraph Goes to War: The Personal Diary of David Homer Bates, Lincoln's Telegraph Operator*, ed. Donald E. Markle (Hamilton, NY: Edmonston, 2003), p. 215.

3 Chandler quoted in James M. McPherson, *The Struggle for Equality* (Princeton, NJ: Princeton University Press, 1964), p. 318; *Their Patriotic Duty: The Civil War Letters of the Evans Family of Brown County, Ohio*, eds. Robert F. Engs and Corey M. Brooks (New York: Fordham University Press, 2007), p. 339; *New York Evangelist*, April 20, 1865.

4 *The Papers of Andrew Johnson*, ed. Leroy P. Graf, Ralph W. Haskins, and Paul H. Bergeron, 16 vols. (Knoxville: University of Tennessee Press, 1967–2000), 7:612, 554 (hereafter *PAJ*).

5 William Robinson quoted in McPherson, *Struggle for Equality*, pp. 314–315; Marquis Adolphe de Chambrun, *Impressions of Lincoln and the Civil War* (New York: Random House, 1952), p. 111.

6 Chambrun, *Impressions of Lincoln*, p. 108; *A Philadelphia Perspective: The Civil War Diary of Sidney George Fisher*, ed. Jonathan W. White (New York: Fordham University Press, 2007), p. 252.

7 *The Selected Letters of Charles Sumner*, ed. Beverly Wilson Palmer, 2 vols. (Boston: Northeastern University Press, 1990), 2:297, 265; *New York Observer and Chronicle*, April 20, 1865.

8 *Independent*, April 27, 1865; George S. Boutwell, *Eulogy on the Death of Abraham Lincoln* (Lowell, MA: Stone & Huse, 1865), p. 10; J. G. Holland, *Eulogy on Abraham Lincoln, Late President of the United States Presented at the City Hall, Springfield, Mass., April 19, 1865* (Springfield, MA: L. J. Powers, 1865), pp. 16–17.

9 Charles Sumner, *The Promise of the Declaration of Independence: Eulogy on Abraham Lincoln* (Boston: Ticknor & Fields, 1865), p. 56; *Letters of Sumner*, 2:297–298.

10 *New York Tribune*, April 24, 1865; "Sherman Blunders at Last," *Ohio Farmer* 14 (April 29, 1865), p. 132.

11 Stanton's condemnation was widely reported. See, for example, *Lowell (MA) Daily Citizen and News*, April 24, 1865; *CW*, 8:330–331.

12 *Memoirs of General William T. Sherman*, 2 vols. (New York: Appleton, 1875), 2:366; *Diary of Gideon Welles*, ed. Howard K. Beale, 3 vols. (New York: Norton, 1960, 2:295–296. Also see Alexander K. McClure, *Abraham Lincoln and Men of War-Times* (Philadelphia: Times, 1892), pp. 216–228).

13 Johnson quoted in Paul H. Bergeron, *Andrew Johnson's Civil War and Reconstruction* (Knoxville: University of Tennessee Press, 2011), p. 76.

14 *Diary of Gideon Welles*, 2:301–304; *PAJ*, 8:599–601.

15 See *New York Times*, December 2, 1865.

16 Banks quoted in Peyton McCrary, *Abraham Lincoln and Reconstruction: The Louisiana Experiment* (Princeton, NJ: Princeton University Press, 1979), pp. 311–312.

17 *Let the Oppressed Go Free, 1861–1867: The Letters of William Lloyd Garrison*, ed. Walter M. Merrill, 6 vols. (Cambridge, MA: Harvard University Press, 1979), 5:299.

18 *PAJ*, 9:466–485.

19 *Advice after Appomattox: Letters to Andrew Johnson, 1865–1866*, ed. Brooks D. Simpson, Leroy P. Graf, and John Muldowny (Knoxville: University of Tennessee Press, 1987), pp. 241–243.

20 *Letters of Sumner*, 2:340; *Advice after Appomattox*, p. 121; *Intimate Letters of Carl Schurz*, ed. Joseph Schafer (Madison: State Historical Society of Wisconsin, 1928), p. 351; *Speeches, Correspondence and Political Papers of Carl Schurz*, ed. Fredric Bancroft, 6 vols. (New York: Putnam's, 1913), 1:355.

21 *Intimate Letters of Schurz*, p. 359; *Advice after Appomattox*, p. 241; *Letters of Sumner*, 2:356, 349.

22 *Hartford (CT) Daily Courant*, December 6, 1865; *Providence Evening Press*, December 6, 1865; *New York Tribune*, December 6, 1865; *Maine Farmer*, December 14, 1865.

23 *Mary Todd Lincoln: Her Life and Letters*, ed. Justin G. Turner and Linda Levitt Turner (New York: Fromm International, 1987), pp. 386–387.

24 Frederick Douglass, "Abraham Lincoln, A Speech," Library of Congress, manuscripts division, available online at http://www.loc.gov/item/mfd.22015/.

See Michael Burlingame, *Abraham Lincoln: A Life*, 2 vols. (Baltimore: Johns Hopkins University Press, 2008), 2:829–831, Eric Foner, *The Fiery Trial: Abraham Lincoln and American Slavery* (New York: Norton, 2011), pp. 333–336, and James Oakes, *The Radical and the Republican: Frederick Douglass, Abraham Lincoln, and the Triumph of Antislavery Politics* (New York: Norton, 2007), pp. 247–287.

25 *Diary of Fisher*, p. 227; *The Collected Works of Abraham Lincoln,* ed. Roy P. Basler, 9 vols. (New Brunswick, NJ: Rutgers University Press, 1953–1955), 5:537.

INDEX